The Decadent Vision in Leopoldo Alas

The Decadent Vision
in Leopoldo Alas

A Study of *La Regenta* and *Su único hijo*

NOËL MAUREEN VALIS

Louisiana State University Press
BATON ROUGE AND LONDON

To my family,
on both sides of the river

Design: Joanna Hill
Typeface: Garamond
Composition: G & S Typesetters
Printing and binding: Thomson-Shore, Inc.

LIBRARY OF CONGRESS CATALOGING IN PUBLICATION DATA

Valis, Noël Maureen, 1945–
The decadent vision in Leopoldo Alas.

Based on the author's thesis, Bryn Mawr, 1975, under
the title: The idea of decadence in the novels of
Leopoldo Alas (Clarín).
Bibliography: p.
Includes index.
1. Alas, Leopoldo, 1852–1901. Regenta. 2. Alas,
Leopoldo, 1852–1901. Su único hijo. 3. Decadence in
literature. I. Title.

PQ6503.A4R3377   1981   863'.5   80-24108
ISBN 0-8071-0769-7

Contents

Acknowledgments   ix
Introduction   3
I Fin de Siècle   7
II *La Regenta*   23
III *Su único hijo*   107
Conclusion   191
Bibliography   195
Index   211

Acknowledgments

I wish to express my appreciation of the encouragement and advice given me by Professor Eleanor Paucker. I am indebted to the Department of Spanish and to Bryn Mawr College for their determined attempts to broaden and sharpen my scholarship and literary perceptiveness. My thanks also to Professor Robert Jackson for his helpful suggestions; to Jackie Wilson for typing the final manuscript; and to the University of Georgia's Research Center for the typing grant given to complete the book.

Some sections of this book appeared in modified form in *Explicación de Textos Literarios, The Comparatist*, and *Modern Language Studies*, whom I gratefully acknowledge for permission to reprint.

The Decadent Vision in Leopoldo Alas

Introduction

Leopoldo Alas, better known to Spaniards as Clarín (1852–1901), wrote in a transitional age, the 1880s and 1890s. It was a period which reflected both the optimism and the despair of a century born of revolutionary fervor and dying, it seemed, in twilight pessimism. It was an age on the brink of another century, simultaneously fearful and curious about the possibilities of the future. In literature, this uncertainty and curiosity were reflected in various attempts to explore the inner recesses of reality, to go beyond the surface presentation of daily existence. In some cases, however, the demands of a confused era proved too much of a strain and resulted in the wish to evade reality.

In Spain, it was the time of the Restoration, a period which presented a façade of tranquillity but which failed to vanquish or even entirely conceal the conflicts, divisiveness, and latent hatreds of a people whose energies were being repeatedly drained away by colonial wars, unfruitful political games, and stultifying, banal frivolities.

Here, the *fin de siècle* desire to penetrate a deeper reality went hand-in-hand with the cognizance of the theatrical illusion, the unreal façade that Spain presented. The historian Melchor Fernández Almagro said of the period that "una inconciencia punto menos que infantil regía el ir y venir apasionado de los españoles en relación con las cuestiones que suscitaba la actualidad inmediata. Nadie miraba a lo lejos. Inconciencia y optimismo." The country was immersed in an "enorme calma chicha."[1] This perverse optimism and gaiety camouflaged Spain's real problems. To some intellectuals of

1. Cited by Pedro Laín Entralgo, *La generación del 98* (Madrid: Espasa-Calpe, 1970), 46.

the day, including Alas, the period seemed empty, the country fraudulent.

Both the urge to plumb the more profound aspects of existence and the wish to evade the historical present of Spain are evident in the two novels of Leopoldo Alas. The first aspect will appear in his efforts to delve deeply into the psychological complexities of his characters and, especially in his second novel, *Su único hijo*, to depict characters in near archetypal fashion. The protagonists of *La Regenta* and *Su único hijo* (Ana and Bonifacio) reveal a dissatisfaction with life and a quest for a deeper reality that will give meaning to their existence. At the same time, both characters are adept at evading reality because their single greatest problem is the failure to come to grips with actual existence. Ana, when not oscillating between her dreams and memories and the temptations of the actual present, wavers between the spiritual and the carnal. Bonifacio is a dreamer who prefers reverie and the make-believe world of the opera to life around him. And, in the fragment "Una medianía," an intended sequel to *Su único hijo*, Antonio Reyes, Bonifacio's son, also indulges in dreams and the reviving of old memories in preference to everyday reality. Worse, he appears, much as his father before him, incapable of working and adapting and is thus depicted as a rather abulic character. In sum, Alas' main characters tend to avoid the nasty sticky-wicket facing them and prefer their own dreams to the restrictive, drab present which was Restoration Spain.

These two kinds of reality—the historical present and the world of dreams and memories—can be seen as two types of decadence. Clarín clearly shows that Restoration Spain was thoroughly corrupt, lax in morals—both public and private—and shallow, if not entirely lacking, in vision. Yet his critical eye does not spare the protagonists' inner world either. The fact that the main characters retreat from reality or indulge in sensual experiences (such as Ana's or Bonis' acts of adultery) in mistaken attempts to heighten reality reveals, from Alas' critical point of view, an unhealthy situation. There is, however, some ambiguity of viewpoint on Alas' part since at times he seems to present the dreamworld in a most favorable light, an indication that evasiveness, or at least dreaming, may not be an entirely negative experience (this is especially the case in *Su único hijo*).

The preoccupation with decadence in Spanish society is paralleled then in the personalities of the main characters. In Ana the author presents the divided soul, a personality in crisis; in Bonifacio Reyes, an anemic soul; and in Antonio Reyes of the fragment "Una medianía," the advanced state of abulia. Expressed in another way, while *La Regenta* conforms largely, though not entirely, to the realist-naturalist conception of decadence in characters and society, Clarín's second novel, *Su único hijo*, develops even further the *fin de siècle* decadent sensibility, which is present in embryonic form in *La Regenta*, to the point of hispanicizing the French decadent typology of the 1880s and 90s.

In Alas, the idea of decadence, as depicted through a corrupt society and degenerate, weak-willed, or fragmented characters, functions as a unifying device in the novels. Although decadent themes, types, and leitmotifs pervade the whole of Clarín's novels, I am not suggesting the notion of a decadent style, but rather the creation of a decadent vision, stimulated in large part by the reigning French literary movements, namely, naturalism and later the decadent movement proper. By appropriating those elements of the French morbid sensibility and concern with decadence which most appealed to Alas personally, the Spanish novelist hispanicizes a theme and preoccupation which had spread from French literary circles to the rest of Europe. Thus, in Restoration Spain, Clarín, while remaining firmly rooted in the Spanish earth, is the writer who most closely resembles his French predecessors.

It is, of course, true that Clarín in his criticism held an essentially hostile position toward *modernismo*, symbolism, and the decadent movement, an attitude which has already been documented and analyzed by several critics and thus needs little further commentary on my part.[2] Nevertheless, the pervasiveness of decadent literature in

2. See José María Martínez Cachero, "Algunas referencias sobre el anti-modernismo español," *Archivum*, III (1953), 311–33, and "Más referencias sobre el antimodernismo español," *Archivum*, V (1955), 131–35; Fernando González Ollé, "Del naturalismo al modernismo: Los orígenes del poema

France and, even in a number of Spanish imitators, could not fail to penetrate and make some impression upon a highly complex and nervous spirit who already was attracted to such decadent precursors as the Goncourts and Baudelaire. Clarín's receptiveness toward the French literary scene, his "literary internationalism," is indisputable and has been so noted by Hans Juretschke and several others;[3] but what needs to be examined now is the manner in which the Asturian writer internalized in his own novels the nineteenth-century obsession with the idea of decadence.

en prosa y un desconocido artículo de Clarín," *Revista de Literatura*, XXV (1964), 49–67; Sergio Beser, *Leopoldo Alas, crítico literario* (Madrid: Gredos, 1968), 201–209; Fernando Ibarra, "Clarín y Rubén Darío," *Hispanic Review*, XLI (1973), 524–40; John W. Kronik, "Rubén Darío y la entrada del Simbolismo en España," in Eleanor Krane Paucker (ed.), *Poemas y ensayos para un homenaje a Phyllis Turnbull* (Madrid: Tecnos, 1976), 95–106; and Lily Litvak, "La idea de la decadencia en la crítica antimodernista en España (1888–1910)," *Hispanic Review*, XLV (1977), 397–412. In *El primer modernismo literario catalán y sus fundamentos ideológicos* (Barcelona: Ariel, 1973), 61–78, Eduard Valentí Fiol seems to place Clarín among religious "modernistas," although he notes his aversion to literary modernists (p. 77). Of related interest is Lisa E. Davis, "Max Nordau, *Degeneración* y la decadencia de España," *Cuadernos Hispanoamericanos*, Nos. 326–27 (1977), 307–23.

3. For an overview of Clarín's position toward French culture, see Hans Juretschke, *España ante Francia* (Madrid: Editora Nacional, 1940), 90–109. Also: Beser, *Leopoldo Alas, crítico literario*, 118–28; and individual studies on Clarín's literary relationships with Baudelaire, Verlaine, Flaubert, the Goncourts, and others, as cited in the bibliography.

I Fin de Siècle

The feeling of being asynchronous with the world is first expressed in modern literature in the romantic artist's isolation from, and hostility to, bourgeois society. Disregarding the romantics' more childish attitudes, which evolve from an exaggerated sense of superiority and egotism, we can see that their early criticism of modern society contains more than a grain of truth. Both the early rebels (*e.g.*, Mariano José de Larra and José de Espronceda), on the one hand, and the Christian romantics (*e.g.*, Félicité Robert de La Mennais and Juan Donoso Cortés), on the other, criticized the growing materialism of the century. The emphasis on the acquisition of things, made easier by advanced industrialization, is only the most obvious example of what traditionalists and nonconformists alike deplored under the blanket concept of "materialism." This exaggerated importance of *things* will also appear in the realist novel, from Balzac on.[1]

Although the romantic will deplore the effects of materialism, it is the realist who will exploit more fully the multiple aspects of the concrete in the nineteenth century. The realist writer is, in the beginning, totally absorbed in the vision of the real; he picks out detail after detail, and lovingly, obsessively lays each one out for the reader to savor. But the realist viewpoint is not one-sided: besides the excessive care and love he reveals in his *detallismo*, the realist is also a critic. Indeed, the realistic tradition is, above all, a critical tradition, as George J. Becker writes: "Critical realism is to be found in Balzac, in Flaubert, in Turgenev and Tolstoy, in fact

---

1. Harry Levin has stated that "etymologically, realism is thing-ism. The adjective 'real' derives from the Latin *res*, and finds an appropriate context in 'real estate' " (*The Gates of Horn*, New York: Oxford University Press, 1966, p. 34).

everywhere that there has been an effort to depict the working of bourgeois society and to show its ugly and repressive aspects."[2] It is frequently stated that the nineteenth-century novel is the novel of, for, and by the middle class, or as Benito Pérez Galdós expressed it: "La clase media, la más olvidada por nuestros novelistas, es el gran modelo, la fuente inagotable."[3] The critical vision of the realist writer focuses precisely upon a middle-class, materialistic society which appears either to repress or distort the world surrounding it. Any simplistic version of an optimistic, progressive nineteenth century must, then, be modified in light of the realists' more critical view of their own society.

As the century draws to a close, moreover, the negative aspects of the nineteenth century's "good life" appear more frequently and in blacker hues in contemporary fiction. A backlash develops in reaction to the accepted doctrines and attitudes of a materialistic age, as the search for more enduring spiritual values results in an attack on, and rejection of, the positivism, scientism, and secularism of previous decades.

In European literature, this reaction manifests itself in a turning away from the naturalism of the 1870s and 80s, a literary movement based on positivistic and scientistic principles, toward a more spiritual, psychological art. E. -M. de Vogüé's *Le Roman russe* (1886), which declared in favor of the Russian novel of spiritual and psychological depths—followed in Spain by Emilia Pardo Bazán's *La revolución y la novela en Rusia* (1887)—is a good example of successful literary propaganda. In his preface, de Vogüé writes: "I am convinced that the influence of the great Russian writers will be salutary for our worn-out art; it will aid it to take flight again, to observe the real better, while looking further away, and above all to rediscover emotion."[4]

2. George J. Becker, "Introduction," *Documents of Modern Literary Realism* (Princeton, N.J.: Princeton University Press, 1967), 21.

3. Benito Pérez Galdós, "Observaciones sobre la novela contemporánea en España," *Ensayos de crítica literaria* (Barcelona: Península, 1972), 122. Originally published in *Revista de España*, XV (1870), 162–93.

4. E. -M. de Vogüé, "On Russian and French Realism," in Becker (ed.), *Documents of Modern Literary Realism*, 342.

Another key book of the period is Paul Bourget's *Le Disciple* (1889), an antipositivistic, antideterministic psychological analysis of a follower of Taine's doctrines. In his preface, which is in the form of a letter to a young man, Bourget makes use of the term "l'Inconnaissable" or the unknowable, a phrase borrowed from Herbert Spencer's *First Principles* (1862). The writings of Bourget and de Vogüé are symptomatic of the *fin de siècle* uneasiness and quest for values other than those of a highly industrialized, materialistic age.

The *fin de siècle* ambience of the past century is not unique. In other places, in other times, men have felt that their world was coming apart at the seams, and that beyond that disintegration, lay either the great "l'Inconnaissable" or, worse, nothingness. All the ills of their time have gained increased momentum, and all seems to be galloping toward general disaster. The theme of decay and disintegration permeated the literature of the final years of nineteenth-century Europe. Spain's relationship to this generally gray and pessimistic mood will be discussed later.

To a certain extent, de Vogüé is correct in analyzing the *fin de siècle* mood as one of ill-founded fears, but what de Vogüé ignored was the irrational strength of a belief and of an emotion. The *fin de siècle* mood was, for such countries as England and France, precisely that: a deeply held feeling that Wagner's *Götterdämmerung* was ready and at hand to envelop the world. In the face of economic prosperity and political stability—England had reached the pinnacle of her empire, and France had recovered speedily from the Franco-Prussian War of 1870—men still insisted, in teleological fashion, on the rending of Western civilization. Indeed, one French novelist, Élémir Bourges, appropriately entitled a book *Le Crépuscule des dieux* (1884), using the Wagnerian opera to structure his story of the corruption and death of a great German aristocratic family.

In one form or another, and from a variety of viewpoints—ranging from the conservative to the liberal—the problem of the decadence of Western civilization pervades intellectual circles. As George Ross Ridge has put it, the idea of decadence "preoccupies, even obsesses, most writers during the second half of the century."[5] A word of explanation is in order here: the preoccupation with decadence and the decadent movement in literature (and the other arts) can be considered, on the whole, as two distinct categories. Quite often, the two categories will overlap, but a writer obsessed with the idea of social, political, moral, and literary decline is not necessarily a member of the decadent literary movement. This is especially true of Leopoldo Alas (Zola also, it might be added), who will borrow devices, themes, and character types from the decadent movement, but who will remain—even in a transitional novel like *Su único hijo*—within the traditional mold of the nineteenth-century critical realist. Indeed, the critical realists and naturalists— the Goncourts, Flaubert, Zola, Galdós, Father Coloma, for example—were as much interested in the idea of decadence as decadents like J.-K. Huysmans, Baudelaire, Oscar Wilde, and the *modernistas*; but not only do the literary techniques differ (with considerable mutual borrowing, one might add): the point of view varies to a great extent also.

In rather simplified terms, the critical realist or naturalist sees decadence from a moral mountaintop, while the decadent revels in the lush valley below. The critical realist, despite his attempts at impersonality and cool objectivity, remains at heart a moralist: whether he presents a case of individual decay and corruption (Galdós' Isidora in *La desheredada* or Zola's Nana) or an entire society fallen out of innocence and into damnation (as in Coloma's *Pequeñeces*, Alas' *La Regenta*, or a representative Zola novel), the critical realist/naturalist has not taken all that trouble to document, structure, and detail with painstaking care for the sake of art alone. He is a giver of messages, except that the medium is the message— *i.e.*, Zola or Flaubert, Galdós or Alas uses his novelistic materials as they constitute a message. Sermonizing may slip in occasionally, but the presentation itself should—indirectly—speak volumes.

The decadent, on the other hand, immerses himself in his ma-

5. George Ross Ridge, *The Hero in French Decadent Literature* (Athens, Georgia: University of Georgia Press, 1961), 1. See also Jacques Lethève, "Le thème de la décadence dans les lettres françaises à la fin du XIXe siècle," *Revue d'histoire littéraire de la France*, LXIII (1963), 46–61.

terial; he loves it, often in a paroxysm of self-identifying ecstasy. Because subject matter and author are more intimately entwined, the decadent tends to be less critical of his material. The sensual, erotic, and frequently abnormal nature of much of the decadent artist's stock-in-trade creates, moreover, an atmosphere of willing complicity on the part of author and subject (and reader for that matter). It is evident, for example, that Huysmans, as much as his decadent hero, des Esseintes—the epitome of the decadent type— savors his own descriptions of the exquisite furnishings with which the protagonist designs his home, or of the extravagant bejewelment of the tortoise's shell.[6]

I am oversimplifying, of course, the differences in point of view, for it is not unusual to find an artist classified in the decadent movement who either is or can be interpreted as a writer of "moral tone." A good example is Baudelaire. It is not my intention here to resolve the moral ambiguities of a poet who has been at various times called everything from an agent of the devil to a supreme Catholic visionary. I merely wish to point out the confluence of the decadent and the moral elements in one writer. Clarín himself considered Baudelaire a Christian poet preeminently concerned with the conflict between good and evil.[7]

Having made the distinction between the two viewpoints, with the caveat that writers of the period will not necessarily fall into such neat classifications, I will now try to dispel one more possible cause for confusion before proceeding to a discussion and tentative definition of decadence in nineteenth-century European literature. The mention of a decadent writer of the 1880s and 90s usually brings to mind a vague and sinister picture of a Dorian Gray–Mr. Hyde composite—*i.e.*, an Oscar Wilde, Paul Verlaine, or early

6. J. -K. Huysmans, *A Rebours* (Paris: Fasquelle, 1970), Chs. 1 and 4. See François Livi, *J. -K. Huysmans, A Rebours et l'esprit décadent* (Belgique: La Renaissance du Livre, 1972); and Michel Lemaire, *Le Dandysme de Baudelaire à Mallarmé* (Montréal: Presses de l'Université de Montréal/ Paris: Klincksieck, 1978).

7. See Josette Blanquat, "Clarín et Baudelaire," *Revue de littérature comparée*, XXXIII (1959), 5–25, for a good exposition of the Clarín-Baudelaire relationship; and Leopoldo Alas, "Baudelaire," in *Epistolario de Menéndez y Pelayo y Leopoldo Alas* (Madrid: Escorial, 1943), 148–85.

Valle-Inclán type. In other words, decadence is first associated with the image of a decadent writer. The idea of decadence is identified with a particular life-style, often with an aesthetic pose, rather than with a society or an ambience. The interpretation is not false, but incomplete. The decadent style of life of an author (which does not, by the way, apply at all to Leopoldo Alas, whose personal life was exemplary) is actually more symptomatic of the period's malaise than a causative agent of it. What then is meant by the term decadence? If one refers to a specific literary movement of the period, the French are represented by Huysmans, Verlaine, d'Aurevilly and company, the English by Oscar Wilde, Ernest Dowson, and Aubrey Beardsley, and the Spanish and Latin Americans by the *modernistas* (*e.g.*, Valle-Inclán and Rubén Darío). Although Huysmans is credited with perfecting the image of the decadent type and decadent book in *A Rebours* (1884), it was Baudelaire who first recognized the importance of decadence in style. In fact, most attempts to circumscribe the decadent movement revolve at first around an aesthetic definition. Thus, in an early statement on decadence, Théophile Gautier writes:

> Le poète des *Fleurs du mal* aimait ce qu'on appelle improprement le style de décadence, et qui n'est autre chose que l'art arrivé à ce point de maturité extrême que déterminent à leurs soleils obliques les civilisations qui vieillissent: style ingénieux, compliqué, savant, plein de nuances et de recherches, reculant toujours les bornes de la langue, empruntant à tous les vocabulaires techniques, prenant des couleurs à toutes les palettes, des notes à tous les claviers, s'efforçant à rendre la pensée dans ce qu'elle a de plus ineffable, et la forme en ses contours les plus vagues et les plus fuyants, écoutant pour les traduire les confidences subtiles de la névrose, les aveux de la passion vieillissante qui se déprave et les hallucinations bizarres de l'idée fixe tournant à la folie. Ce style de décadence est le dernier mot du verbe sommé de tout exprimer et poussé à l'extrême outrance.[8]

This rather lengthy but useful quotation from Gautier reveals some of the manifestations of decadence: a highly ripened, subtle,

8. Théophile Gautier, "Notice," in Charles Baudelaire, *Les Fleurs du mal* (definitive ed.; Paris: Calmann Lévy, 1900), 16–17.

and exotic style which delves into the psychologically abnormal and perverse. Holbrook Jackson, in his well-known study of the "yellow nineties," lists the characteristics of decadence in this fashion: 1) perversity, 2) artificiality, 3) egoism, and 4) curiosity. He then goes on to say that "these characteristics are not at all inconsistent with a sincere desire 'to find the last fine shade, the quintessence of things; to fix it fleetingly; to be a disembodied voice, and yet the voice of a human soul.'"[9] Jackson has pointed out the elusive refinement typical of decadent writers such as Verlaine, Huysmans, and Valle-Inclán. At this juncture I do not intend to plumb the depths of the relationship between the decadent and the symbolist movements, but it would appear evident that the decadents do share in the symbolists' love of suggestiveness and allusion, artificiality, and the quest for a reality deeper than their quotidian surroundings.

The decadent movement gained adherents so easily because it appealed, like romanticism before it, to the artist's sense of alienation in the face of what seemed to be an intolerable middle-class complacency and narrow conventionality. The artist needed an escape valve, something which decadent art provided through its sexual and verbal exoticism; or as the critic Brandreth observes:

> The Decadent movement was the expression of this malaise which, most notably in the world of letters, but in painting and music as well, was an effort to escape, by any means that offered, from a world of reality which had become intolerable. Thus the artificial had always to be preferred to the natural; the real world was ugly and beauty could only be created by the artist.[10]

Huysmans's artificial paradise in *A Rebours* was the epitome of what will often prove to be the descent into the artificial, the unreal, or the perverse. The Gustave Moreau paintings of Salomé and the highly symbolic art of Odilon Redon offer pictorial parallels to the

9. Holbrook Jackson, *The Eighteen Nineties* (orig. pub. 1913; New York: Capricorn Books, 1966), 64. Jackson is quoting from Arthur Symons' "The Decadent Movement in Literature" (*Harper's New Monthly Magazine*, November 1893), 862. See also Jacques Lethève, "Un mot témoin de l'époque 'fin de siècle': Esthète," *Revue d'histoire littéraire de la France*, LXIV (1964), 436–46.

10. Henry R. T. Brandreth, *Huysmans* (New York: Hillary House Publishers, Ltd., 1963), 55–56.

verbal artificiality and sinister but exotic refinement of decadent literature.

Thus far, the discussion of decadence has been confined to its expression in the decadent movement proper of the 1880s and 90s. Several critics (Arthur Symons, Paul Bourget, Havelock Ellis), taking as their cue Gautier's definition of the decadent style, defined this movement as a stylistic one. It is a supremely aesthetic explanation of the literary preoccupation with decadence which, within a limited context, is a valid notion, but two problems appear: the stylistic disparities among writers classified as decadents are too great; and the idea of a decadent style precludes a broader view of decadence as a theme and a preoccupation. In this connection, A. E. Carter has suggested a division of the obsession with decadence into three phases:

> The first is the late Romantic phase . . . when the moody, introspective and fatal hero of 1830 adopts the cult of the artificial and the abnormal; then the Naturalist phase, marked by the influence of psychopathology, which leads to an interpretation of decadence in terms of nervous disease; finally the *fin de siècle* phase, when there is a return to the monstrous characters of late Romanticism. The first period goes from 1830 to the beginnings of Naturalism; the second from Naturalism to 1884 (the Goncourts and Zola to *A Rebours*); the last from 1884 to the first years of the new century—from the nerve-storms of Des Esseintes to the emotional garbage of *Monsieur de Phocas* and *Le Jardin des supplices*.[11]

Here, Carter has considerably broadened the base of the definition of decadent literature. The decadent movement of the 1880s and 90s becomes merely one of three stages in the general evolution of the theme. What all three phases, while remaining distinct, have in common are: the cult of the artificial; and the rejection of ideal love. Both points are in opposition to the romantics' love of nature and cult of ideal love. Carter's stress on the unnatural and the perverted is in basic accord with Holbrook Jackson's previously

11. A. E. Carter, *The Idea of Decadence in French Literature, 1830–1900* (Toronto: University of Toronto Press, 1958), 27.

mentioned list of decadent characteristics (perversity, artificiality, egoism, and insatiable curiosity).

It is important to retain the notion of Carter's three-part classification of the preoccupation with decadence since it is implicit in my analysis of Clarín's novels. Roughly speaking, I place *La Regenta* in the naturalist phase while pointing out the beginnings of a *fin de siècle* sensibility (third phase) which emerges here and there in the novel. *Su único hijo*, while clinging to vestiges of a naturalist aesthetic and demonstrating the persistence of Clarinian realistic irony, reflects in its characters and situation the decadent typology of the 1880s and 90s (a typology which derives from romantic characters).

The decadent movement proper, as a manifestation of the *fin de siècle* malaise is, by itself, the expression of a minority group, but taken in a larger context, decadent literature of all types points to a more generalized condition, the obsession with decadence in its multiple social, political, moral, religious, and literary forms. Here, decadence may be considered as a nonaesthetic phenomenon. G. L. Van Roosbroeck has pointed out the confusion which arises when aesthetic and nonaesthetic definitions of decadence are indiscriminately mixed.[12] The nineteenth century displays a bewildering variety of nonliterary types of decadence. Nietzsche thought decadence was Christianity; Max Nordau identified it with mental disease and physiological degeneration, Bourget with individualism. Few writers agreed on a definition of decadence in the social and moral sphere; but decadence in its broadest resonances implies social deterioration, the defeat of a society, or in individual cases, pathological degeneracy or the descent of a healthy personality into mental or spiritual instability.

The literary treatment of the theme can, in that case, differ widely, ranging from the critical realist and naturalist tradition to the more "idealist," psychological in-depth structure. One of the many fascinations this particular period offers is its transitional nature; thus, an author usually classified as a realist or naturalist (Zola, for

12. G. L. Van Roosbroeck, *The Legend of the Decadents* (New York: Institut des Études Françaises, Columbia University, 1927), 19.

example) may suddenly (or fairly consistently in Zola's case) exploit a symbolic device (such as the transcendent myths of death and cosmic renewal of the earth's forces in *La Terre*)[13] or make use of "decadent types" such as the androgyne, the domineering female, or the weakling male counterpart (as we shall see in Alas' *Su único hijo*).

From the mid-1880s to the end of the century, writers might retain the residues of the realist-naturalist genre while consciously or unconsciously imbibing the decadent and symbolist quest for a deeper reality. Whether the writer aggressively attacks the social structure through realistic satire or naturalistic exaggeration or merely slips quietly away into a fictitious, more agreeable dreamworld, either route indicates a profound dissatisfaction with the reality of the period. It is then that the term *decadence* transcends mere style or literary movements and takes on the significance of a world view. In other words, the literary treatment of the idea of decadence expresses the pervasive concern in intellectual circles with the theme of societal and individual decay. It becomes a particular vision of a society in decline, expressed through such literary movements as naturalism or decadentism (the decadent movement proper).[14] The literary movements themselves are not decadent, but rather, through a variety of types, devices, and leitmotifs, they manifest a preoccupation with decadence.

It has been said that the decadence of the last two decades of the nineteenth century is symptomatic of a "tired mood," a feeling expressed with gentle resignation by Ernest Dowson in his poem "Spleen": "I was not sorrowful, but only tired of everything that ever I desired."[15] It is this minor tone of surfeit that the English poet strikes which is very characteristic of the decadent period when it is not engaging in frenetic excess and exaggeration.

It is true the period is abulic—or at least seems so in contempo-

13. See Philip Walker, "Prophetic Myths in Zola," *PMLA*, LXXIV (1959), 444–52, for an elucidation of this very Zolaesque use of myth.

14. See Ridge, *Hero in French Decadent Literature*, 22.

15. Jackson, *Eighteen Nineties*, 66; Ernest Dowson, *Poems and Prose* (New York: Modern Library, 1919), 42.

rary literature—but, as Jackson has convincingly written, "it should not be forgotten that the effort demanded by even the most ill-directed phases of decadent action suggests a liveliness of energy which is quite contrary to the traditions of senile decay."[16] It would be an oversimplification to see in the decadent period nothing but a draining away of energy, of the vital forces, because decay and corruption may also provoke vigorous resistance to them.

Indeed, this very preoccupation with the idea of decadence in Spain incited Spanish intellectuals (including Alas) to attack abulia and preach regeneration with aggressive fervor. The problem of Spain's decadence is an old one. As Ortega y Gasset has written: "De 1580 hasta el día cuanto en España acontece es decadencia y desintegración."[17] Since Spain has been pursuing her downhill course in decay from the seventeenth century on, it is certainly legitimate to question how long a country must take to disintegrate and precisely when the fall (decadence obviously implies one) occurred. It is usual to identify the starting point of Spain's troubles as 1588, the year of the defeat of the Armada; from there everything, hindsight tells us, just went downhill. And yet the decay was not immediately evident to Spanish contemporaries. We know now that while economic and financial debility occurred at an early date, the military decline was postponed until the 1640s. By then, Spanish morale had nearly reached its nadir; and yet during all these troublesome times Spain experienced a literary and artistic flowering unequaled before or since.

The movement of Spanish history does not record a single episode of such dramatic weight and intensity as to cause the total collapse of the empire, but rather a constant, apparently inevitable wearing-away of its somewhat precarious prosperity and stability. Ortega y Gasset has come to the conclusion that the Spanish Empire was, in reality, only a brief moment of glory for his country, and that actually Spain has never been well, has always been "decadent." He realizes of course that this would imply no real decadence at all

16. Jackson, *Eighteen Nineties*, 65.
17. José Ortega y Gasset, *España invertebrada* (orig. pub. 1921; Madrid: Revista de Occidente, 1967), 63.

since decadence must be compared to a previous state of well-being; hence, he chooses to call Spain's problem "defectos de constitución." And yet, whether one opts for "decadence" or "defectos de constitución" as a description of the Spanish situation, the fact remains that "España se va deshaciendo, deshaciendo . . . Hoy ya es, más bien que un pueblo, la polvareda que queda cuando por la gran ruta histórica ha pasado galopando un gran pueblo."[18]

I do not intend to try to probe this question in all its ramifications, but merely to suggest that Ortega's remarks reveal, *inter alia*, an important fact about Spain: alienated by force and by choice from the rest of Europe, she has never conformed to the historical pattern of other Western European nations. As a result of this separation, an undue schism was created between the forces of tradition and those of progressive liberalism. The problem of the "two Spains" waxes hotter and hotter throughout the nineteenth century, and as the period draws to a close, it becomes evident that attempts to reconcile the opposing forces—there was, for example, a movement called *armonismo* which preceded the Revolution of 1868—[19] have failed.

The reestablishment of the Bourbon dynasty in the person of Alfonso XII under a constitutional monarchy in 1874 preserved only the mere façade of harmony between conservatives and liberals. Ortega y Gasset labeled the period of the Restoration "esa senilidad, esa desintegración fatal de los partidos vigentes, esa conducta de fantasmas que llevan los organismos de la España oficial frente a la nueva." A few lines later he continued: "La Restauración significa la *detención de la vida nacional*." And with the finality of the last act of a drama, he clinched his denunciation of the period with this: "Este vivir el hueco de la propia vida fue la Restauración."[20] The Restoration appeared as a theatrical contrivance not only to

18. *Ibid.*, 152–53, 70.
19. Donald L. Shaw, "Armonismo: The Failure of an Illusion," in Clara E. Lida and Iris M. Zavala (eds.), *La Revolución de 1868: Historia, pensamiento, literatura* (New York: Las Américas Publishing Company, 1970), 351–61.
20. José Ortega y Gasset, *Vieja y nueva política* (orig. pub. 1914; Madrid: Revista de Occidente, 1963), 31–33.

Ortega, but to the earlier generation of intellectuals such as Leopoldo Alas.

The problems of the Restoration period were multiple and longstanding. The historian Raymond Carr, in his analysis of nineteenth-century Spain, probes deeply into her political, economic, social, and religious difficulties, and points out how Spain, in the political sphere, was racked by electoral corruption, the hypocrisy of the *turno pacífico*, the abuses of *caciquismo*, and the weakness of over-centralization in a country composed mainly of impoverished *patrias chicas*, indifferent to, and ignorant of, the capital's powers and limitations.[21] The economic difficulties were rooted in Spain's poverty, characterized by undercapitalization, exploitation by foreign capital, and an agricultural economy which was plagued with rural overpopulation and the limited capacity of land development. Finally, the society itself was ideologically and religiously divided. Beneath the seeming placidity of the Restoration lurked the turmoil of a people internally at war with itself, a disquietude which surfaced in the acrimonious debates of Spanish intellectuals, in the anarcho-terrorist acts which occurred with increasing frequency by the turn of the century, in the violent anticlericalism and just as fanatical religiosity of the *beatas* and ultra-Catholics.

Many of Spain's difficulties can be traced to the fact that she was a backward country, a reality which makes her, in that respect, less unique than ardent Hispanists would have her be. Her backwardness was exacerbated by a strong sense of isolation from the rest of Europe and by the extremely divided character of her people, a condition born of the special circumstances of her history.

It is customary, though not accurate, to credit the Generation of 1898 with the discovery of Spain's decadence and the need for regeneration, but older members of the Restoration period were well aware of Spain's state of decay. Núñez de Arce, for example, in the preface to his *Gritos del combate* (1875), deplores the pitiful ruin which Spain has become: "Triste, desengañado y abatido, siento cierta especie de melancólico orgullo en mirar desde las regiones de

21. Raymond Carr, *Spain, 1801–1939* (London: Clarendon Press, 1966), Chs. 9–11.

la poesía, los desvaríos, las impurezas, el rebajamiento moral de esta época, tan exhausta de caracteres viriles como de virtudes cívicas." He then cites "el fango agitado de nuestras costumbres públicas" and the "grosero materialismo de nuestra Edad descreída."[22] These very points will be made likewise during the same decade about France by intellectuals as disparate as Ferdinand Brunetière and Émile Zola.

Indeed, Núñez de Arce embraces Spain and France together in a devastating criticism of both countries' decadence:

> Pueblos sin ideal, marchan al azar, haciendo siempre tentativas infructuosas, cambiando a cada instante de postura sin hallar ninguna que mitigue sus dolores, devorados por la fiebre, consumados por la impotencia, faltos de energía para salvarse, porque no tienen fe; sin resignación para sufrir su suerte, porque no tienen esperanza.[23]

The indecisiveness, lack of will power and faith, and general ambience of confusion and chaos enumerated here are characteristics which intellectuals in all parts of Western Europe would catalog in order to describe what they believed to be the malaise and state of eclipse of Western civilization. Zola's Rougon-Macquart series, for example, which is a denunciation of Napoleon III's Second Empire, of its corruption and moral laxity, contains in *Nana* (1880) a symbol of the monstrous putrefaction of French society embodied in the prostitute Nana herself, the "Golden Fly" who saps the energies of the rich and of the aristocrats and thus avenges herself and the poor.[24]

In addition to Núñez de Arce's condemnation of Spanish society, Benito Pérez Galdós contributed his share of criticism not only in his novels but in his essays and discourses. In his acceptance speech made to the Spanish Royal Academy, he noted that "las grandes y

22. Gaspar Núñez de Arce, "Prefacio," *Gritos del combate* (orig. pub. 1875; Madrid: Fernando Fe, 1914), 32–33.

23. *Ibid.*, 39.

24. See especially the final description of the rotting corpse of Nana, which is an almost operatic climax in the Wagnerian sense to the decline and fall of a putrescent civilization (*Nana*, Paris: Charpentier, 1928).

potentes energías de cohesión social no son ya lo que fueron," and he continued:

> Las disgregaciones de la vida política son el eco más próximo de ese terrible rompan filas que suena de un extremo a otro del ejército social, como voz de pánico que clama a la desbandada. Podría decirse que la sociedad llega a un punto de su camino en que se ve rodeada de ingentes rocas que le cierran el paso. Diversas grietas se abren en la dura y pavorosa peña, indicándonos senderos o salidas que tal vez nos conduzcan a regiones despejadas . . . [pero] los más sabios de entre nosotros se enredan en interminables controversias sobre cual pueda o deba ser la hendidura o pasadizo por el cual podremos salir de este hoyo pantanoso en que nos revolvemos y asfixiamos.[25]

Leopoldo Alas will sound the same note of pessimism in the face of the closed society of Restoration Spain.

The directionless and confused society which Núñez de Arce and Galdós depict points indirectly to a more profound problem: the difficulty of determining what a nation or a people's essence is. It is this problem of defining *lo español* which will preoccupy the Generation of 1898 and which older writers like Galdós, Núñez de Arce, and Alas also perceived. The attempt to describe the unique customs and characteristics of a people in the process of losing them (in which the early *costumbrista* writers were engaged) and the torment of a Larra who saw himself as a member of a "cuasi" nation are earlier manifestations of the same obsession.[26] The fear of *afrancesamiento* likewise indicates the depth of the Spaniard's uncertainty regarding his sense of identity.

This quest for identity is intimately linked to the question of Spain's historical decadence. In fact, almost all nineteenth-century Spain can be viewed from the perspective of an ever-increasing

---

25. Benito Pérez Galdós, "La sociedad presente como materia novelable," *Ensayos de crítica literaria* (orig. pub. 1897; Barcelona: Península, 1972), 177.

26. Thus, José F. Montesinos writes that one of the central themes of Spanish *costumbristas* is that "España comienza a dejar de ser" (*Introducción a una historia de la novela en España en el siglo XIX*, Madrid: Castalia, 1955, p. 122).

trend toward dissolution. Not only did the nation as a whole, its government and its policies, periodically fall apart but individuals did not cohere to the social body. The ripping apart of the social fabric implied isolationism among Spaniards themselves, or as Unamuno described his nineteenth-century countryman: "Vive cada uno solo entre los demás en un arenal yermo y desnudo, donde se revuelven pobres espíritus encerrados en dermatoesqueletos anémicos."[27] This isolation and solitude of the individual in Spain can be interpreted as a result of excessive pride and egoism, but it can also be seen as a fearful, protective reaction to the encroachments of others upon the individual's personality. All these difficulties point to a crisis in self. And, what is most interesting in Spain's nineteenth century is the fact that national decay and loss of national characteristics seem to go hand in hand with the loss of unity in the individual personality, a parallel downhill course toward degeneration and dissolution which can be observed in Leopoldo Alas' novels.

27. Miguel de Unamuno, "Sobre el marasmo actual de España," *En torno al casticismo* (Madrid: Espasa-Calpe, 1968), 140.

II *La Regenta*

It is not the purpose of this study to tie a neat label of "decadent" onto *La Regenta* (1884–1885) in the same fashion as one might easily dispose of *A Rebours* or *The Picture of Dorian Gray*. In the first place, the term *decadent*, as we have seen, is not an easily disposable item. And, in the second place, to call *La Regenta* a novel of decadence is not so much a definitive explanation as a modest endeavor to enlarge upon what is the essential theme and subject matter of the work, *i.e.*, decadence. By no means does one exhaust the thematic and stylistic range of *La Regenta* by so limiting and delineating the contours of a study such as this.

I should emphasize at this point that I shall be discussing decadence not only as a theme and unifying novelistic device but as a *fin de siècle* literary preoccupation which encompassed certain character types, motifs, and images. In his presentation of Spanish decadence—both collective and individual—Alas sometimes makes use of decadent types and allusions which appear in romantic and naturalistic writings and anticipate the full flowering of the decadent movement proper. These artifices do not predominate in *La Regenta* but, rather, complement a host of other thematic and stylistic devices which intensify the movement of decline and fall in the novel. I am not at all suggesting that *La Regenta* is an example of the aesthetic-decadent novelistic pattern; it obviously conforms in large part to the realist tradition, but its author does resort to a number of decadent expressions common to the period of the 1880s. The recourse to decadent types and situations is greatly intensified and expanded in *Su único hijo* while in *La Regenta* their appearance can probably be described as a fortuitous supplement to the general delineation of the theme of decadence. For this, after all, is the substance of *La Regenta*: a novel which depicts through the decline and fall of an individual the profound pervasiveness of evil and decay in Spanish Restoration society.

Decadence as a social-moral-political manifestation and decadence as a literary expression in *La Regenta* will frequently merge and be extremely difficult if not impossible to distinguish. This is another way of stating that "forme et fond" then achieve an artistic oneness in the novel. Indeed, no higher compliment of the aesthetic realization of *La Regenta* could be devised than to declare its structural integrity and unity.

How then, does Alas express the theme of decadence in *La Regenta?* What, first of all, is represented as in a state of decline and from what former position of glory and power has it slipped? Decadence implies a contrast between two distinct modes of existence, between a positive past and a negative present. The key word here is *contrast*: much of *La Regenta*'s composition is built on either an implicit or explicit contrast between what was and what is, between a higher form and a lower form of existence.

One of Alas' most effective and often subtle literary treatments is what can be called the mirror technique of reverberation and reflection. I mean that the novel teems with the techniques of allusion, contrast, satire, and parody, devices by which the author can demonstrate how Restoration society is a degenerate form of life in comparison to Spain's past. (That the Hispanic past was in all likelihood no utopian scheme is irrelevant; that it appeared glorious and, at any event, better than the present, is the point at issue.) Clarín is adept at creating echoes, reverberations of past modes, lifestyles, religious attitudes, and literary movements in the inauthentic posturing of contemporary Vetustans. The characters' romantic attitudinizing, for example, is precisely that: an awkward, utterly false imitation of the true romantic. Religious endeavors to approach the mystical state of perfection betray either an evident self-consciousness, a none too subtle hypocrisy, or sexual overtones. All attempts at re-creating the Spanish past—its religious fervor, mysticism, literary glories, *etc.*—result in gross distortions, the deformed images of twisted fun-house mirrors. There is an acrid strain of grotesquerie, of ridiculousness (often derisive, sometimes pathetic, and even bathetic) in the allusive, satiric, and parodic intent of Alas. Indeed, it is this harsh, mocking approach which precludes tragedy in *La Regenta*, though not the makings of it. Without Alas' pervasive irony and habit of picking away at and tearing down his characters' pretensions, much of Ana Ozores' predicament, for example, could be seen in a tragic light.

In this frequently brutal treatment of contemporary Spanish reality, two subject areas most thoroughly covered are: literature, in particular romanticism; and religion. The two elements, in fact, are often cleverly woven together to produce a devastating attack on Vetustan inauthenticity. An example of the interpenetration of religion and literature is found in the first chapter of *La Regenta*. Indeed, Chapter 1 serves as a useful illustration not only of the decay of Spanish religiosity but of the decline of Spanish society as a whole. Furthermore, it contains good examples of Alas' techniques of allusion and contrast, description and satire. In brief, one might almost call this introduction to the Vetustan universe a compendium of Alas' presentation of decay in Restoration society.

An Approach to La Regenta: *The First Chapter*

How does Chapter 1 begin? Vetusta is presented in a quiescent state of drowsiness; she is, in short, sleeping off the effects of gastronomical incursions. The city is dormant: "La heroica ciudad dormía la siesta." The juxtaposition of the adjective "heroica" with the phrase "dormía la siesta" ironically demonstrates the gap between reality and illusion. The only activity discernible in the perhaps once heroic city's landscape is the lazy movement of the clouds and the rustling of bits of dust, old rags, papers, and other debris in the deserted streets:

> El viento Sur, caliente y perezoso, empujaba las nubes blanquecinas que se rasgaban al correr hacia el Norte. En las calles no había más ruido que el rumor estridente de los remolinos de polvo, trapos, pajas y papeles, que iban de arroyo en arroyo, de acera en acera, de esquina en esquina revolando y persiguiéndose, como mariposas que se buscan y huyen y que el aire envuelve en sus pliegues in-

visibles. Cual turbas de pilluelos, aquellas migajas de la basura, aquellas sobras de todo se juntaban en un montón, parábanse como dormidas un momento y brincaban de nuevo sobresaltadas, dispersándose, trepando unas por las paredes hasta los cristales temblorosos de los faroles, otras hasta los carteles de papel mal pegados a las esquinas, y había pluma que llegaba a un tercer piso, y arenilla que se incrustaba para días, o para años, en la vidriera de un escaparate, agarrada a un plomo.[1]

In this first paragraph the author brings out two points of interest for the description of the Vetustan milieu: the sense of inaction; and the impression of abandonment, of relinquishing the stage to the mere rubbish of history. The passivity of the town is accentuated by this human desertion: nothing is visible but the remains of things, the debris of human experience. Clarín has succeeded in creating in the very first paragraph the moral landscape of Vetusta, the mood of stagnation and surrender to the worthless elements in life.

To strengthen and clarify the purpose of the first paragraph Alas introduces in the second the historical contrast between contemporary Vetusta and the Vetusta of the distant past:

Vetusta, la muy noble y leal ciudad, corte en lejano siglo, hacía la digestión del cocido y de la olla podrida, y descansaba oyendo entre sueños el monótono y familiar zumbido de la campana de coro, que retumbaba allá en lo alto de la esbelta torre en la Santa Basílica. (p. 71)

Here, the ironic opposition between a noble past, left chronologically imprecise, and a base present interested only in digestion and sleep is quite clear as the moral implication of decay seen in the introductory paragraph crystallizes in the second.

After carefully establishing the moral circumference of the Vetustan milieu, Alas proceeds to describe in the second paragraph the one object of sublime majesty which remains of the city's aureate past: the tower of the cathedral. Alas' own latent romanticism surfaces in one of the few passages of authentic lyricism untinged by

1. Leopoldo Alas, *La Regenta*, ed. Gonzalo Sobejano (Barcelona: Noguer, 1976), 71. All subsequent quotations are taken from this edition and will be cited hereafter in the text.

ironic nuance: "La torre de la catedral, poema romántico de piedra, delicado himno, de dulces líneas de belleza, muda y perenne, era obra del siglo dieciséis" (p. 71). Then, in a play of opposites he describes the tower: "Mejor era contemplarla en clara noche de luna, resaltando en un cielo puro, rodeada de estrellas que parecían su aureola, doblándose en pliegues de luz y sombra, fantasma gigante que velaba por la ciudad pequeña y negruzca que dormía a sus pies" (p. 72). The antithesis of light and shadow, giant (the tower) and pigmy (the city), is characteristic of one of Alas' favorite romantic writers: Victor Hugo.[2] A perusal of Hugo's *Notre-Dame de Paris* (1831; 1832, definitive edition) reveals a number of similarities and parallels, as well as obvious differences in style and structure, with *La Regenta*: notably, the description and significance of the cathedral and its tower, the contrast between the grotesque and the sublime, and the presence of the priest figure.

For Alas the cathedral tower is a "poema romántico de piedra, delicado himno" just as for Victor Hugo Notre-Dame de Paris is a "vaste symphonie en pierre." Both novelists also see the symbol of the Faith as a giant dominating the city environs: there is indeed something monstrous visible in the majestic and massive proportions of these cathedrals. Clarín calls his tower a "fantasma gigante"; Hugo sees Notre-Dame as a two-headed sphinx and even as a prodigious elephant. Both writers also emphasize the antithesis of shadow and light which hover about the cathedrals in *tenebrista* fashion. Alas' "pliegues de luz y sombra" are an echo of Notre-Dame's black silhouette cutting across a starry heaven or of the dramatic brilliance of the rosette flashing amidst the obscurity of the naves and arches.[3]

But the resemblance ends there. In the French poet-novelist's work the cathedral of Notre-Dame takes on the grandiose and gi-

2. Clarín considered Victor Hugo as one of his "padres del espíritu" ("Camus," *Obras selectas*, Madrid: Biblioteca Nueva, 1966, p. 1126); and in a letter dated December 5, 1887, he writes to Galdós: "Tengo en mi cuarto de trabajo a mi poeta favorito, Víctor Hugo" (*Cartas a Galdós*, ed. Soledad Ortega, Madrid: Revista de Occidente, 1964, p. 245).

3. Victor Hugo, *Notre-Dame de Paris* (Paris: Garnier-Flammarion, 1967), 197, 275, 379.

gantic proportions of a figure out of a primitive epic myth. Indeed, not only the cathedral but nearly all the characters and Paris itself are depicted as larger than life; they are endowed with that romantic exuberance for which Victor Hugo is well known. The novelist immerses himself and the reader in the very heart of the Middle Ages: the enveloping puissance of the Church.

In contrast to Hugo's vigorous and deliberate reconstruction of a distant past, Alas adheres to the present. The past, however, consistently intrudes as a subtle and sometimes not so subtle reminder of what was once the splendor of imperial Spain. The cathedral tower functions in this manner, and yet at the same time it is not a dead vestige of another century; it is the symbol of a still potent force within Spanish society. This power is at first only implied in the poetic image of the spiritual but massive spire of the cathedral which dominates the rest of the city. As the novel advances, the very secular and corrupt grip which the clergy exercises over the congregation becomes evident.

The architectural sublimity of the spire suffers a strong contrastive shock in *La Regenta* in the abrupt presentation of the church bell-ringer and acolyte, Bismarck and Celedonio. The grotesque element now comes into play and effectively extinguishes the delicate lyric overtures and, in fact, one could say that henceforth it will be the grotesque, the grossly realistic, which predominates in the rest of *La Regenta*.

The introduction of the grotesque in these first pages is yet another reverberation of Hugoesque romantic realism. In his "Préface de Cromwell," in which he discusses the role of the grotesque in modern times, Hugo declares that the grotesque now predominates over the sublime.[4] Although he gives no precise definition of *grotesque*, he does apply the word to that which is ridiculous, comic, deformed, ugly physically and morally, strange, or monstrous. The best example of grotesqueness in Hugo's work is, of course, Quasimodo. It is Quasimodo who in his physical ugliness and malicious ignorance presents a striking contrast to the sublimity of Notre-

4. Victor Hugo, *Cromwell* (Paris: Garnier-Flammarion, 1968), 75.

Dame de Paris. Hugo likens the hunchback to a "reptile naturel de cette dalle humide et sombre" and, more specifically, to a lizard. The novelist consistently applies animal images to Quasimodo: he is, for example, a monkey and a chamois; and in another instance he approaches the monstrous being described as a bizarre centaur, half man, half bell.[5]

The function of the grotesque in the opening scenes of *La Regenta* is delegated to Bismarck and Celedonio. Bismarck's very name is resonant with ironic connotations: he is an "illustrious delinquent" ("un pillo ilustre") who in the cathedral adulates the acolyte Celedonio and in the street bullies him. Celedonio calls him a "mainate," a "bobo"; it is interesting to note that the term *mainate* also signifies magnate, or the "powers that be" in Vetusta. In fact, Bismarck, of a cheerful character actually, is quite leery and fearful of the "mainates," in particular, of Fermín de Pas, the magistral. Thus, Bismarck is a cowardly and none too intelligent bullying and droll rascal who offers a somewhat comic aspect to the reader. Clarín, in addition, dehumanizes this secondary character by comparing him to a clock: "Cuando *posaba* para la hora del coro . . . sentía en sí algo de la dignidad y la responsabilidad de un reloj" (p. 73).

With the arrival of Celedonio the mood and tone change, as Clarín immediately associates the acolyte with something unclean. His cassock is dirty and threadbare; from the heights of the cathedral, he spits with contempt upon the square below and sometimes throws small stones at occasional pedestrians, but when he assumes the beatific expression of the priest, Celedonio is at his worst. His hypocritical attitude of official piety appears grotesque and nauseating to Clarín. Celedonio's "cara de chato" assumes an affected and artificial air which, far from seeming humble, gives an "intención lúbrica y cínica a su mirada, como una meretriz de calleja, que anuncia su triste comercio con los ojos, sin que la policía pueda reivindicar los derechos de la moral pública" (p. 77). The parodistic imitation of the servant only emphasizes the unnatural character of Celedonio. Clarín takes this artificial nature a step further and predicts Cele-

5. Hugo, *Notre-Dame*, 171, 172, 176.

donio's future sexual proclivities, a description which for its day and for Spanish realism is most audacious in its morbidity and sexual frankness:

> Así como en las mujeres de su edad se anuncian por asomos de contornos turgentes las elegantes líneas del sexo, en el acólito sin órdenes se podía adivinar futura y próxima perversión de instintos naturales provocada ya por aberraciones de una educación torcida. Cuando quería imitar, bajo la sotana manchada de cera, los acompasados y ondulantes movimientos de don Anacleto, familiar del Obispo . . . Celedonio se movía y gesticulaba como hembra desfachatada, sirena de cuartel. (p. 77)

Thus in Celedonio's case the grotesque becomes the sexually perverted, an example of latent homosexuality. Because of his essentially optimistic romanticism, Victor Hugo does not stress sexual perversion as one more aspect of the grotesque side of nature, for Quasimodo, though unnatural in his physical deformity, does not possess a perverted soul. In contrast, Celedonio, an unclean and effeminate hypocrite, reflects the later European preoccupation with decadence—to be more precise, with the decadent motif of unnatural love and sexual abnormalities. Nineteenth-century French literature abounds with examples of the "love that dare not speak its name": from Gautier's *Mademoiselle de Maupin* and Balzac's *La Fille aux yeux d'or* to Baudelaire's "Femmes damnées" and Huysmans' *A Rebours*, with later manifestations in Verlaine, Rachilde, Jean Lorrain, Péladan, and Mirbeau. Spanish literature contemporary with Clarín, however, displays more discretion in such matters; while neurotics and madmen are not unheard of,[6] the presentation

6. For examples: Galdós' *La desheredada, Lo prohibido, La familia de León Roch,* and *Ángel Guerra.* Next to Clarín, Valle-Inclán comes closest perhaps to the French morbid delectation in the perverse. In his *Sonatas* (1901–1905), he dallies suggestively with the idea of incest and even necrophilia, but these are essentially provocative hints. The Marqués de Bradomín is a womanizer with no real interest in homosexual love, although he does not object to it on moral grounds: "Aquel bello pecado, regalo de los dioses y tentación de los poetas, es para mí un fruto hermético. El cielo, siempre enemigo, dispuso que sólo las rosas de Venus floreciesen en mi alma y, a medida que envejezco, eso me desconsuela más."

of sexually abnormal types is considered a breach of good taste. Even though Celedonio is but a secondary character, his role will become significant in the final scene of the novel in which he plants a cold and viscous kiss on the insensible Ana's lips.

Celedonio, it should be noted, is not an exception in *La Regenta*. Clarín implies sexual deviations, mostly latent, in a number of secondary characters. Paco Vegallana, for example, is also described as effeminate but, contrary to the acolyte's physically womanish cast, his unmanliness is of the soul:

> La fantasía de Paco, sus costumbres, la especial perversión de su sentido moral le hacían afeminado en el alma en el sentido de parecerse a tantas y tantas señoras y señoritas, sin malos humores, ociosas, de buen diente, criadas en el ocio y el regalo, en medio del vicio fácil y corriente. (p. 238)

Effeminacy is insinuated in the numerous priests who glide in and out of the Vetustan scenario. De Pas, frustrated by the confining role of the priesthood, inwardly criticizes the sacerdotal costume which feminizes the priests (p. 438). And Don Álvaro, envious of the influence the clergy exercises over the female population, imagines the three most elegant priests as a trio of beautiful nuns who could easily attract the opposite sex. Álvaro interprets the admiring glances of the women toward the three handsome priests as "declaraciones inconscientes de la lascivia refinada y contrahecha" (p. 609).

Secondary female characters are not exempt either from Alas' prying into their unnatural souls. Early in the novel, the minor character Camila, Ana's English governess, is depicted as possessing the countenance of an "anafrodita." Giving the impression of a sexless creature, her ruling passion is, nevertheless, lechery; but, writes

---

Presiento que debe ser grato, cuando la vida declina, poder penetrar en el jardín de los amores perversos. A mí, desgraciadamente, ni aún me queda la esperanza" (*Sonata de estío, Sonatas,* New York: Las Américas Publishing Company, 1961, p. 98). And in the *Sonata de otoño,* the Marqués declares that "bien sabe Dios que la perversidad, esa rosa sangrienta, es una flor que nunca se abrió en mis amores. Yo he preferido siempre ser el Marqués de Bradomín a ser ese divino Marqués de Sade" (p. 143).

Clarín, "La lujuria, satisfecha a la inglesa: una lujuria que pudiera llamarse metodista si no fuera una profanación" (p. 150). *Marimachos* can be found in the figures of Doña Paula (de Pas's mother) and the *beata* Doña Petronila. Doña Paula, who dominates the magistral, is almost as tall as her son, broader in the shoulders than de Pas, and smokes, though only in private. Doña Petronila, who possesses the head of a corpulent friar, is nicknamed "el gran Constantino." Finally, latent lesbianism is perceived in Obdulia Fandiño's lustful attitude toward the spectacle of Ana's Nazarene: "Sentía Obdulia en aquel momento así . . . un deseo vago . . . de . . . de . . . ser hombre" (p. 778).

Returning now to Celedonio and Bismarck, one can state that the two function in ironically parodistic fashion as servants to the master de Pas, that they are grimmer versions of the Siglo de Oro valets. Just as the *gracioso* has his little love affair which runs parallel to the nobleman's, so Celedonio attempts to ape de Pas's amorous activities, except that in this instance he kisses the mistress, not the maid. The result is a perversion of the *gracioso*'s role. It is also interesting to note that Hugo included the *gracioso* as an example of "le grotesque."[7]

The subordinate, often mimetic position in which Celedonio and, to a lesser degree, Bismarck stand before the magistral runs parallel to Quasimodo's association with the priest figure, Claude Frollo. The function of the bell-ringer is shared by Bismarck and the hunchback. But the more significant relationship resides in the pair Celedonio/Quasimodo–de Pas/Frollo. Here, as already noted, Celedonio attains what de Pas has been denied: to kiss Ana Ozores. In this situation, greatly perverted and modified, Alas reproduces the Quasimodo-Frollo-Esmeralda triangle. In Hugo's novel, it is Frollo who plants upon the unconscious Esmeralda a burning kiss, but it is Quasimodo who ultimately triumphs, though in true romantic irony only by passing through the agony of death. In the final chapter entitled "Mariage de Quasimodo," two skeletons (Esmeralda and Quasimodo) are engaged in an eternal embrace and

7. Hugo, *Cromwell*, 74.

"quand on voulut le [Q.] détacher du squelette qu'il embrassait, il tomba en poussière." [8]

In the final scene of *La Regenta*, Celedonio's venture into heterosexual experience echoes Frollo's kiss. Although Celedonio's lips are described as viscous and cold and, in contrast, Frollo's are burning, the physical contact for both Esmeralda and Ana is an abhorrent sensation. The acolyte's gesture is, in addition, a twisted parody of the final scene in *Notre-Dame de Paris*. There is something of the sublime in the grotesque ending of Hugo's novel because there is something of the sublime in Quasimodo's soul. Hugo was obviously drawing on the universal appeal of the beauty and the beast fable when he depicted scenes of Quasimodo's tender and pathetic protectiveness toward the defenseless Esmeralda. The intent was simple: to indicate the naissant beauty of Quasimodo's inner being.

The situation is completely perverted in *La Regenta*. Here, Celedonio's soul is as filthy and abnormal as his cassock and effeminate bearing; and the kiss, which implies the momentary triumph of the subordinate over the master and of the latent heterosexual over the homosexual drive, destroys any vestige of Ana Ozores' romantic, idealizing soul. Romantic love is dead while the grotesque gloats and smirks. Even the status of pariah that both sets of characters share is distorted in *La Regenta*: the will-o'-the-wisp Esmeralda is outcast from society for her gypsy style of life; Quasimodo for his physical deformities. But both Celedonio and Ana are outsiders for a far more ignoble reason: their sexual proclivities. He is cut off from normal society for his homosexuality while Ana is scorned for her adulterous misadventure.

After delineating the character of the two grotesques, Alas proceeds to give his first and longest description of the priest, the magistral Fermín de Pas, master of the two *graciosos*. It is the portrait of a corrupt and powerful man. And yet the first two notes struck prior to the lengthy descriptive passage present a somewhat different picture. We see de Pas first through Celedonio's eyes and next through Bismarck's. Arrogantly looking through the window, Cele-

8. Hugo, *Notre-Dame*, 509.

donio spots de Pas down below in the street, and he seems the size of a black beetle ("un escarabajo"); in this gesture of contemptuous disdain, Celedonio is actually imitating an attitude which is characteristic of de Pas himself when, from the tower, he stares down upon the tiny human figures below ("También él [de Pas] veía a los vetustenses como escarabajos," p. 82).[9]

Bismarck, on the other hand, sees only the underskirts of the priest ("los bajos"); it is a lowly view which is appropriate to the menial position that Bismarck holds in church affairs. He notices that the priest's feet are as dainty as a lady's and that his shoes, though simple in style, are of exquisite workmanship and elegant appearance. These seemingly trivial details that Alas inserts throughout the novel are indicators of character. In public, de Pas is a dandy in dress, as much as he is able to be given the severe restrictions of his vocation. The dainty feet may seem at first misleading; one might jump to conclusions and think that de Pas too is effeminate and weak. Not so. Clarín frequently alludes to a certain feminine quality inherent in ecclesiastical garb. The swaying, sometimes mincing walk and the swishing robes of the priest suggest slyness and cant, apparently "feminine" qualities. The priests, however, are not depicted as weaklings; on the contrary, they wield a corrosive influence upon the secular branch of society. Their effeminate qualities imply a subtle corruption in morality but no draining of power.

Clarín now moves on to an analysis of de Pas's remarkable face:

> Si los pilletes hubieran osado mirar cara a cara a don Fermín, le hubieran visto, al asomarse en el campanario, serio, cejijunto; al notar la presencia de los campaneros levemente turbado, y en seguida sonriente, con una suavidad resbaladiza en la mirada y una bondad estereotipada en los labios. Tenía razón el delantero. De Pas no se pintaba. Más bien parecía estucado. En efecto, su tez

9. Later, Celedonio also mimics de Pas's viewing of Vetusta through a telescope ("El acólito, de puntillas, sin hacer ruido, se había acercado por detrás al Provisor y procuraba seguir la dirección del catalejo," p. 79). Quasimodo, likewise, reproduces Claude Frollo's intent gazing from the tower upon the dancing Esmeralda ("[Frollo] vit Quasimodo qui, penché à une ouverture de ces auvents d'ardoises qui ressemblent à d'énormes jalousies, regardait aussi lui, dans la place," p. 274).

blanca tenía los reflejos del estuco. En los pómulos, un tanto avanzados, bastante para dar energía y expresión característica al rostro, sin afearlo, había un ligero encarnado que a veces tiraba al color del alzacuello y de las medias. No era pintura, ni el color de la salud, ni pregonero del alcohol; era el rojo que brota en las mejillas al calor de palabras de amor o de vergüenza que se pronuncian cerca de ellas, palabras que parecen imanes que atraen el hierro de la sangre. Esta especie de congestión también la causa el orgasmo de pensamientos del mismo estilo. En los ojos del Magistral, verdes con pintas que parecían polvo de rapé, lo más notable era la suavidad de liquen; pero en ocasiones, de en medio de aquella crasitud pegajosa salía un resplandor punzante, que era una sorpresa desagradable, como una aguja en una almohada de plumas. Aquella mirada la resistían pocos; a unos les daba miedo, a otros asco; pero cuando algún audaz la sufría, el Magistral la humillaba cubriéndola con el telón carnoso de unos párpados anchos, gruesos, insignificantes, como es siempre la carne informe. La nariz larga, recta, sin corrección ni dignidad, también era sobrada de carne hacia el extremo y se inclinaba como árbol bajo el peso de excesivo fruto. Aquella nariz era la obra muerta en aquel rostro todo expresión, aunque escrito en griego, porque no era fácil leer y traducir lo que el Magistral sentía y pensaba. Los labios largos y delgados, finos, pálidos, parecían obligados a vivir comprimidos por la barba que tendía a subir, amenazando para la vejez, aun lejana, entablar relaciones con la punta de la nariz claudicante. Por entonces no daba al rostro este defecto apariencias de vejez, sino· expresión de prudencia de la que toca en cobarde hipocresía y anuncia frío y calculador egoísmo. . . . La cabeza pequeña y bien formada . . . descansaba sobre un robusto cuello, blanco, de recios músculos, un cuello de atleta, proporcionado al tronco y extremidades del fornido canónigo. (pp. 78–79)

A number of features in this masterful description contribute to the overwhelming impression of unnaturalness and corruption in a powerful but evil nature: 1) the whitewashed or stucco effect of the complexion; 2) the lewd, congested redness of the cheeks; 3) the green, snuff-flecked lichen eyes; and 4) the fleshiness of the eyelids and nose.

Unnatural pallor in diabolical and/or neurotic protagonists (male

or female) is a device used in both romantic and decadent literature. Deriving in part from such Gothic types as Mrs. Radcliffe's
Schedoni of *The Italian* (1797), Byron's Corsair and Giaour are
good examples of the pale satanic hero who would proliferate in
romantic literature. As the century wore on, the Byronic hero gave
way to a far more depraved, definitely unheroic protagonist. Vestiges of the Byronic hero remain in Barbey d'Aurevilly's character
M. de Mesnilgrand in "À un Dîner d'athées" (*Les Diaboliques*,
1874); and in the monomaniacal baron Saturne of Villiers de l'Isle-
Adam (*Contes cruels*, 1883), but at the height of the obsession
with decadent themes and subjects, the 1880s, the heroic, passionate pallor of the Byronic type has become the anemic lackluster of a
des Esseintes (*A Rebours*). One critic described the decadent type
as "fatally pale, disquietingly pale." [10] This bloodless visage reflects
a corruption which supposedly has penetrated to the very marrow,
the very soul of the protagonist. At the same time, however, his
paleness reveals a vague yearning for an unexpressed ideal, something which refutes the rank materialism of the age. Pallor, then, is
soul, spirituality.

Where does Fermín de Pas's pasty, stuccoed visage fit into all
this? As in Barbey d'Aurevilly, Alas also appears to incorporate a
trait or two of the Byronic satanical hero (and of Lewis' *The
Monk*). De Pas *is* evil. An aura of diabolical mystery cloaks his
person; but he inspires fear and aversion in most of his parishioners
and colleagues, not admiration. There is no heroic grandeur in his
satanical nature. His cruelty is founded on a hypocritical and supremely egotistical character.

Clarín also indicates a certain inclination in de Pas toward the
perverse, toward the sexually corrupt. His face *appears* cosmetically
artificial. The contrast between the unnatural pallor and the lewdly
red cheeks comes very close to the decadent's fascination with cosmetics and with the artificial in general. Originating in Baudelaire's
"Éloge du maquillage" (1863) and Gautier's "Notice" (1868),
the heavy use of cosmetics in both men and women is seen, for ex-

10. G. L. Van Roosbroeck, *The Legend of the Decadents* (New York:
Institut des Études Françaises, Columbia University, 1927), 1.

ample, in Mallarmé's *Hérodiade*, Zola's *Nana*, Bourges' *Le Crépus-cule des dieux*, and Huysmans' *A Rebours*. The use of cosmetics is identified, in the nineteenth century, with decadence. Even the mere suggestion of painting his face stains de Pas's nature with a tint of perversion. Thus, the priest shares with the decadent type of the 1880s the unnatural countenance which suggests evil and corruption. De Pas does not, however, participate in the least in the pale soul's search for the ideal.[11]

The stamp of deep corruption and evil is further accentuated by de Pas's eyes. First, they are green. Green eyes, as Mario Praz points out, are frequently to be found in sadistic characters of popular romantic literature.[12] Some of Barbey d'Aurevilly's characters in *Les Diaboliques* also have green eyes: the violent Major Ydow in "À un Dîner d'athées" and the murderess the Comtesse de Stasseville in "Le Dessous de cartes d'une partie de whist." The device of green eyes as indicators of cruelty and sadism continues to the end of the century in such literary trash as Octave Mirbeau's *Le Jardin des supplices* (1899). Fermín's eyes are another example of the literary tradition of green-eyed characters of sadistic and cruel inclination, as is borne out in the rest of *La Regenta*.

The green malevolence of the eyes is further stressed by the allusions to the snuff-like flecks and the lichenous quality of the priest's eyes. The snuff image is another instance of the deliberate insertion of the artificial as a delineator of de Pas's character. Here Alas is making a subtle association of one of civilization's peccadilloes, snuff, with the suggestion of corruption and unnaturalness. This is

11. Pallor as a sign of spirituality is especially marked in the paintings of the Pre-Raphaelites Burne-Jones and Dante Gabriel Rossetti, who inspired the later decadent painters Gustave Moreau, Fernand Khnopff, and Jean Delville. See Philippe Jullian's *Dreamers of Decadence: Symbolist Painters of the 1890's* (New York: Praeger Publishers, 1974).

12. Mario Praz, *The Romantic Agony* (New York: World Publishing Co,. 1968), 313. In addition, green, besides being naturally linked with vegetation (see, for example, Verlaine's "Green," in *Romances sans paroles*), is associated with the idea of death and lividness (J. E. Cirlot, *Dictionary of Symbols*, New York: Philosophical Library, 1962, p. 51). The decadent predilection for the color green, especially in Oscar Wilde, is parodied in Robert Hichen's *The Green Carnation* (1894).

one example of how drugs, alcohol, and tobacco, as artificial and corrupting products of civilization, made possible the identification of civilization with decadence in the nineteenth century.

The final interpolation of the lichen image is the culmination of the descriptive chain green-snuff-lichen. Lichen is an extremely unattractive flowerless plant, composed of a symbiotic relationship between an alga and a fungus, which grows on bare rocks, tree stumps, and waste places and which produces an acid that softens soil and dissolves rock. Lichen is also any of several skin diseases characterized by an eruption of flat papules, which, in *Lichen Planus*, are covered by a horny glazed film. There is, in addition, a *lichen green* which is a light greenish gray. Lichen, then, summons up images of the loathsome, deformed, and monstrous. It is a "flower of evil."

The Baudelairean metaphor of the "fleurs du mal" attains new heights in the decadent novel *A Rebours*. Chapter 8 contains the horticulturist's dream of monstrous tropical plants which are so deformed and unnatural in appearance that they seem more artificial than fake flowers themselves, the precise effect which des Esseintes desired. The image of the garden of evil appears even earlier in Zola's *La Curée*. Here again, monstrous tropical plants growing profusely and luxuriantly in a hothouse are described in detail but with a different intent in mind. While Huysmans, without denying the obvious sexual connotations of such flowers, links disease (especially syphilis and smallpox) with the deformed and ugly plants, Zola stresses the sensual and heady atmosphere of the conservatory. In other words, with characteristically Zolaesque hyperbole, he exploits scenes of sexual depravity amidst a heavy and sinister tropical setting. In brief, plants that deviate from the natural are associated with the artificial, the diseased, and the sexually corrupt.

Clarín's use of the lichen image, then, is fraught with suggestive meanings. Cruelty and repressed sexuality in de Pas have already been noted in the green eyes and the contrasting white-red of the complexion. The artificial is expressed in the cosmetic appearance of the face and the image of the snuff-flecked eyes. The "suavidad de liquen" in Fermín's eyes, with its suggestions of depravity and deformity, further accentuates the implied diseased nature of the priest.

That de Pas has a cruel nature is manifestly proven in the dense pages of *La Regenta*. Revengeful and calculating, he machinates the downfall of his enemies, whether clerical or secular. In the grip of an overwhelming jealous rage, he vindictively helps to crush the object of his sexual desires, Ana Ozores. Much of de Pas's cruelty originates either in frustrated ambition or thwarted sexual experiences. The first restraint results in a crafty hypocrisy; both the first and the second in a sadomasochistic view of himself and the universe. At bottom, de Pas's sense of superiority in himself rests on a rather shaky foundation of insecurity and an inferiority complex.[13] The feeling of not having accomplished his highest ambitions of power and prestige, of being under the heel of his domineering mother, of being imprisoned in his ecclesiastical robes, all these impressions of failure and mediocrity foster the priest's cruelty. Self-castigation is externally transmuted into the punishment of others; but this play of superiority-inferiority in Fermín's nature remains an enigma in this first description. We only perceive from the initial portrait the almost cowardly cruelty of a mysterious, diabolically powerful priest. We do not know at this point why he is so.

Undoubtedly, Alas' portrait of de Pas also derives from the Spanish realistic tradition. The fleshy nose and eyelids which contribute their share to the image of corruption reflect the earthy quality of Spanish realism. The hyperbolic description of the priest's nose inevitably brings to mind the incomparable "archinariz" of Quevedo from his sonnet, "A un hombre de gran nariz." [14] Clarín's satirical bent well matches Quevedo's in this instance. The limitations of this essay, however, preclude any lengthy investigation of Alas' work as seen in the light of Spanish realism.

13. In one scene of self-contempt, Fermín's inner monologue culminates in these words: "Y las propias habilidades ¡qué ruines, qué prosaicas! Su carácter fuerte y dominante ¡qué ridículo en el fondo! '¿A quién dominaba él? ¡A escarabajos!' " (p. 381).

14. Francisco de Quevedo, *Obras completas* (Barcelona: Planeta, 1968), I, 546.

Before concluding the study of this passage from Chapter 1, a glance at another description of Fermín from the same chapter confirms and reinforces the impression of corruption and artificiality in the priest protagonist:

> El manteo que el canónigo movía con un ritmo de pasos y suave contoneo iba tomando en sus anchos pliegues, al flotar casi al ras del pavimento, tornasoles de plumas de faisán, y otras veces parecía cola de pavo real; algunas franjas de luz trepaban hasta el rostro del Magistral y ora lo teñían con un verde pálido blanquecino, como de planta sombría, ora le daban viscosa apariencia de planta submarina, ora la palidez de un cadáver. (pp. 92–93)

The first sentence stresses the dandyesque element of de Pas's nature, of necessity essentially sober and restrained, recalling the austere, British style of dress which Charles Baudelaire adopted. The emphasis on elegance in dress is another sign of the artificial in Fermín. And, as A. E. Carter demonstrates in *The Idea of Decadence in French Literature*, "artificiality, in fact, is the chief characteristic of decadence as the nineteenth century understood the word."[15]

The second sentence of this passage condenses in a striking image what Alas' introductory page-long description subtly implied: the identification of the priest with a "flower of evil." The inconstant light flickering on Fermín's face creates a watery effect, giving him first the lichen-green tint of a lustreless plant, then the viscous appearance of an aquatic organism, and finally the pallor of a corpse.[16] These are flowerless plants, which suggest sterility, disease, and culminate in death. The sickly greenish hue that hovers over de Pas's features is a mark of his unredeemed, corrupt nature which bears no seeds but fruits of evil.

This discussion began by drawing a parallel between Victor Hugo's *Notre-Dame de Paris* and Alas' novel, noting the dominating presence of the church architecture (the sublime) and the entrance of the acolyte and bell-ringer (the grotesque). The third ele-

15. A. E. Carter, *The Idea of Decadence in French Literature, 1830–1900* (Toronto: University of Toronto Press, 1958), 25.

16. The words *viscoso*, *submarino*, and *cadáver* function as leitmotifs throughout *La Regenta*.

ment of comparison is the priest figure (Fermín de Pas and Claude Frollo).[17] Although both priests are filled with sexual longings which ultimately lead to a catastrophic ending, Frollo's essentially austere and intellectual nature, which includes a generous share of compassion for his younger brother and Quasimodo, contrasts strongly with de Pas's baser ambitions and sexuality. The strong moral conflict in Frollo is lacking in de Pas. One can say that the difference between the two men points to the larger difference between romanticism and realism. In his description of Frollo's fall from grace, Hugo, in a characteristic hyperbolic outburst, magnifies the diabolical, inhuman qualities of the priest figure. De Pas, though supremely evil and also diabolical, is far more depraved than Frollo; his inhumanness reduces him. The evil is no less intense, but it is compressed within the less noble confines of a more calculating and hypocritical nature.

Pedro Penzol has already pointed out the similar stance of superiority and aloofness which both de Pas and Frollo assume before the world.[18] This attitude is dramatically visualized in the view from the cathedral tower which the two priests enjoy. Each is seen in a remote and physically domineering stance which represents his position in society. The priest is simultaneously, then, a part of society as one of its leaders and separated from it by virtue of his power and superiority. Neither the enormous influence that the Church exercised in the Middle Ages nor the political and spiritual authority that Frollo evidently possesses interests the archdeacon at the moment in which all of Paris lies at his feet. Staring fixedly down from the heights of the cathedral tower upon the square below, Frollo's vision narrows until it focuses upon one figure alone, the dancing

17. Pedro Penzol in his "Parentescos" (*Archivum*, II, 1952, pp. 421–26) discusses the proliferation of the priest figure, especially the adulterous type, in nineteenth-century literature (Hugo's *Notre-Dame*, 1832; Zola's *La Faute de l'abbé Mouret*, 1875; Eça de Queiroz's *O Crime do Padre Amaro*, 1875; Alas' *La Regenta*, 1884–85). In the introduction to his edition of *La Regenta*, Gonzalo Sobejano remarks on parallels between Fermín de Pas and the priest in Zola's *La Conquête de Plassans*, published in 1874 (p. 17).

18. Penzol, "Parentescos," 422.

gypsy Esmeralda. Thus, what we see is an extremely telescoped and reduced point of view as seen through the archdeacon's eyes. The survey of the city, which is fully developed from the authorial point of view in Book III, Chapter 2, is ignored in the scene from Book VII.

In *La Regenta*, however, it is the city which engages the rapt view of the magistral.[19] The bird's-eye view ("a vista de pájaro" = "à vol d'oiseau") is similar to the panoramic sweep which Victor Hugo offers in his chapter, "Paris à vol d'oiseau" (Book III, Chapter 2), but the effect differs. In *Notre-Dame de Paris*, the novelist reconstructs medieval Paris in architectural terms while indirectly criticizing modern-day Paris' aesthetic and artistic deficiencies. Clarín, on the other hand, uses the device of the tower view for two purposes: to delineate the relationship between de Pas and the city; and to review, not in aesthetic terms, but within the social and historical context, the past and present of Vetusta. The bond between de Pas and the city is comparable to that between an animal and his prey. It is a brutal image: "Vetusta era su pasión y su presa . . . Lo que sentía en presencia de la heroica ciudad era gula" (p. 81). In another passage: "devoraba su presa, la Vetusta levítica, como el león enjaulado los pedazos ruines de carne que el domador le arroja" (p. 82). And again: "Era una presa que le disputaban, pero que acabaría de devorar él solo" (p. 82).

This emphasis on devouring, on gross animal appetite is a running leitmotif through *La Regenta*, but for the moment it is sufficient to note the early insertion of the theme and to comment on the animalistic description given Fermín de Pas. The zoological

19. See Frank Durand's study of the tower scene as an example of the changing point of view in Alas ("A Critical Analysis of Leopoldo Alas's *La Regenta*," Ph.D. dissertation, University of Michigan, 1962), Ch. 3. The critic notes that "in this beginning chapter, then, the groundwork of the entire novel is established by the omniscient author through the use of Fermín's point of view" (p. 83). By emphasizing the subtle use of viewpoint in order to characterize, Durand anticipates and confirms some of my own preliminary observations. See also Michael Nimetz, "Eros and Ecclesia in Clarín's Vetusta," *MLN*, LXXXVI (1971), 242–53, for an analysis of sex and religion amid the antithetical images first presented in Chapter 1 of *La Regenta*.

classification of the priest not only dehumanizes him but, more significantly, corrupts him. The picture of a caged lion devouring putrescent pieces of meat—thus Vetusta is also depicted as something corrupt—evokes popularized images of ancient Roman practices. It is not necessary here for Alas to develop further such an association of images because the one image presented and repeated several times already possesses enough suggestiveness of an aura of decay.

There is yet another association which Alas makes between de Pas and Vetusta; the priest is seen in the guise of a conqueror, and the city as the prize. The magistral consciously thinks of himself as a conquistador: "¿Qué había hecho él? Conquistar" (p. 82). The fact that the domain fought over does not measure up to his boyhood dreams of glory and power is discounted by the thirty-five-year-old de Pas, who has largely given up his youthful illusions and ideals. Hence the word *conquest* refers here to a very limited sphere of action; worse, the booty is scarcely worth the taking. Nevertheless, as the gap between illusion and reality, between what one desires and what one settles for widens, the capacity for self-delusion adjusts itself accordingly. Moreover, to grasp the desired object, no matter the paltriness of it, whets the appetite to acquire more, or in Alas' words, to devour more. It is also significant that this gluttony of ambition takes on a voluptuous cast.

The word *conquistar* also summons forth historical connotations. The implied contrast between a distant Siglo de Oro with its vast empire of foreign possessions and the insignificance of Vetusta as de Pas's realm, his "imperio natural," as Clarín terms it (p. 88), points not only to the reduced expectations of the priest's original ambitions but, on a collective scale, to the decay of a once-great nation.

Another instance in which Spain's golden-age past is obliquely referred to is the image of the magistral figuratively lifting the roofs of Vetusta's edifices in order to scrutinize more closely its inhabitants:

El Magistral . . . paseaba lentamente sus miradas por la ciudad escudriñando sus rincones, levantando con la imaginación los techos, aplicando su espíritu a aquella inspección minuciosa, como el naturalista estudia con poderoso microscopio las pequeñeces de los cuerpos. (p. 81)

Clarín renovates a traditional literary device, which both Quevedo in *Los sueños* and Vélez de Guevara in *El diablo cojuelo* used, by comparing the priest who is also a confessor, to a naturalist, a not surprising analogy given the nineteenth-century preoccupation with the sciences and especially with recent biological discoveries and hypotheses (Darwin, Wallace, and Huxley). It is instructive to note how felicitously Clarín manages to tie together the image of the conquering priest and the naturalist who examines the native population by means of the tower view. From the heights de Pas feels himself a conqueror, and by right of conquest, justifies his prying into the affairs of the inhabitants. Thus, the golden-age motif of conquering and the image of spying by figuratively lifting the rooftops are given a new ironic twist by being applied to a modern-day conquistador of diabolical character.

After exploring the relationship between de Pas and the city, Alas proceeds in straightforward exposition to describe the various sectors of the city and its environs. Clarín, in following the slow movement of the spyglass which de Pas focuses upon the city, is able to control and delimit the eye of the glass, the viewpoint which, in this case, is that of the author, who permits Fermín's thinking to intrude now and then in the form of the third person. The major purpose of this close investigation is to define clearly the sharp differences in the social structure of Vetusta and, by so doing, to indicate the historical direction of the city's past and present.

The magistral first concentrates on the Encimada, the oldest and noblest section of Vetusta, in which the most aristocratic and the most ragged cohabit in long-accustomed economic injustice. The streets are narrow, tortuous, humid, and obscure. Grass is growing in some of the streets, a sign of neglect and human surrender to the passing of time. The buildings of this neighborhood, which recount the history of the privileged classes and, by implication, Spain's past, are dominated by the presence of churches and convents, but they are ecclesiastical remnants which "gloriosamente se pudren poco a poco víctimas de la humedad y hechas polvo por los siglos" (p. 90). But the implication is there that the changing tides of history and social transformations have managed to sweep away and largely undermine the influence of these ancient bastions of the Faith. It would be more precise perhaps to state that the secular power of the Church, which is evidenced in the vulgar and new religious edifices constructed in the *indianos*' district, has grown in strength, but that the spiritual authority of the Church, represented by those crumbling, decaying vestiges of the Reconquest, Santa María and San Pedro, has alarmingly diminished. This suggestion of a decline in spirituality is later borne out by the external commitment to religious practices and the internal spiritual vacuity of the Vetustans themselves.

In contrast to the quiet Encimada's ruined past, its aristocratic insularity, and choked, squeezed-in, impoverished lower classes, the Campo del Sol, in which the miners and factory workers reside, and the Colonia, the *indianos*' community, bustle with activity and hints of Spain's future. But the workers, rebellious toward secular and religious authority alike, occupy a minor place in *La Regenta*, appearing only once more in Chapter 9 when Alas draws attention to their habit of nighttime strolls in imitation of the more affluent *señoritas* and *caballeros*.

This parodying of the aristocracy, which naturally results in a more degenerate form of behavior, occurs much more frequently in the *indianos*, the nouveaux riches returning emigrants. The decadence of the nobility, which is amply illustrated later in the mores of the Marquesa de Vegallana and her friends, is of long standing with its roots in the Spanish past, while the *indianos*' corruption is more recent and, more significantly, derivative in nature. That is, the *indianos*' imitation of the manners and morals of the aristocrats results in a layer of decadence arising out of an even deeper layer of decadence in the upper classes. One form of corruption erupts out of another which is more thoroughly ingrained than the *india-*

nos' gaudy pastiche of the New and the Old Worlds. The *indianos qua indianos* play no real role except as an object of satire on Alas' part, but as imitative continuators of the aristocrat's way of life they slide in and out of the novel. In his description of the Colonia, Alas emphasizes the affected, showy vulgarity of the *indianos'* architecture, their apery of the nobility, and the possessive pride which de Pas experiences when he gazes down upon one of his personal fiefdoms, "un Perú en miniatura, del cual pretende ser el Pizarro espiritual" (p. 89). One notes again, in passing, the reference to de Pas as a conquistador, this time of a domain which is even more miserable than the Encimada because of its inhabitants' cheap counterfeit behavior.

Although this initial description of the Vetustan milieu covers all major sectors of the city, in most of the novel Alas is only concerned with the Encimada and its residents, the very neighborhood which is not growing, which is, in fact, gradually dying as can be seen in the decaying churches, moldering houses and gardens, and the narrow streets invaded by grass. The expansion of industry and the dynamism of the growing, commercial middle class are touched on briefly and in passing in Clarín's allusion to the smoke and machine whistles, indications of factories and business, but are almost entirely neglected in the rest of the novel. *La Regenta* is, in truth, a one-sided presentation of Spanish Restoration society since Alas has deliberately chosen to forego certain aspects of the social structure and to concentrate his art precisely on those groups which show the most signs of decay, corruption, and unease.

The device of the tower view, which we have seen is used to delineate de Pas's character and to dissect the social composition of the town is, in addition, needed to emphasize the physical contrast between the heights and the depths. What Hugo presents in simple, graphic terms Alas does more subtly, for de Pas will experience a fall—not from grace since he lost that long ago, but from power. In addition, Ana Ozores will descend from the height of her social position and her supposedly unassailable virtue to the degradation of social ostracism and an irremediable sense of guilt. Thus, Alas is already preparing with this first view from the cathedral tower the pattern of descent from the heights which is the predominant movement of the novel.

The view from above is also significant for the play of opposites it engenders. We see from a distance the corruption of a society, the moral decline of a social microcosm which is Spain itself. More interesting, we perceive these beetles, these insignificant beings who, for the most part, appear morally unsalvageable in later chapters, through the viewpoint of a man who himself is thoroughly corrupted by power and unclean desires. The fact that the first conception of the Vetustan universe that we obtain is derived from a morally questionable priest intensifies the ironic thrust behind the first chapter (and succeeding ones, to be sure).

But Alas is not yet satisfied with the tower device as it now stands. He proceeds one step further and establishes a viewpoint which is superior in distance and in moral tone to that of Fermín de Pas: his own. The ironic distance which the tower view technique creates is precisely the aloof position which Alas himself takes before his characters. The reader gradually becomes aware that an invisible hand maneuvers the man from the heights who holds the threads to the social fabric of Vetusta below. In this sense, Alas plays the role of God to de Pas's mere mortality, a function which is analogous to the priest's relationship with the city. The device of the tower view, then, symbolizes the authorial stance throughout the novel.[20]

In brief, the focus from above which will converge upon the city below provides the key to the interpretation of the rest of the novel. Disregarding for the most part Hugo's aesthetic antithesis, Alas will concentrate on the moral and metaphysical landscape of the Vetustan depths. As de Pas is likened to a curious naturalist so is Alas; he too spies upon the native population. In fact, he frequently

20. It is a technique which, curiously enough, breaks down to a certain extent in Clarín's analysis of Ana's inner turmoil; here, the author appears much closer in spirit and sympathy to the ill-fated *regenta* than to the swarm of Vetustans elsewhere.

plunges right into the bowels of the organism, dissecting and exposing the signs of decay and putrefaction. In this sense, Alas' contrastive use of height-depth is a deliberate vulgarization of the more poetic and lyrical Hugoesque antithesis. And, as we have seen in the case of Fermín, the debasement of this play of opposites is pursued even more intently when superior positions taken by the characters themselves are shown to be either spurious (Don Álvaro's bravado) or morally tainted (de Pas's show of strength from the tower) and when aspirations toward the ideal are undermined by confused values (Ana's attempts at mysticism) or by no fixed and real values at all (Víctor's risible efforts in Christian piety or his pathetic conformity to an honor code to which he has heretofore paid only an actor's allegiance). Indeed, one can draw the conclusion that there are no values of goodness and ethical strength which are morally efficacious in *La Regenta*. The only good (the aspiration toward the things of the spirit) that exists in the novel is there for ironic distance. The good is sought after but continually eludes the grasp of the seeker who lacks a stable moral universe in which to act (Ana is the prime example). But the depths of corruption prevail.

In this first half of Chapter 1 we have seen how Alas refashions and refills an older literary mold, the romanticism of that arch-romantic himself, Victor Hugo, by deliberately distorting the simpler lines of the 1832 novel. The use of a well-known literary pattern now demodé, which is deposited upon the original stratum of reality created in *La Regenta*, produces the photographic effect of the superimposition of one overlay (a twisted romanticism) placed upon the original, primitive layer of Spanish realism. The result is striking. One literary mode complements another, enriches Alas' basic realism with its romantic reverberations and allusions.

The romantic situation whose archetype is found in Hugo is, however, but a foil to the insertion of the grotesque, the decadent, the corrupt elements which ultimately determine the moral ambience of the novel. In effect, what one perceives in *La Regenta* is the decay of romanticism, the loss of aesthetic antithesis which is replaced by the predominance of the grotesque. In *La Regenta*, all has become Quasimodo, and the sublime perverted. In similar fashion, the echoes of Siglo de Oro history and literature are subjected to a pitiless distortion through Clarín's mirror technique; that is, the original image of the golden-age motif is reflected off the misshapen mirror of nineteenth-century Restoration society.[21]

In the above instance it is the author who imposes a particular literary pattern upon the living Spanish reality, but in the second half of Chapter 1 and in many other cases in *La Regenta*, it is the characters themselves who view life through the illusive looking glass of literature. This aspect of Alas' novelistic technique has been remarked upon by several critics.[22] Here, the subtle allusive approach often turns into a more direct satire or even parody.

The first example found in Chapter 1 is that of Don Saturnino Bermúdez, self-appointed archeologist and conservationist of Vetusta's architectural glories. In Bermúdez' Christian name, Alas makes a sly, ironic comment on the antiquarian's nature. *Saturnine*, which means moody, sullen, and even devilish, though far removed from Saturnino's real character, nevertheless obliquely refers to his dress habits which always give him the semi-clerical appearance of a man in mourning. Saturnino could also allude to Saturnalia, the ancient Roman festival of unrestrained revelry; in this instance, the reference is frankly hilarious because it reflects Bermúdez's vain efforts to be a Don Juan, a man of the world who takes his pleasures at will and with the proper spirit of devilish insouciance. Don Saturnino models his imagined life of sensualism on Parisian love stories and romantic daydreams, which are translated into caricaturized romantic posturings such as his skulking around at night, dis-

21. Alas' use of light is analogous to the mirror approach: rays of light strike different objects and produce distorted images of them. See pages 92 and 94 of *La Regenta*.

22. See, for example: Albert Brent, *Leopoldo Alas and La Regenta* (Columbia, Missouri: University of Missouri, 1951); Frank Durand, "Characterization in *La Regenta*: Point of View and Theme," *Bulletin of Hispanic Studies*, XLI (1964), 86–100; and Robert M. Jackson, " 'Cervantismo' in the Creative Process of Clarín's *La Regenta*," *Modern Language Notes*, LXXXIV (1969), 208–27.

guised in a voluminous cape and hat, in order to stand in mute adoration before the house of the unsuspecting Ana Ozores. Imagining himself misunderstood by the Vetustan female population but in reality too timid to plunge headlong into sin, Saturnino compensates for the lack of satisfactory amatory experiences by congratulating himself on his manly resistence to temptation which then allows him, in a paroxysm of voluptuous idealism, to indulge in sensuous reveries in his bed.

The mixture of idealism, approximating a convoluted sort of mysticism, and sensual romanticizing in Saturnino is in actuality a parody of the attitudes of the novel's major character, Ana Ozores. We have already seen how, for example, Celedonio imitates de Pas's gestures and posture and how the *indianos* copy the manners and morals of the aristocracy. The inferior mirrors the superior (relatively speaking); one reflection springs from another just as, earlier, we noticed that one literary mode rebounds off another. In Saturnino the behavior patterns which parodically imitate Ana's actions do not originate in a conscious mimicking of the *regenta*'s conduct and thoughts. Rather, the author himself draws the parallel in order to indicate the level of debasement to which romanticism has sunk. The Saturnino caricature also devaluates Ana's own romanticizing and idealizing because, once again, it offers a shallow but twisted reflection of the *regenta*'s soul. Saturnino is good only because he is too afraid of doing evil; likewise, Ana's virtuousness stems in part from fear and vacillating timidity. Like Don Saturnino, she takes refuge in her bed, which becomes the setting for voluptuous daydreaming and lascivious nightmares. And also like Don Saturnino, who focuses his amorous attention upon the lewd Obdulia, Ana will transfer her starved affections to the dissolute Don Álvaro Mesía.

Obdulia Fandiño is also introduced in the first chapter. The stress on the artificial and the corrupt, which is seen in Fermín, is similarly a characteristic of Obdulia. One is first struck by the overpowering impact of her scent, "el olor mundano de que había infestado la sacristía desde el momento de entrar. Era el olor del billete, el olor del pañuelo, el olor de Obdulia con que el sabio [Saturnino] soñaba algunas veces" (p. 102). She dresses flashily, preferring scarlets and carmines which are closely molded to her body; and she dyes her hair ("rizos y más rizos de un rubio sucio, metálico, artificial"). Using the confessional as though it were her dressing room, Obdulia even tries to seduce Fermín. The accouterments of civilization—the articles of dress, the perfume, the dyed hair—which are intimately linked to the toilet-table setting reveal her depraved nature. Again, Alas is making the identification civilization-artificiality-corruption which was to obsess naturalists and decadents alike.

In summary, Chapter 1 of *La Regenta*, by presenting romanticism and past Spanish glories through a glass darkly, manages to show the slimy underside of the Vetustan reality. The use of the tower device, which functions as a critical authorial viewpoint, allows us to perceive the absence of goodness by stressing the pervasive presence of the depths of evil. The ironic play of opposites, of heights and depths, which the tower viewpoint promotes, indicates that the depths and descent into the depths will prevail in *La Regenta* and, thus, Clarín's ethical stance from the tower prepares the ground for a critical view of the characters' lack of moral fiber and corruption.

By depicting the residents as either unnatural and artificial (De Pas, Celedonio, Obdulia) or affected and imitative (the *indianos*, Don Saturnino), the author betrays an interest in the various manifestations of decadence as the nineteenth century interpreted them. The immoral, even perverted elements displayed in Chapter 1 are neatly tied to the theme of the debasement of religion and romanticism by metamorphosing the original Hugoesque romantic situation into a far more decadent scenario; and, as a humorous leavening agent, the Don Saturnino parody—which is also permeated with corruption though of a less melodramatic stripe—is juxtaposed to the more sinister presence of Fermín de Pas. Clarín will further develop this preliminary glimpse into Vetustan corruption and decay by presenting a decadent universe of animalized sensation seekers whose cruel and egotistical competitiveness even succeeds in dragging some of the characters into that final dissolution, death itself.

Vetusta: A Darwinian Universe

The frequent use of animal images to characterize human beings in La Regenta has been noted by Durand and others, who have pointed out that the technique results in a dehumanization of the Vetustans.[23] Taken within a larger context, however, animal imagery may be regarded as the signpost to a particular interpretation of the Vetustan universe. The combined influence of Darwinian science and Zolaesque naturalism propelled many nineteenth-century writers to see their world as a conflict-ridden, Breughelian big-fish-eat-little-fish society. Life was more than competitive; it was a divisive, fragmented existence in which one man was pitted against another in frequently unequal struggle, in which the desires of the self were thrown against the larger, more powerful interests of the group.

Clarín could not fail to perceive that the Vetustan world did indeed greatly conform to this popularized version of the Darwinian hypothesis. All was struggle. But Vetusta is a society on the way down, engaged in the desperate writhings of a dying organism. Self against self, individual against individual, group against group, the fragmentive force of selfishness tears asunder the none too secure underpinnings of the Vetustan moral fabric. The members of a society which is in decline act egotistically, in pursuit of their own interests and in isolation from one another. There is no real friendship, no real love in a world where survival and gain prevail to the exclusion of those virtues of goodness, decency, and compassion which we like to think are innate to humankind. The disintegration of the individual not only points to the breakdown in society but contributes substantially to it.

23. Examples: De Pas is a lion; Pompeyo Guimarán a bear; Ripamilán a bird; Santos Barinaga a dog, and his daughter a snake; and Visitación a magpie. The device does not, of course, originate in Alas; instances of animal imagery applied to humans can be found in Hugo, Balzac, Zola, Galdós, and Flaubert, to name but a few nineteenth-century writers.

The word which provides the key to Vetustan life is *devorar*. The verb is used with such alarming frequency and in a variety of contexts that it soon becomes apparent it is a leading leitmotif in the novel. *Devorar*, as noted before, is first applied in Chapter 1 to Fermín de Pas's savage and ambitious character. Like the caged lion, he devours without distinctions everything within his sight and grasp. Fermín is not the only character to be obsessed with insatiable ambitions, desires, and hatreds. A good illustration is found in Chapter 13, in which one group of guests has been invited to dinner at the Marquesa de Vegallana's house and the other group excluded. Clarín describes this division of the insiders and the outsiders thus:

> La aparente cordialidad y la alegría expansiva de todos los presentes ocultaban un fondo de rencores y envidias. Aquellas señoras, clérigos y caballeros particulares estaban divididos en dos bandos enemigos en aquel instante: el bando de los envidiados y el de los envidiosos; el de los convidados a comer, que eran pocos, y el de los no convidados. (p. 401)

The priest Glocester is one of the unprivileged ones "que fingía atender a lo que le decían los pollos insulsos, *devoraba* con el rabillo del ojo a los del grupo" (p. 401, italics mine). The hostilities which instantly spring up and the devouring envy and resentment which gleam in every eye are signs of a festering social sore of long standing that is only partially disguised by the habitual mask of hypocrisy which nearly everyone assumes.

Another of the ways in which their devouring nature is revealed is through the image of the marketplace, which permeates the religious, political, social, amorous, and economic spheres of the Vetustan world. In the same way that characters are constantly jockeying for a better position in the social sphere, they compete in a marketplace of one-upmanship. The clergy is by no means excluded, dickering and haggling in the bureaucratic atmosphere of the Bishop's Palace where de Pas carries through the directives of his mother Doña Paula, the invisible hand behind clerical intrigues. In this vein Alas writes:

De Pas se vio cogido por la rueda que le sujetaba diariamente a las fatigas canónico-burocráticas: sin pensarlo, contra su propósito, se encenagó como todos los días en las complicadas cuestiones de su gobierno eclesiástico, mezcladas hasta lo más íntimo con sus propios intereses y los de su señora madre. (p. 389)

And then: "Nunca había puesto los pies allí doña Paula. Pero su espíritu parecía presidir el mercado singular de la curia eclesiástica" (p. 389).

For de Pas, everything is business, even salvation itself: "La salvación era un negocio, el gran negocio de la vida. Parecía un Bastiat del púlpito" (p. 375). The reference to the French economist is pertinent since Bastiat advocated economic individualism, laissez-faire, and free trade. In other words, Fermín is recommending self-interest as the Christian way of life, good works and charity as insurance against the Day of Judgment.

Politics in the notorious form of the *turno pacífico* is also business. Curiously, the political arena is perhaps the least fraught with strife and hostilities. Although the two nominal heads of the conservative and liberal parties are the Marqués de Vegallana and Álvaro Mesía respectively, in reality Mesía is the true *cacique*. He makes all the decisions for both parties. Politics is "business as usual." The deep hatreds and divisiveness of Vetustan society go beyond mere political labels. *Not* ideological struggles, but the personal grasp for power *qua* power and absolute self-interest motivate Vetustans. *La Regenta* has been interpreted as the work of a liberal, progressive, anticlerical novelist who attacks a conservative, status quo, pietistic society.[24] In one sense, of course, this is an accurate statement. But Alas' acerbic pen devastates liberals and conservatives alike in *La Regenta*. What Alas demonstrates is a society that has slipped so far into the depths of decadence that it has lost all belief, whether secular or religious. If God does not exist for the Vetustans, neither does ideology. Nothing matters but personal gain and the selfish struggle to attain it.

24. Eugene Savaiano, *An Historical Justification of the Anticlericalism of Galdós and Alas* (Wichita, Kansas: University Studies No. 24, February 1952).

Critics have commented on the fact that Clarín seemed to have in mind the depiction of Vetusta as a collective protagonist.[25] And this is superficially true, particularly when the collective body masses itself in an attack against the individual, as in the case of the social ostracism of Ana Ozores. Groups unite only when they hold in common the same hatreds (the cabal which Glocester and his allies constantly devise against de Pas) and vices (Don Álvaro's clique of aspiring dandies who dream of sexual conquests), or when the collective goal serves the individual concerns of the members (Fermín's cooperation with the *beata* Doña Petronila's religious confraternity in order to form closer ties with the *regenta*). But a society which is fragmented by egotistical interests does not cohere as a whole; it has lost its sense of community because it lacks a common good.

The image of the "mercado" infiltrates not only religion and politics but friendships and love, and is graphically illustrated in Chapter 9 during Ana's evening stroll through the calle del Comercio, "el núcleo de estos paseos nocturnos y algo disimulados":

> Los caballeros van y vienen por la ancha acera y miran con mayor o menor descaro a las damas sentadas junto al mostrador. Con un ojo en las novedades de la estación y con otro en la calle, regatean los precios, y cazan lisonjas y señas al vuelo. (p. 292)

Vetustans window-shop—they purchase and are purchased.[26] The calle del Comercio is the scenario for prospective love affairs, possible marriages, and innumerable flirtations. Clarín thus adroitly welds together the buying and selling image of wares and flesh which takes place under the protective and suggestive mantle of night.

25. See, for example: Brent, *Leopoldo Alas*, 20; J. A. Balseiro, *Novelistas españoles modernos* (New York: Macmillan Company, 1933), 353; Mariano Baquero Goyanes, *Prosistas españoles contemporáneos* (Madrid: Rialp, 1956), 138; and Segundo Serrano Poncela, "Un estudio de *La Regenta*," *Cuadernos Americanos*, CLII (1967), 229.

26. In another chapter, Álvaro's set of cynical friends are called "compradores de carne humana" (p. 504). Michael Nimetz in his article, "Eros and Ecclesia in Clarín's Vetusta," also remarks that "clergy and aristocracy regard womankind as chattel or hand-me-down" (p. 243).

And finally, the marketplace symbol is strikingly evoked within the natural and appropriate context of business itself. The sordid incident in which de Pas has ruined and driven to drink a fellow business competitor, Don Santos Barinaga, demonstrates clearly Fermín's and his mother's rapacious desires for money. Money is a serious affair with them; indeed, it is treated with a religious reverence in which "parecía ella una sacerdotisa y él un acólito de aquel culto plutónico" (p. 470). The travesty of the classical reference is, by the way, a device to which Alas will have recourse a number of times.

The miserable end to which Barinaga comes is the culmination of this dog-eat-dog episode in which the stronger de Pas has devoured the weaker member of society. His death and funeral mark the conclusion to which all such mortal struggles are destined, for the annihilation of one party, the destruction of the weaker (Santos, Víctor, Ana) is presupposed. Before Don Santos suffers his last, however, he must endure the indignities to which his snake-like, verminous *beata* daughter Celestina subjects him ("era una beata ofidiana . . . y trataba a su padre como a un leproso que causa horror"; "tenía facha de sabandija de sacristía," pp. 476–77). The struggle for existence is here translated into an unending series of rows between the drunken anticlerical and his pietistic daughter. The likeness to a reptile and to vermin which dehumanizes Celestina—the name is an ironic allusion to "celestial," not a particle of which quality she possesses—furthers the Darwinian ambience of one member of the human species savaging another.

Barinaga's death agonies are shot through with Clarinian irony: Don Santos is dying of hunger and neglect as his fellow Vetustans parade in and out of his house, offering commiserations but no bread. The grotesque situation is intensified as a stream of meaningless verbiage in the form of banalities and clichés spews forth from the visitors who protest indignantly that Don Santos is dying like a dog, but do nothing to alleviate the critical situation. Barinaga's death is trivialized, its sacredness utterly obliterated by the overwhelming meaninglessness and meanness of Vetustan behavior. The fact that "moría como un perro" is without doubt a cliché of the most worn-out sort does not detract from the grim reality that Santos does die a dog's death. Repetition of the cliché, which Alas deliberately exploits as such and exposes as a commonplace used by the town's population, heightens the dehumanizing effect of the scene. Don Santos' humanity, the meaning of his existence, is crushed by the onslaught of lethal trivialities.

The cliché itself is made concrete by the presence of a dying old dog who, along with Don Pompeyo Guimarán, is the sole witness to Barinaga's death. During the funeral procession, the dog's head which appears from the balcony is like a stab at Fermín's conscience who looks at it with terror. The dog is forgotten, abandoned in the ruined house: he seems like the ghostly shadow of Don Santos himself. The commonplace is repeated during the funeral when curious spectators come to mock the service.

Reference is also made to the breach in the cemetery wall through which dogs and cats may penetrate to profane the resting place. The squalid setting, the heavy downpour, the indistinctive, dissolving appearance of the wet, gray landscape, all these descriptive elements contribute to the image of a hopelessly dismal conclusion to a battered existence. The breach in the wall makes an especially strong impression on Don Pompeyo, who dreams later that night that he himself is the wall with a gaping hole in it through which dogs and cats and other creatures enter and exit ("Soñaba que él era de cal y canto y que tenía una brecha en el vientre y por allí entraban y salían gatos y perros, y alguno que otro diablejo con rabo," p. 700).

The nightmare is rather humorous in its first effect and, yet, one consequence of the funeral might cause one to pause and reflect that the ultimate intent Clarín had in mind is serious: Don Pompeyo later dies, never having fully recovered from the chill he took on the day of the funeral (see Chapter 26). Thus, the dream of rift in the body of Guimarán represents the triumphant invasion of death into the weakened human citadel. A more brutal conception of death effectively extinguishes the Christian significance of dying.

The origin of de Pas's and Doña Paula's avarice and urge for power, which results in the downfall and death of Don Santos, is related by Alas in Chapter 15. In this chapter, which is positioned

exactly halfway between the two parts of the novel and which therefore can look both forward and backward upon the novelistic material, the author re-creates the Genesis theme as the Darwinian
struggle for survival. Here, the symbol for the origins of man is not
the Garden of Eden, but the caves out of which emerge the black-
ened, despairingly blasphemous miners. De Pas's mother develops
in the sordid, rapacious ambience of the mines into which her
father habitually descends. Matalerejo is a town of literally subterranean men who, by identifying the bowels of the earth only
with money, exploit its inner recesses. Matalerejo's only real resource is greed: "El dinero estaba en las entrañas de la tierra; había
que cavar hondo para sacar provecho. En Matalerejo, y en todo su
valle, reina la codicia, y los niños . . . parecen hijos de sueños de
avaricia" (p. 457).

Thus, Paula's last name, Raíces, appropriately fits within the
context of the caves and miners; one must dig deeply into the roots
("raíces") of the earth to make good in this life; and that is precisely what Doña Paula proceeds to do. The valuable metal concealed underground becomes, to use Clarín's phrase, incrusted in
the very insides of Paula Raíces's being ("semilla de metal que se
incrusta en las entrañas y jamás se arranca de allí," p. 457).

The image of the cave into which brutalized, darkened men descend and emerge in order to make their fortunes is the means by
which Alas furthers his contrastive leitmotif of heights-depths
which he had already introduced in Chapter 1. In this instance, the
motif suffers some modification by becoming one of descent-ascent;
yet the analogy to the heights-depths antithesis remains. Subterranean beings struggle to clamber out of the earth's bowels, to
ascend the economic ladder in order to escape grinding, debasing
poverty. This is exactly what both Doña Paula and her son strive
to accomplish.

Yet one should not be deceived by the motif descent-ascent into
believing that the image implies a moral amelioration of the human
condition. The contrast is purely ironic just as the heights-depths
play of opposites is. Men are no better after they emerge into the
bright sunlight and fresh air than before when they exist as under-

ground moles—they are only economically less burdened. Clarín demonstrates most effectively this fact in the setting of the tavern which Doña Paula opens after previous business ventures have failed miserably. The vicious and violent ambience of the tavern encourages and is encouraged by the animalized nature of the miners. Doña Paula likens the horde of workers to wild animals, "fieras," and "osos de la cueva," conceiving of herself as a sort of wild animal tamer. The comparison is only partially accurate since much of the time Fermín's mother is forced to defend herself strenuously from the sexual attacks of these human animals. The miners view Doña Paula as easy prey for conquest; one notes once again the reference to "conquista" and "presa," the same debased golden-age context in which the son Fermín sees himself. Just as the economic struggle for existence is reduced to animal terms so is sex become a Darwinized conception.

The allusions to the miners' brutal appetites—both gastronomical and sexual—stress their devouring nature. Interestingly enough, this same quality is affixed to the determined way in which Doña Paula and her son seek to crash through the educational barrier; they devour books (" [De P.] devoraba los libros"; "ella devoraba libros"). The quest for knowledge, however, is not undertaken for knowledge's sake alone, but to escape the mines and all that they stand for—poverty, ignorance, and brutality.

That this particular conception of existence is not confined to the more primitive sphere of the mines alone becomes quite clear when we penetrate beyond the veneer of civilization with which polite society masks its own basic needs and desires. The cave image, for example, is used to describe the Bishop's Palace. De Pas feels a sense of relief when he is at last able to escape its cavernous confines.

The idea of being underground is also analogous to that of being submerged by the heavy rains which cover Vetusta a good part of the year. Clarín describes it as "aquella vida submarina" to which the people resign themselves until about April. They become "an-fibios que se preparan a vivir debajo de agua la temporada que su destino les condena a este elemento" (p. 479). The physical sense of being covered by a sea of rain and mud is also representative of the submerged state of mind and moral ambience of the city. The Vetustans live underwater like amphibians because they, just as the miners do, live below, in the darkened reaches of existence. The fact that two elements of nature, earth and water, produce the sensation of existing holed-in does not mean that nature itself is responsible for the Vetustan character. It is the Vetustans themselves who choose to deny the multifaceted possibilities of life and to limit themselves to the condition of underground or underwater creatures.

De Pas, whose discerning intellect is quite aware of the true nature of the Vetustans, also perceives the city's life as subterranean: "El Magistral conocía una especie de Vetusta subterránea: era la ciudad oculta de las conciencias" (p. 329). The priest equates the Vetustans' inferior sense of morality to a heap of garbage ("un montón de basura," p. 330), an image which recalls the initial reference to debris in Chapter 1 and which is implied in the scraps and crumbs remaining after dinners and feasts.

Devorar, it will be shown, can be understood in both sexual and nonsexual terms. Love, as already noted, is treated as a commercial enterprise by native Vetustans. It should not, therefore, surprise us to see it further debased by being conceived as a kind of animal appetite and nothing more by nearly all the characters. The link between *devorar* and *apetito* is supplied by this ignoble conception of love as an object to be ravenously devoured. The relationship is intensified by the frequent intermingling of food and sex which Alas effects in a number of scenes.

A revealing scene which illustrates the Vetustan appetite takes place, appropriately enough, in the Marquesa de Vegallana's luxurious kitchen. Obdulia, whose lascivious character has already been well established, and Visitación de Cuervo have temporarily appropriated the Marquesa's kitchen in order to make some special dessert. Clarín first delineates Visitación's nature by pointing out one of her characteristics: in other people's houses she is an "urraca ladrona," that is, she constantly pilfers small objects, bits of food, everything but money. Her hands are always sticky or greasy, and she always talks with something in her mouth. The thieving magpie is a glutton, a fact which everyone knows and tolerates.

Clarín takes advantage of the culinary setting and devotes a solid paragraph of description in good Dutch still-life manner to the glorious foodstuffs and delicacies with which the Vegallana's pantry is stocked. The delights of eating are in no way denied. But Obdulia's behavior modifies the hearty atmosphere when Don Álvaro and Paco Vegallana enter, as she commences sexual overtures toward Paco. Sexual stimulation has metamorphosed the gastronomic urge into an equally basic need. The use of the kitchen scene neatly combines both kinds of appetite, and in this way, we perceive the clear link between food and sex in the novel.

The close association between food and sex contributes to the creation of a morally polluted atmosphere in *La Regenta*. Two scenes, in particular, illustrate the extent to which the novel's characters are tainted by the continual stress on appetite: the dinner at the Marquesa's house in Chapter 13 and the banquet scene in Chapter 20.

Before analyzing in detail the dinner party, it would be well to establish the pre-dinner scene which sets the tone of Chapter 13. In the opening view of the Marquesa's salon Alas' description gives the impression of a light-hearted, innocent, and festive occasion ("Si entraban raudales de luz y aire fresco, salían corrientes de alegría, carcajadas," p. 397). In the first paragraph, the author alludes to the affected hair style which the Marquesa wears: she powders her hair and adorns it with natural flowers that seem, nevertheless, artificial. Doña Rufina, continues Alas, reigns over a society "donde canónigos reían, aristócratas fatuos hacían el pavo real, muchachuelas coqueteaban, jamonas lucían carne blanca y fuerte, diputados provinciales salvaban la comarca, y elegantes de la legua imitaban las amaneradas formas de sus congéneres de Madrid" (p. 397). The greater emphasis is on the artificial, the affected airs which Vetusta's smart set assumes while following the rules of the game as set forth by the capital. The local dandies are not alone in imitating the mores of Madrid society—nearly all the privileged members of Vetusta look to the capital as the ideal model for the latest fashions, clichés, and poses. In reality, the provincials' mirroring of Madrid is but a paler reflection of Parisian customs since the Spanish capital slavishly copies the French one.

The image of mannered posturing which tinges the gay, fresh air with a breath of something less pure and wholesome crystallizes in the second paragraph in the frame which Alas creates around the trio Doña Rufina, Glocester, and Obdulia Fandiño. The poses of the three characters are comparable to the deliberate attitudinizing one might see in a stilted, unnatural painting of morals and manners.

This group and others scattered throughout the house are depicted as discussing, in the midst of laughter, shrill screams, and tasteless, worn-out jokes, such philosophical and moral subjects as the relative merits of the married woman as opposed to the bride of the church, or the question of virtue itself. The extremely secular and affected tone of the gathering perverts the supposed seriousness of such discussions; and indeed, the whole affair seems like a deliberate travesty of the Platonic dialogue, just as later we shall see that the banquet scene in Chapter 22 is a parody of past modes.

When the dinner hour arrives, Alas, like the good realist he is, hastens to describe the physical setting of the dining room. An interesting aspect of this description is the reference to the paintings, all of poor quality, which are hung on the walls and which nearly all allude to hunting or to related culinary subjects. The first example depicts a feudal scene of hunters and the hunted; the second, a romantic scene à la Feuillet of a huntress closely followed by a lover also in hunting garb. Yet another painting shows a disorderly table; and finally, a scene of a rather nauseating eating-house.[27] Ordinarily, a realistic description of this sort would appear like one more filling-in of the surface detail. In this case, however, the pictorial background functions as a visual comment on the behavior

27. There is also a portrait of Jaime Balmes which, juxtaposed to the pictures of hunting and food, evokes a humorous reaction for its incongruity.

and attitudes of the dinner guests. The stress on hunting and eating in the backdrop parallels and explicates in the guise of a mute witness what is occurring center stage.

The tone of the dinner party is established initially as one of frivolous, wine-inspired gaiety. To indicate this Alas resorts to a description of a garden in which "todo era contento: allá en la huerta rumores de agua y de árboles que mecía el viento, cánticos locos de pájaros dicharacheros . . . perfumes traídos por el airecillo que hacía sonajas de las hojas de las plantas. Los surtidores de abajo eran una orquesta que acompañaba al bullicioso banquete" (p. 415). Thus, nature outside, like the silent paintings inside, serves as an expressive adjunct to the mood and ambience of the dinner party. Clarín also brings in the added touch of the two servant-girls, Pepa and Rosa, who appear as fresh and graceful as nature itself. The air of contentment arising out of the natural determines the initial sense of apparent order which the scene communicates.

But then a nuance of a different variety insinuates itself into the scene: Don Álvaro's insistent preoccupation with the prospective seduction of Ana Ozores. For the local Don Juan the banquet is only a means to an end—sexual victory over the *regenta*—an occasion to excite his prey by the stimulus of physical touch. All this sly flirtation whets his appetite ("por más que pinche el apetito"), a reaction which he shares with Paco Vegallana and his cousin Edelmira, Obdulia, and Joaquinito Orgaz. These couples also use the pretext of the dinner to indulge in coquetry. The only character who is excluded by nature and by consensus from the games of flirtation is the bathetic Saturnino Bermúdez, whose ludicrous idealistic comments on the female species underline Alas' satiric intentions in this scene.

Clarín describes the conclusion of the banquet in one compact paragraph:

Se acabó la discusión, sin causa, o por causa de los vapores del vino, mejor dicho. Todos hablaban; Paco quería también secularizar a las monjas; Joaquinito Orgaz comenzó a decir chistes flamencos que hacían mucha gracia a la Marquesa y a Edelmira. Visitación llegó a levantarse de la mesa para azotar con el abanico abierto a los que manifestaban ideas poco ortodoxas. Pepa y Rosa y las demás criadas sonreían discretamente, sin atreverse a tomar parte en el desorden, pero un poco menos disciplinadas que al empezar la comida. Pedro ya no se asomaba a la puerta. Se habían roto dos copas. Los pájaros de la huerta se posaban en las enredaderas de las ventanas para ver qué era aquello y mezclaban sus gritos gárrulos y agudos al general estrépito. (p. 420)

The key word in this account is *desorden*. A sense of disorder which is revealed in the simultaneous speech, the off-color jokes, Visitación's indiscriminate use of her fan, even in the less disciplined servants, and especially in the two broken wine glasses, permeates the scene. The birds, which at first had appeared gay and bubbly, now emit sharp and garrulous cries paralleling the human breakdown in restraint inside. The garden itself, nature's domain, will be perverted by human contact when the guests' attempts to imitate children's games result in rather scandalous behavior.

The scene has moved from order to disorder, from restraint to moral permissiveness. It is a movement analogous to the fall which Ana experiences as she passes from a state of rigid inhibition to moral laxity. It is also significant that Ana's seduction occurs shortly after a somewhat disorderly dinner (Chapter 28). But, on a larger scale, it is indicative of the profound moral taint which penetrates every aspect of Vetustan life. In this dinner scene it would be difficult to say whether it is the sexual appetite drive which pollutes the act of eating or appetite which excites sexuality. The two are inextricably entwined in this instance as one reacts upon the other.

When the dinner party and the games have ended, Alas neatly summarizes in the last paragraph of the chapter the food-sex relationship in the final sentence:

De Pas vio una mano enguantada que le saludaba desde una ventanilla. Era una mano de Obdulia, la viuda eternamente agradecida. No saludaba con las dos, porque la izquierda se la oprimía dulce y clandestinamente Joaquinito Orgaz, quien jamás hizo ascos a platos de segunda mesa, en siendo suculentos. (p. 432)

Here, infused with Clarinian irony, the image of food has become the sex object Obdulia.

This blend of food and sex, both of which impulses are united to one another through the common verb *devorar*, is also noted in the masterly presentation of the banquet scene in Chapter 20. It is interesting to note, by the way, that the practice of banqueting was apparently quite habitual in Spanish Restoration society.[28] The custom of honoring writers, actors, journalists, and other *distingués* personalities of the day eventually was abused, as Alas' friend, Luis Taboada, humorously pointed out in his book of personal reminiscences, *Intimidades y recuerdos*.[29] Thus the dinners and banquets which appear frequently in *La Regenta* reflect the very real custom of Spanish Restoration society; and the banquet scene in Chapter 20, especially, might also be considered a satire on the abused practice of paying homage to anyone who could offer a barely suitable pretext for celebrating.

The critic Guido Mazzeo has also correctly pointed out that the banquet which is offered in honor of Don Pompeyo Guimarán, the town atheist, is an irreverent caricature of the Last Supper.[30] The presence of twelve free-thinking friends, the substitution of the non-believer Guimarán for the Christ figure, the secularity and materialism of the scene, all indicate a deliberate travesty of the da Vinci Last Supper setting.

But the banquet scene also has its roots in an even older tradition in which lasciviousness, irreverence, and a luxuriant repast are the

28. The custom parallels what Roger Shattuck has called the "Banquet Years" of Paris' *belle époque* of the last century in which "the banquet had become the supreme rite" (*The Banquet Years*, Rev. ed., New York: Random House, 1968, p. 3). By the 1880s formal dinners of the Spanish upper classes had also become increasingly more French in culinary refinement and elaborateness (Fernando Díaz-Plaja, *La vida española en el siglo XIX*, Madrid: Prensa Española, 1969, p. 63).

29. Luis Taboada, *Intimidades y recuerdos* (Madrid: Administración de "El Imparcial," 1900), 143–44.

30. Guido Mazzeo, "The Banquet Scene in *La Regenta*, a Case of Sacrilege," *Romance Notes*, X (1968), 68. See also Frances Weber's "The Dynamics of Motif in Leopoldo Alas's *La Regenta*," *Romanic Review*, LVII (1966), 188–99.

principal ingredients: the Trimalchion banquet in Petronius' *Saty-ricon*, which is itself a parody of the Platonic dinner discussion. Indeed, one could state that the entire *Satyricon* as a depiction of Roman decadence in manners and morals offers parallels with the moral corruption found in Vetusta. The differences in tone and ambience are obvious—Petronius writes a vivid, roisterous satire of the full gamut of Roman perversions while Alas' satire, of a more restrained and less audacious sort, exposes less shocking scenes of corruption because of the camouflage of hypocrisy. Nevertheless, both authors base their views of human nature on a skeptical reluctance to accept the disinterestedness of good and a firm belief in the innate propensity to do evil.

Such a position results in satire in both writers. But Petronius' point of view reveals that the author takes considerable undisguised pleasure in depicting vice and perversion. Thus, one of the archetypes of Roman decadence, *The Satyricon*, which romantic, naturalist, and decadent writers were to adopt as a pattern of degeneration, was to leave the door open to two different approaches to the theme of decadence: satire with its moral implications and aesthetic enjoyment with its rejection of a moral stance. Clarín chose the first approach, but many decadent writers—Huysmans, Verlaine, Rachilde, Albert Samain, etc.—were fascinated by the tainted image of the legend of imperial Rome, enough so that they made correlations between decadent Paris and decadent Rome or sometimes went directly to the archetype itself, the Latin image of corruption.

Hence, it is not surprising that Alas too, who knew well his classical literature, should see parallels in the Roman decline and fall and the Vetustans' moral descent. Clarín is careful not to suggest openly such similarities, but the implication is present, especially in such a scene as the banquet in honor of Don Pompeyo Guimarán. The opening description is similar to that of the Vegallana dinner party: the provincial restaurant displays a gay, fresh, and promising setting of a table "aun pulcra, correcta, intacta." When, under the influence of spirits, the conversation turns to the subject of women, however, the supposed noble and serious purpose of the banquet vanishes, never to appear again, to the chagrin of Don Pompeyo.

From women the topic passes to the question of morality, which is very quickly established by the majority as relative and by Foja as nonexistent. Man is a creature of habits, he says; "Homo homini lupus," chimes in Bedoya. That's the struggle for survival, pontificates Joaquinito. Nothing exists but matter, adds Foja. And the chorus: Power and matter, matter and money. Here, as in Santos Barinaga's death scene, the use of the cliché is an excellent vehicle to demonstrate the moral vacuity of the Vetustans. This little chorus of commonplaces sets the stage for the rest of the discussion and celebrating. The conversation will then return to the subject of women and love affairs, switching toward the end to religion and the question of God's existence.

There is, of course, nothing exceptional in an all-male scene of frank and even brutal allusions to women and their honor—Alas is merely evoking an extremely realistic picture of male customs. But, by this time, the reader of *La Regenta* also knows that whenever Alas depicts a dinner scene, the question of sex almost automatically accompanies it. Moreover, when sex and food mix, the intention is not innocent. Thus, at Don Pompeyo's banquet, it is no mere fortuitous circumstance that the topic of sex is discussed amidst cigar ash, bread crumbs and sausage, and wine stains. Sex is as sullied as the dinner itself. The previously intact and clean table cloth is now soiled and messy—so is the human spirit in this scene. Debris is the symbolic expression of the Vetustan universe.

It is Don Álvaro Mesía who dominates the discussion of women and sex; he is the "Master"—replacing Don Pompeyo as the central figure in the scene—to whom all listen with respect and envy. Clarín makes sure that the reader has caught the irreverent stance of Álvaro's "misticismo báquico" by likening the scene to Leonardo da Vinci's *Last Supper*. Álvaro's lengthy disclosures of numerous love affairs, a sacrilegious parody of the confessional, create an atmosphere of sexual gluttony. The listeners greedily suck in one story after another and insatiably crave for more. Here is Alas' description of the titillated sexual curiosity of the banqueters:

De vez en cuando el silencio era interrumpido por carcajadas estrepitosas; era que una aventura cómica alegraba al concurso, sacándole de su estupor malsano y corrosivo. Entre la admiración general serpeaba la envidia abrazada a la lujuria: las tenias del alma. Los ojos brillaban secos.

El arte del seductor se extendía sobre aquel mantel, ya arrugado y sucio; anfiteatro propio del cadáver del amor carnal. (p. 618)

To intensify the picture of the group's unhealthy and corrosive stupor Alas has created two extremely expressive and compact images which concentrate in themselves all the degenerate vileness of Vetusta. The first one—"las tenias del alma"—is worthy of a *conceptista*.[31] Envy and lust, intimately entwined, are the tapeworms of the soul. It is highly appropriate for an image that reveals the debased soul of a society—its resentments, hatreds ("envidia"), and excessive sexual appetite ("lujuria")—to be a parasitic worm that indicates sickness in the host organism. The tapeworm, which attaches itself to the alimentary tract of the host, is characterized by the growth of long, undifferentiated segments of tissue. The image thus associates digestion with the idea of something growing unhealthily within the organism. Lust and envy, like the tapeworm, feed on the weaknesses of the human condition. Hence the soul is seen as an organism infected by the growing desires of sexual gluttony and jealousies.

In the second image, the tablecloth, now dirty and wrinkled, is visualized as an "anfiteatro propio del cadáver del amor carnal." Again, implied by the presence of the soiled tablecloth, the digestive process is linked to sex, the "cadáver del amor carnal." It is insinuated that, by listening avidly to Álvaro's amorous adventures, the men, like worms, are feeding on the remains of love. Love is, then, nothing but carrion. In this way Alas neatly combines the subjects of food and sex under the shared heading of debris.

The topic of religion winds up the banquet. By this time no one

31. The tapeworm image of the soul reappears in Chapter 23 when Ana compares her wicked, disorderly impulses to a tapeworm which devours her good intentions (p. 711). I have since noted a similar image in Balzac's *Le Père Goriot*: "Cette vie extérieurement splendide mais rongée par tous les *toenias* du remord" (ed. Pierre-Georges Castex, Paris: Garnier, 1963, p. 174).

should be surprised when one of the group declares that "la cuestión de si hay Dios o no lo hay, no se resuelve . . . se disuelve" (p. 622). If morality is relative or nil, and love nothing but appetite, that God is dissolving into nothingness follows naturally. The incident of Joaquinito performing an irreverently mocking flamenco dance afterward is the logical consequence of dismissing religion as a moral rudder in contemporary society.

The entire banquet scene, like the Vegallana supper party, has passed from a state of order to disorder. The sense of order, however, is only apparent, for it resides merely in the physical arrangement of things, and disorder, in the form of moral laxity, sexual gluttony, and religious indifference, constitutes the very essence of men's souls in *La Regenta*. The banquet scenario symbolizes the profound sense of disorder which has penetrated the Vetustan universe.

The gluttony, sexual and gastronomical, which characterizes the banquet cannot in any way equal the degenerate and perverted events of *The Satyricon* (very few books, one might add, come up, or down, to *The Satyricon*'s level of decadence). Indeed, sexual inversion and other abnormalities are mostly talked about in *La Regenta* rather than enacted. After he has dined particularly well, Paco Vegallana, for example, loves to display his knowledge of what he calls "lecturas técnico-escandalosas." He claims that the abnormal in sexual affairs is rarely appreciated and desired—"y sin embargo, las damas romanas de la decadencia"—and that, anyhow, sexual aberrations have always been the same in all periods of history. All true. But what is important here is precisely what is not being said. The clichés, the apparently bored and jaded attitude strike the reader first, but the very fact that Paco and his group of friends take to reading and discussing pornography and sexual abnormalities reveals a deep abiding interest in the subject.

Preoccupation with corrupt sexual practices does not always uncover an actual de Sade. Clarín's characters, when they do think about sex (which is more often than not), engage for the most part in a kind of morbid daydreaming, akin to the vague desires of a d'Albert (*Mlle de Maupin*) who rarely puts into practice what he dreams. Sexual inversions, such as Celedonio's and Obdulia's, remain latent. But the odor of sex permeates the Vetustan scene; few acts or thoughts remain unaffected by it. Even heterosexuality, the predominant sexual tendency, is tainted. No sexual gesture is innocent, because the depravity lies in the Vetustan mind itself.

Thus, the banquet in Chapter 20 affords a kind of vicarious pleasure to the group's sexual urges while at the same time it reveals the polluted spirit of humankind in Vetusta. Although Don Pompeyo's dinner is but a poor reflection of Trimalchio's banquet, the Roman archetype does function as the original image to which the Vetustan fête alludes. Clarín was well aware that he could not hope to improve upon or even equal Petronius' invention. On the contrary, the banquet archetype would be better served if it were but palely echoed in a dim, wobbly reflection of the original.

This weaker, duller version of the banquet not only offers more nineteenth-century verisimilitude but reveals the essentially insignificant and unoriginal character of the Vetustans. Petronius' characters may actually carry out their caprices and fantasies, but Clarín's are only allowed to discuss sex. Trimalchio is able to overwhelm his guests' palates by stuffing them with one sumptuous course after another, while the Vetustans are constrained by the gastronomical resources of the day.

Yet the irreverence, the lasciviousness, and general tone of amorality, if not immorality, obtain in both banquet scenes. A belief in a kind of gross materialism is especially evident. In *The Satyricon*, however, man's materiality emerges in a potent expression that dwarfs the pale, unimaginative clichés of the Vetustans: "What are men anyway but balloons on legs, a lot of blown-up bladders?" Just as the Vetustans declare that God is dead and that power and money are sovereign, so one of Trimalchio's guests comments that "the gods have got a finger in what's happening here. And you know why? Because no one believes in the gods, that's why." And later, Trimalchio explains that his household gods are "Fat Profit, Good Luck, and Large Income."[32] The absence of any

32. Petronius, *The Satyricon*, trans. William Arrowsmith (New York: New American Library, 1959), 50, 52–53, 67.

moral values makes it quite easy, therefore, for religious rites to be mocked, as in the case of the sacred saffron which is squirted at the guests' faces. This sacrilegious gesture parallels the burlesque flamenco dance Joaquinito performs in *La Regenta*.

We have also noted that the Spanish scene passes from a state of order to disorder, a movement that echoes the increasing sense of chaos which prevails in *The Satyricon* banquet. Finally, as the narrator Encolpius declares, "the whole business had by now become absolutely revolting."[33] The chapter ends in utter confusion as firemen mistakenly thinking there is a fire within smash down Trimalchio's doors. In *La Regenta*, the guest of honor, Don Pompeyo, eventually becomes disgusted with the banquet. He too stumbles home in a drunken stupor just as Giton, Ascyltus, and Encolpius do. In the Spanish novel it is dawn by the time the banquet breaks up. In *The Satyricon*, however, the crowing of the cock is a false alarm. Both examples allude to the Platonic device of ending a long discussion and banquet with the coming of the dawn, as seen in the *Symposium*.

Moreover, if sex is debased, so is the underlying sacredness of food itself. The banquet scene clearly reveals how the rite of feasting has been profaned. The act of eating is part of the essence of life itself. Such an attitude unconsciously harks back to the most primitive instincts in man when food and the gods were one. Clarín only needed to turn to the example of the Bible to see the religious significance of food displayed directly in feasts and indirectly in parables, or to the rite of Holy Communion itself.

What conclusions can be reached about the nature of men's appetites in *La Regenta*? The most significant point to be made about "el apetito" is that it is essentially not healthy in Alas' novel. Appetite is not a sign of wholesomeness but a symptom of degeneration because it indicates an insatiable craving for sensation. Don Álvaro, who pursues the chaste *regenta* precisely because her virtuousness offers him a new kind of pleasure, is not alone among the novel's characters who need new thrills to prick jaded emotions. De Pas

33. *Ibid.*, 84.

views his relationship with Ana as something new which will pick up his flagging spirits.

In another example, Visitación, already characterized by her unappeasable sweet tooth, takes an intensely voluptuous pleasure in watching Ana's fall from virtue. Spying on her friend's drawn-out struggles to maintain her integrity is like tasting a brand-new kind of candy for Visitación. Clarín describes the effect this secret and piquant sensation has on her commonplace and flat life:

> Ella, Visita, no quería renunciar al placer de ver a su amiga caer donde ella había caído; por lo menos verla padecer con la tentación. Nunca se le había ocurrido que aquel espectáculo era fuente de placeres secretos intensos, vivos como pasión fuerte; pero ya que los había descubierto, quería gozar aquellos extraños sabores picantes de la nueva golosina. . . . Visitación sentía la garganta apretada, la boca seca, candelillas en los ojos, fuego en las mejillas, asperezas en los labios. "Él [Mesía] dirá lo que quiera, pero está *chiflado*", pensaba con un secreto dolor que tenía en el fondo una voluptuosidad como la que produce una esencia muy fuerte; aquellos pinchazos que sentía en el orgullo, y en algo más guardado, más de las entrañas, los necesitaba ya, como el vicioso el vicio que le mata, que le lastima al gozarlo; era el único placer intenso que Visitación se permitía en aquella vida tan gastada, tan vulgar, de emociones repetidas. El dulce no la empalagaba, pero ya le sabía poco a dulce; aquella nueva pasioncilla era cosa más vehemente. (p. 484)

It is evident that in Visitación's case the new sensations she needs to feel derive in large part from an obscure sadomasochistic drive. Some of this same instinct is present in the crowds gazing intently upon the spectacle of Ana dressed as a Nazarene self-consciously martyrizing herself through the muddy streets on Holy Friday. Ana's bare feet also evoke an even more primitive reaction: lust. The people are depicted as devouring her with their eyes (p. 777). Obdulia's response is more extreme:

> "¿Cuándo llegará?", preguntaba la viuda, lamiéndose los labios, invadida de una envidia admiradora, y sintiendo extraños dejos de

una especie de lujuria bestial, disparatada, inexplicable por lo ab-
surda. Sentía Obdulia en aquel momento así . . . un deseo vago . . .
de . . . de . . . ser hombre. (p. 778)

As in the example of Visitación, Obdulia's thirst for a new stimu-
lant to a boring, monotonous life leads to perversion, at least in
thought if not in practice.

Illustrations of sensation-seeking are numerous in *La Regenta*,
ranging from individual pursuits of selfish pleasure to collective
curiosity for the same sorts of new sensations (the Holy Friday
crowds, the guests at the frequent Vegallana gatherings, and the
banqueters in the scene just discussed). A world in which spiritual
and moral values are debased leaves human nature open and vulnerable to the temptations of the senses. An experiment with one
sensation makes one crave another or, as Holbrook Jackson puts it,
"to kill a desire, as you can, by satisfying it, is to create a new desire."[34] This is, in essence, a last-ditch stance since once the higher
values of mankind are denied, nothing remains but matter and
sensation. The healthier and more balanced view of man's dual
nature vanishes.

Before leaving the subject of sensation and appetite in *La Regenta*, I would like to extract one more illustration of the manner
in which Alas imbues the act of devouring with sexual overtones
and thereby unifies the two impulses. The example, a particularly
good one which is found in both naturalist and decadent works of
the period, is the incident in which Fermín de Pas, stimulated by
the receipt of a letter from Ana Ozores, voluptuously bites into a
rosebud. The scene is infused with Clarinian irony by the fact that
Fermín stubbornly deceives himself into believing that his passion
for the *regenta* is free from carnal desire. Deeply aroused, de Pas's
sensuality is gratified by the touch and smell of a rose:

El Magistral arrancó un botón de rosa, con miedo de ser visto; sintió placer de niño con el contacto fresco del rocío que cubría aquel

34. Jackson, *Eighteen Nineties*, 65.

huevecillo de rosal; como no olía a nada más que a juventud y frescura, los sentidos no aplacaban sus deseos, que eran ansias de morder, de gozar con el gusto, de escudriñar misterios naturales debajo de aquellas capas de raso . . . El Magistral . . . tiraba al alto el capullo que volvía a caer en su mano, dejando en cada salto una hoja por el aire; cuando el botón ya no tuvo más que las arrugadas e informes de dentro, don Fermín se lo metió en la boca y mordió con apetito extraño, con una voluptuosidad refinada de que él no se daba cuenta. (p. 638)

This morbidly voluptuous experience is still sustained when de Pas becomes enraptured in the cathedral with a group of young girls learning the catechism. There is an aura of perversity which surrounds this scene: the thirty-five-year-old supposed celibate devours with his penetrating eyes girls ranging in age from eight ("anafroditas las más, hombrunas casi en gestos, líneas y contornos," p. 641) to fifteen ("casi todas iniciadas en los misterios legendarios del amor de devaneo, muchas próximas a la transformación natural que revela el sexo," p. 641). The priest regards the girls as his "roses" whose heads he is privileged to stroke just as he caresses the petals of a flower. All the girls emit "aromas espirituales de voluptuosidad quintiesenciada con cierta dentera moral que les encendía las mejillas y los ojos" (p. 641). Biting into a rosebud and visually devouring one of his own rosegirls are vicarious sexual experiences, a kind of sexual conquest.

The particularly morbid stress on "voluptuosidad" which is seen in the de Pas–rose incident is rooted in the Baudelairean tradition of the "flowers of evil." This idea which associates flower images with the sensuality and corruption of men finds its way into naturalistic and decadent writing of the nineteenth century. There is, for example, in Zola's *La Curée* (1872) a moment of jealous passion in which one of the main characters, Renée Saccard, "l'esprit perdu, la bouche sèche et irritée, prit entre ses lèvres un rameau de Tanghin [a plant of Madagascar] qui lui venait à la hauteur des dents, et mordit une des feuilles amères." The image persists to the very end of the century when it reappears in Mirbeau's *Le Jardin des supplices* (1899). Here, the degenerate Clara bends over a thalictrum plant and later is seen running away, "le visage tout jaune de pollen, la tige de thalictre entre les dents."[35] In all these examples the accent is on the degenerate response which the plant evokes in the character.

It is of especial interest that Alas chose the rose rather than some monstrous, exotic plant out of a Zola or Huysmans garden. The rose, since the Christian era, has been associated with the blood of martyrs, Christ's five wounds, and mystic perfection; it has also symbolized the fragility and impermanence of human life.

But Alas, though he may very well be implying a perversion of the religious significance of the rose, is reverting to an older tradition in the flower's history: the use of the rose in Roman customs. References to roses are frequent among Latin writers. Roses adorned the heads of Roman revellers. Besides being used at festivals and public games, roses, noted Martial, decorated Roman banquets. At one feast the degenerate emperor Heliogabalus is said to have suffocated several guests by smothering them with thousands of rose petals. Beds of roses were not uncommon.[36] Thus, the rose in the time of the Roman Empire was readily equated with voluptuousness. Clarín makes the same identification. Furthermore, if one recalls the description of de Pas given in Chapter 1 as a flowerless underwater plant with lichenous eyes, then the association with a flower of sensuousness serves to tighten the close metaphorical relationship between the priest and plants.

The use of the term *voluptuosidad* in the rose incident ("voluptuosidad refinada," "voluptuosidad quintiesenciada") is characteristic of the Spanish novelist who displays the word and its syntactical variants with great frequency throughout the novel. Clarín usually associates it with the concrete, physical attributes of

35. Émile Zola, *La Curée* (Paris: Fasquelle, 1969), 66; Octave Mirbeau, *Le Jardin des supplices* (Paris: Charpentier, 1929), 171.

36. In *La Faute de l'abbé Mouret* (1875), Zola combines the device of the bed of roses with the Heliogabalus incident when the heroine Albine chooses to die of suffocation in a bed of roses and other flowers.

sensuous enjoyment, as in the above examples in which "voluptuosidad" is experienced through olfactory and tactile sensations.

Gustatory sensations, naturally enough, also engender voluptuousness (*viz.* the rose–de Pas incident). A particularly good example occurs at the end of Chapter 21 when de Pas, enjoying the otiose pleasures of summer, breakfasts daily with the servant girl, Teresa, by sharing a biscuit dipped into a cup of hot chocolate:

> Don Fermín, risueño, mojaba un bizcocho en chocolate; Teresa acercaba el rostro al amo, separando el cuerpo de la mesa; abría la boca de labios finos y muy rojos, con un gesto cómico sacaba más de lo preciso la lengua, húmeda y colorada; en ella depositaba el bizcocho don Fermín, con dientes de perlas lo partía la criada, y el *señorito* se comía la otra mitad. (p. 666)

This scene is very similar to an earlier one of Zola in which Nana and her friend Satin eat a pear together:

> Mais Satin, qui avait pelé une poire, était venue la manger derrière sa chérie, appuyée à ses épaules, lui disant dans le cou des choses, dont elles riaient très fort; puis, elle voulut partager son dernier morceau de poire, elle le lui présenta entre les dents; et toutes deux se mordillaient les lèvres, achevaient le fruit dans un baiser.[37]

Although Zola's scene is more daring because the two characters are women, both examples exude lasciviousness, albeit of a more refined sort in Alas' case. It is also possible to view Fermín's gesture as a profanation of the act of Communion; in that case, the scene attains an added perversity.

Without presuming to establish a direct influence, one wonders whether Alas' generous use of the word is in any way a reflection of Charles-Augustin Sainte-Beuve's novel *Volupté* (1834). But Sainte-Beuve, while still retaining the original stress on sensuous pleasure, develops his own special definition of *volupté*. In his preface, the French critic and novelist explains the purpose of his book as an analysis of a "penchant, d'une passion, d'un vice même, et de tout le côté de l'âme que ce vice domine, et auquel il donne le

---

37. Zola, *Nana*, II, 107–108.

ton, du côté languissant, oisif, attachant, secret et privé, mystérieux et furtif, rêveur jusqu'à la subtilité, tendre jusqu'à la mollesse, voluptueux enfin."[38] Sainte-Beuve has enlarged the scope of the noun to include two other terms, reverie and *impuissance* (later to be called abulia).

Sometimes one senses that Alas is attempting to infuse into the word *voluptuosidad* shades of meanings other than that of mere physical sensuous enjoyment. Hence, we find associated with *voluptuosidad* such qualifiers as *refinada, quintiesenciada*, and the frequent juxtaposition of voluptuousness and mysticism or religious fervor. The word is sometimes used in what would appear to be a deliberately vague context as though Alas were seeking to expand the suggestiveness of the term. The voluptuousness of reverie is evoked in this example:

> Ella se dejaba columpiar dentro de la blanda barquilla en aquel navegar aéreo de sus ensueños . . . Y, mientras los personajes de su fantasía se decían ternezas, ella les preparaba un suculento almuerzo en un jardín de fragancias purísimas y penetrantes. Ana aspiraba con placer voluptuoso los aromas ideales de sus visiones turgentes. (pp. 179–80)

It would be difficult to decide which element, the ideal or the sensual, predominates in this instance. If "los aromas ideales" subtly modifies "visiones turgentes," the reverse is also true. The voluptuousness of the senses is etherealized, enveloped in the vague contours of the dream. Clarín comes closest to Sainte-Beuve's definition of the word in his second and last novel, *Su único hijo*.

Examples of sexual appetite and the preoccupation with sensation and sensuousness, a few of which have been given here, are abundant in *La Regenta*. Juan Ventura Agudiez sees in the Clarinian obsession with sensuality a reflection of an earlier novelist, Barbey d'Aurevilly, in whose unclassifiable works is perceived an aura of refined decadence and sensuality.[39] There is a strong possibility,

38. Charles-Augustin Sainte-Beuve, *Volupté* (Paris: Garnier-Flammarion, 1969), 37.
39. Juan Ventura Agudiez, "La sensibilidad decadentista de Barbey

as Agudiez suggests, that Alas was quite familiar with d'Aurevilly's opus and possibly influenced by the French critic-novelist. But some of the examples that Agudiez cites as evidence of a possible d'Aurevilly influence, in particular those of satanism and sensualism, could be found elsewhere in both romantic and realistic writers of the past century.

Agudiez specifically comments on the use of silks, animal skins, and other accouterments which delight and stimulate the sensual imagination. He notes that this literary device, which Barbey was one of the first to exploit, was new to Spanish writers with the exception of Clarín, who "con bastante maestría, tocará algunas notas correspondientes a esta estética, virgen en España antes de *La Regenta*." [40] The particular example given by the critic is the often-mentioned tiger skin in Ana's bedroom. The *regenta* uses it as an unconscious substitute for sexual fulfillment:

> Después de abandonar todas las prendas que no habían de acompañarla en el lecho, quedó sobre la piel de tigre, hundiendo los pies desnudos, pequeños y rollizos en la espesura de las manchas pardas. Un brazo desnudo se apoyaba en la cabeza algo inclinada, y el otro pendía a lo largo del cuerpo, siguiendo la curva graciosa de la robusta cadera. Parecía una impúdica modelo olvidada de sí misma en una postura académica impuesta por el artista. Jamás el Arcipreste, ni confesor alguno, había prohibido a la Regenta esta voluptuosidad de distender a sus solas los entumecidos miembros y sentir el contaco del aire fresco por todo el cuerpo a la hora de acostarse. Nunca había creído ella que tal abandono fuese materia de confesión. (p. 130)

In using the somewhat exotic device of the tiger skin, Alas relies upon a literary tradition which, in the nineteenth century, first appears in the romantics. A good example can be found in Théophile Gautier's story "Une Nuit de Cléopâtre" (1838). There, two of the queen's attendants lift her gently from her bed and "la posèrent

---

d'Aurevilly y algunos temas de *La Regenta*," *Revista de Occidente*, XXXIII (1971), 355–65. See also Matías Montes Huidobro, "Riqueza estilística de *La Regenta*," *Revista de Estudios Hispánicos*, II (1969), 49.

40. Ventura Agudiez, "La sensibilidad decadentista de Barbey d'Aurevilly," 362.

précieusement à terre, sur une grande peau de tigre dont les ongles étaient d'or et les yeux d'escarbouches." But even naturalists used the device. Zola displayed bear skins instead of tiger pelts, but the effect of voluptuousness remained the same. And Octave Mirbeau, whose combined excesses of decadent and naturalistic literature culminated in *Le Jardin des supplices*, continued the tradition in his decadent heroine, Clara, who "divinement calme et jolie, nue dans une transparente tunique de soie jaune . . . était mollement couchée sur une peau de tigre." [41]

The pleasure derived from tactile sensations is characteristic of *La Regenta*'s ambience. Man is first of all a physical creature, a tenet of the naturalists which Alas accepts unreservedly though without denying the existence of man's soul (Ana's tortured psyche is proof of that); but when Alas stresses the animality of human beings, he extracts as much of the perverted and degenerate tendencies of that animality as he possibly can without exceeding the limits of propriety. Thus, when he describes tactile sensations, he emphasizes the aura of decadence which envelops them, as seen in the examples of de Pas caressing the rose and Ana reclining voluptuously on a tiger skin. Even the *regenta*'s tender rubbing of the satiny bed sheets against her cheeks, which only partially satisfies the maternal longings of a neglected child, is initially expressed in sensual terms: "Abrió el lecho. Sin mover los pies, dejóse caer de bruces sobre aquella blandura suave con los brazos tendidos. Apoyaba la mejilla en la sábana y tenía los ojos muy abiertos. La delectaba aquel placer del tacto que corría desde la cintura a las sienes" (p. 130).

The desire for tactile gratification sometimes forces the darker passions of the soul to emerge, namely a masochistic urge to wound oneself. This is particularly true in Ana's case. The self-martyrdom she displays as she walks like a Christ-figure in the religious procession in Chapter 26 reveals a strong masochistic drive in her personality. In another scene, frustrated and afraid of her sexual desires, she disrobes and, seizing some foxtails normally used for dusting, she indulges in an act of self-flagellation:

41. Théophile Gautier, "Une Nuit de Cléopâtre," *Le Roman de la momie, précédé de trois contes antiques* (Paris: Garnier, 1963), 29; Zola, *Nana*, II, 82; Zola, *La Curée*, 246; Mirbeau, *La Jardin*, 101.

> Ana, desnuda, viendo a trechos su propia carne de raso entre la holanda, saltó al rincón, empuñó los zorros de ribetes de lana negra . . . y sin piedad azotó su hermosura inútil, una, dos, diez veces . . . Y como aquello también era ridículo, arrojó lejos de sí las prosaicas disciplinas, entró de un brinco de bacante en su lecho; y más exaltada en su cólera por la frialdad voluptuosa de las sábanas, algo húmedas, mordió con furor la almohada. (pp. 713–14)[42]

Ana's self-punishment, which can also be interpreted as a perversion of the ascetic ideal, produces a bizarrely voluptuous reaction which, again, is based on a tactile sensation, that of the cold sensuousness of the sheets. In brief, Clarín has inserted two decadent motifs: the act of self-flagellation and sensual delight in the soft physical contact of fabrics and textures.

The stress on unnatural and/or bestial appetites in human nature is shared by naturalist and decadent writers alike. Naturalists like Zola and his followers saw men in Darwinian terms (one of Zola's novels is entitled *La Bête humaine* or *The Beast in Man*). Greatly influencing this conception of man was the spate of medical publications on the subject of psychopathology which appeared during the second half of the century. In nearly all of them, the view most commonly held was that nineteenth-century man was decadent—a creature of low instincts, easily perverted and loving to pervert. This holds true, for example, in all the social classes presented in the Rougon-Macquart series. Animal appetites, though frequently camouflaged by a veneer of refinement, also prevail in such decadent characters as the early, transitional Chevalier d'Albert (*Mlle de Maupin*, 1834), des Esseintes (*A Rebours*, 1884), and Otto (*Le Crépuscule des dieux*, 1884).

Human nature is corrupt in both kinds of works. A major difference resides in the fact that decadent characters self-consciously exploit their degeneration: the aura of evil which surrounds them

42. Ana's frenzied biting of the pillow is another example of the connection between devouring and sexuality, which is further tightened by the allusion to Ana as a Bacchante. Elsewhere, Ana's hysterics are also described as bacchantic; and a sensual daydream about the Bacchantes occurring moments before her seduction presages her almost vampirish future relationship with Don Álvaro.

is a deliberate ingredient of their personalities. They are premeditated seekers after sensation. As we have seen, decadence as expressed through animalized, unhealthy appetite also plays a large part in Alas' novel, but like Zola's creations, Clarín's characters do not participate in a decadent sensibility per se. They do not self-consciously construct a decadent personality to justify their egotistic pursuit of pleasure. They are already corrupt.

Although some of his characters obviously take great though frequently disguised pleasure in their animal appetites, Alas himself is highly critical, not because he is puritanically minded, but because he perceives that the Vetustans in their obsession with unhealthy desires debase themselves and hence become lower-order creatures. The excessive interest in sensation which the decadents self-consciously and somewhat defiantly extoll becomes a main point in Alas' criticism of Vetustan society because it demonstrates the bankruptcy of positive values. Here, Alas clearly continues the tradition of the critical realists and naturalists.

But the emphasis on the morbid quality of the Vetustan sensation-seekers brings Alas much closer to the decadent sensibility of French literature than any other Spanish novelist of his generation. Indeed, as in Zola's case, one senses that Alas perhaps dwells too long and too often on his characters' morbid appetites, that he is as fascinated by sexual corruption as are his characters. In lingering on the decadence of the Vetustans Clarín unconsciously betrays an undue interest in the subject and thereby compromises his original ironically detached viewpoint. The same thing may be said of Zola's writing. Yet it is not difficult to see why both writers are to a certain extent ambiguous in their treatment of the theme of decadence, since the subject itself possesses all those simultaneously fascinating and repulsive qualities which evil frequently exerts over man.

The Sickly Soul

Given the foregoing concentration on the collective aspects of Vetustan decadence, it is appropriate to consider now the predicament of the individual in *La Regenta*. I have noted that a society ruled by the absolute of self-interest and devoid of moral values does not cohere, its members scattering in individual pursuit of pleasure or power. Thus in this sense, *La Regenta* is a novel of individuals whose shallowness and inauthenticity destroy the characteristic of being separate and different personalities.

Characters in *La Regenta* are either secure in their complacency, ignorance, and false or artificial posturings or insecure for a variety of reasons. Self-satisfied, superficial types such as Paco Vegallana or Álvaro Mesía are cardboard targets for Alas to knock down and expose as individuals who lack individuality. The more vulnerable characters usually conceal their precariousness of spirit either through assuming a superior attitude or by attempting to avoid the problem altogether through religion, literature, daydreaming, or sex. But their sense of individuality is compromised by feelings of deficiency or by an inner turmoil.

It is this question of the wholeness of personality which is paramount in an analysis of the principal feminine character, Ana Ozores. Through her crises in personality we also see the depths of degeneration to which the Spanish society as a whole has sunk. It is my contention that the pattern of Ana's life forms a psychological and symbolic parallel to the life of her country and that her downfall represents the final moral and spiritual collapse of Spanish Restoration society.[43]

To understand Ana's psyche it is necessary to unveil the secrets of her childhood and youth, which is precisely what Alas does in Chapters 3, 4, and 5. The setting is her bedroom, or to be more exact, her bed. Ana's bed is frequently the focal point of her daydreaming, reminiscences, and sensual experiences, all three activities often indiscriminately meshed together. Chapter 3 contains Ana's first bedroom scene and is undoubtedly the most significant of all of them. The softness of the pillows transmits to Ana a sense of the

---

43. Robert M. Jackson has also observed that "Clarín, directly in the tradition of his contemporary Galdós, has constructed simultaneous private and public existences not only for the individual characters but for their collective story as well" ("*La Regenta* and Contemporary History," *Revista de Estudios Hispánicos*, XI, 1977, p. 288).

maternal and prepares her for the subsequent recollection of a child-hood episode which represents the turning point of her life, after which the *regenta* imagines her existence as split into two parts. The incident is simple enough in its bare outlines: ten-year-old Ana, ne-glected by her father and orphaned by her mother, and a twelve-year-old boy named Germán, decide to run away together in a small boat and search for her father, who supposedly is off "matando moros." She and Germán are detected and brought home, but the episode becomes tainted by the vile aspersions which Ana's English governess and the townspeople of Loreto cast upon the children's adventure.

How can one interpret this incident? The psychological under-pinnings which support and bind the episode are planted deep in Ana's unconscious. The most significant factor to be noted here is Ana's unsatisfactory relationship with her parents. While searching for her father, she joyfully replies to Germán's innocent statement that they are now man and wife: "¡Yo soy una mamá!" Germán appears to be substituting for the father whom Ana desperately needs, but he also plays the part of a husband in this little drama. There is, in my view, a subtle implication of incestuous behavior being suggested here. This becomes particularly important when one considers how deeply ingrained is her confusion about this episode.

Ana's maternal obsession has been duly noted by every reader of *La Regenta*, but this early scene reveals that her preoccupation with motherhood is ultimately rooted in a quest for her father. The two drives are inextricably linked together here. The very instrument used for the seeking of the father figure is an object frequently as-sociated with the maternal image: the boat. The distinguished Jung-ian Erich Neumann has observed that the central symbol of the feminine is the vessel. The maternal is perceived as a containing ele-ment whose most elementary function is to protect. Clarín estab-lishes a trio of maternal images: 1) the bed and 2) the boat which suggests 3) a rocking cradle. To complete the vessel symbolism Alas mentions the gentle sound and movement of the water sur-rounding the boat. Such "containing water," writes Neumann, "is the primordial womb of life."[44] Thus, the boat is analogous to a womb cradled by the soft lapping of its protective fluid.

Ana never overcomes this unconscious fixation with her father. Her real father, Don Carlos, is a politically liberal émigré who returns disillusioned and ruined by his conspiratorial misadventures. His failure runs parallel with that of the country (p. 150). Ana pursues the idealized image of the dashing, romantic military figure by superimposing this image on other men whose real characters unfortunately fall far short of her romantic imagination. The *regenta* conceives of Don Víctor as a moral fortress for her own inner weaknesses, "la muralla de la China de sus ensueños" (p. 201). The magistrate, with whom Ana enjoys a father-daughter relationship, physically suggests the image of a venerable and even heroic general; but Víctor is impotent in both spirit and sex. Ana romantically conceives of Álvaro Mesía, a second-rate, cynical, and aging Byronic *poseur*, as a Count Almaviva and, later, as King Amadeo. The operatic image indicates that Álvaro is but a mere façade; and the political image furthers this idea. By being compared to the figurehead Amadeo, Álvaro is identified with both political incompetence and impotence. Finally, the religious ballast which the *regenta* naïvely thinks to find in her spiritual protector, Fermín de Pas, is given a rough jolt by the sudden revelation of de Pas's very carnal passion for her.

In all three cases—Víctor, Álvaro, de Pas—Ana attempts to find in a source outside her own inner reserves the sense of security and stability which an unhappy childhood stripped from her. What Ana seeks is a governing principle which will calm and direct the chaos of her soul.[45] This inner anarchy is perceived as a kind of fragmentation of Ana's self. The unconscious incestuous feelings for her father are chaotically mixed up with the dreadful knowledge of personal wrongdoing; and the vague desires to be simultaneously

44. Erich Neumann, *The Great Mother: An Analysis of the Archetype* (Princeton, N.J.: Princeton University Press, 1972), 39, 47.

45. The *regenta* (regir = rule, govern) is unable to govern herself; and Don Víctor is no victor. (The use of deliberate misnomers is a frequent ironic device in Clarín.)

mother and wife for her father become confused. The two roles are never united and thus create a definite split in Ana's psyche.

Ana's obsession with the father image forms a tight relationship to her recollections of the past. Like the liquid maternal containment of the father previously discussed, the mnemonic process in Ana is closely associated to the sense of the fluidity of water: memory is fluid and flows from one dissolving image to another. When, for example, the image of Don Álvaro begins to disappear from Ana's daydreaming, Alas depicts the fading image in these terms:

> La imagen de don Álvaro también fue desvaneciéndose, cual un cuadro disolvente; ya no se veía más que el gabán blanco y detrás, como una filtración de luz, iban destacándose una bata escocesa a cuadros, un gorro verde de terciopelo y oro, con borla, un bigote y una perilla blancos, unas cejas grises muy espesas . . . y al fin sobre un fondo negro brilló entera la respetable y familiar figura de su don Víctor Quintanar con un nimbo de luz en torno. (p. 138)

This dissolving effect of the vanishing picture not only presages future cinematic techniques but, more to our purposes, is comparable to swirling waters which blot out one image in order to allow a fresh one to surface, albeit only momentarily. Indeed, it is in the very nature of these memories and daydreams that Ana is unable to hold onto them, that, despite the rich psychological sediment they reveal, they slip away like will-o'-the-wisps. Memories haunt her, they even chain her, often unconsciously, to the past; they do not allow her to breathe freely in the present. And when she tries to live on and through them by daydreaming and reminiscing, she fails utterly. She only succeeds in temporarily escaping drab reality, but she has not learned how to live either with or without her past.

There are in reality two pasts in the *regenta*'s life: the nimbus-crowned golden age of happiness and heroism; and the subsequent fall from innocence which is represented by the adventure with Germán and the boat. Ana mentally reconstructs the period before her misadventure with Germán, her childhood in Loreto, its green meadows and woods, as a latter-day Garden of Eden. Much later, when the adult Ana is convalescing from a serious illness, she returns to the countryside and tries to recapture that pre-Christian sense of youthfulness (Chapter 27). She even resumes childhood readings in mythology. The pagan stories of gods and goddesses reflected the child's state of guiltlessness. The young Ana also perceives the exuberance of childhood in epic, Homeric dimensions. There is, therefore, an intense need for heroes—*i.e.*, an idealized image of her father, Don Carlos—which Ana finds in the unsuspecting Germán.

In conclusion, both pasts exercise a strong influence on Ana's adult predicament. First, Ana is unable to relinquish the imaginative and nostalgic hold of this original state of grace which is her childhood; but second and most important, the decisive episode in Germán's boat succeeds in irrevocably tainting Ana's soul and her sexual nature. She retains a confused understanding of her own sexuality and a corrupted image of sex itself. In addition, her inner mainspring is broken, an event which is further exacerbated by the loss of parental authority.

Earlier I suggested that Ana's psychological history might provide a clue to the collective dilemma of Spanish Restoration society. By so intimating, I do not mean rigidly to equate the *regenta*'s psychological patterns of childhood trauma and subsequent neurosis to the social and moral behavior of Spain herself. There is no strict identification in itself. Rather, there exist a number a parallels in the quandary in which Ana and Spanish society find themselves. As in Ana's case, the past exercises both a nostalgic and a repressive grip over Vetustan society. The collective past is closely bound to the idea of a golden age, often pastoral in concept, which Vetustan characters endeavor to recapture, sometimes through memory, but more frequently through vulgar imitation of past modes. The attempt to summon forth the past is first perceived in individual terms and then linked to the collective awareness of the past. Before analyzing this particular aspect of the past, let us first note the repressive side of the collective past.

In Vetusta the past soars visibly before the inhabitants in the sublime form of the cathedral spire. The power and the glory of the Spanish Church are apparent in the graceful yet solid architecture. The dominating, unchanging view of the tower symbolizes the serene transition of ecclesiastical authority from one age to another. The Spanish past of sacerdotal splendor is inviolate, it seems to tell us; but the reality is other. The iron hold of the priesthood over Vetusta represents a past which has become morally polluted because the original ideals and spiritual grandeur have vanished. This is precisely the meaning of the anemic Christ figure which Alas describes in Chapter 1:

> Delante del retablo estaba un Jesús Nazareno de talla; los ojos de cristal, tristes, brillaban en la oscuridad; los reflejos del vidrio parecían una humedad fría. Era el rostro el de un anémico; la expresión amanerada del gesto anunciaba una idea fija petrificada en aquellos labios finos y en aquellos pómulos afilados, como gastados por el roce de besos devotos. (p. 92)

Religion in Vetustan society has been drained of its spiritual blood, like the face of the anemic Christ, so that no traces of vitality remain. Instead, the mannered expression suggests the petrifaction of religious ideals, *i.e.*, that the true religious spirit has become ossified and then gradually worn smooth as old bones by repetition and routine. The spiritual vigor of the past, then, has visibly declined, but the very real power of the priests, while of a purely secular and corrupt nature, persists.

The past endures in a variety of other ways too. We have already seen in Chapter 1 that the past modes of romanticism and Siglo de Oro literature and attitudes persist in the *modus operandi* of several characters. Don Saturnino Bermúdez, for example, is a perfect caricature of the romantic hero. He models his life on fictional standards which he finds in cheap French novelettes. This interpenetration of life and literature points to a larger problem in Vetustan society: the inability to evolve patterns of behavior and codes or beliefs which are appropriate to the present and are not mere vestiges, often deformed, of the past. Don Saturnino, like Ana's maiden aunts and the *regenta* herself, lives through a romantic pose. Their present is thus an inauthentic rendering of the past.

Spanish romanticism itself has often been described as a second-rate throwback to golden-age literature, so mimicking the romantic generation is, in effect, a double-layered imitation. *La Regenta* contains a great many references to Siglo de Oro history and literature. The most evident illustration of living one's life through a set of fictional beliefs dating from the seventeenth century is Don Víctor's ardent yet pathetic Calderonianism. The revelation of Ana's adultery in Chapter 29 forces Víctor to acknowledge the unfitness of a seventeenth-century code of honor in nineteenth-century Spain. Nowhere in *La Regenta* are the agony and utter abasement of self so melancholy and pitiable as in those moments of Víctor's self-realization that he is unable to continue his life as though he were an actor strutting and swaggering on stage. Yet he does not know what to do. Without the code he has no inner reserves of moral fortitude. He wishes fervently that he might grow roots and branches and become a thing of nature. "Vegetar," he thinks desperately, "era mucho mejor que vivir" (p. 883). But knowing this to be impossible is equivalent to accepting the human condition. Don Víctor has been forced to discover that it is always difficult to be human. That is the human predicament: one must first realize and then acknowledge the real core of authenticity that lies concealed by layers of posturing and false beliefs and, finally, one must act on that revelation. But Don Víctor, though he now knows he has been playacting, is not strong enough either to withstand the pressures of external reality (society's contempt for the cuckold) or to deny the inner vacuity which he senses within himself. He assumes the role of the outraged, betrayed husband, goes through the motions of a duel, and is killed for his pains.

The strong hold of the Siglo de Oro past manifests itself in other forms of Vetustan behavior. The private conduct of the upper classes is a case in point. More specifically, I refer to the frequent games indulged in by the aristocrats and their guests while visiting the country. The insistence on deliberately childish games such as hide-and-seek is, first of all, a rather corrupt echo of childhood itself. The need to amuse oneself, to dispel boredom is paramount, and playing the role of a child offers an enticing, refined aura of decadence. The games are not only a reflection of the personal or individual past of the characters but of an historical-literary past., The games, which function as ersatz lovemaking, generally take place in a rural setting, although occasionally the Vegallanas' house also serves the purpose. The bucolic scenario of gardens and thick woods echoes the Siglo de Oro vogue of *novelas pastoriles*, of *Dianas*, and *Dianas enamoradas*. The priest Ripamilán certainly perceives, although perhaps a trifle too idealistically, these rustic outings in golden-age pastoral terms:

> Ripamilán . . . iba en sus glorias; no por su contacto con el Gran Constantino, sino por ir entre damas, bajo sombrillas, oliendo perfumes femeniles, y sintiendo el aliento de los abanicos; ¡salir al campo con señoras! ¡la bucólica cortesana, o pocos menos! El bello ideal del poeta setentón, del eterno amador platónico de Fílis y Amarilis con corpiño de seda, se estaba cumpliendo. (p. 430)

But the Platonic charm and endearing youthfulness of the games which are idealized amorous catch-as-catch-can devices in the pastoral novels are completely defiled in *La Regenta*. Here, what might superficially appear as a nostalgic yearning to return to innocent golden days of youth (both personal and collective) is, in reality, a corruption of the past by the present. As in the Vegallana dinner scene, Platonism is made lascivious.

Allusion to the pastoral element occurs in yet another context. De Pas's early life was spent as a shepherd, a fact upon which the priest's memory likes to dwell. Whenever he telescopically surveys the city from the lofty distance of the tower, his mind returns to his earliest recollections of childhood. Like Ana, "prefería las más veces recrear el espíritu contemplando lo pasado en lo más remoto del recuerdo" (p. 83).[46] In the tower scene, de Pas mentally tele-

---

46. De Pas's history offers another parallel with that of Ana's. Like the *regenta*, he is chained to his past through a parental figure (his mother). In addition, the priest, like Ana, sometimes experiences the sensation of being two: the outer, public de Pas characterized by his ambition, pride, and simony; and the inner, passionate de Pas who is known only to himself (pp. 643-44). For a discussion of the split in self, see Matías Montes Huidobro, "Riqueza estilística de *La Regenta*," 43-59; Franklin Proaño, "Presencia y problemática del yo en los personajes de 'Clarín,' " *Boletín del Instituto de Estudios Asturianos*, XXVIII (1974), 313-21; and Franklin Proaño, "Di-

scopes the past and the present into a single image: "Desde aquella infancia ignorante y visionaria al momento en que se contemplaba el predicador no había intervalo; se veía niño y se veía Magistral; lo presente era la realidad del sueño de la niñez y de esto gozaba" (p. 84). He sees his childhood dreams of glory and ambition realized in the power he possesses over Vetusta (elsewhere, however, de Pas's dissatisfaction with the prize of Vetusta runs deep and generally predominates over this more positive reaction). The lonely shepherd now has a much larger flock of sheep to guard, the Vetustan congregation; but the lamb of God has become a lion, as the pastoral image gives way to the fixed resolve of conquest. De Pas remembers his youthful aspirations as though they were "recuerdos de un poema heroico leído en la juventud con entusiasmo" (p. 81). Conquest, as has already been noted, is a reflection of the military grandeur of Spain's golden age, but it has degenerated into a Darwinian struggle for survival. The need for conquest occurs not only in the religious sphere but in affairs of the heart. Don Álvaro, for example, is a corrupt version of the Siglo de Oro Don Juan Tenorio who enjoys the reputation of an "audaz e irresistible conquistador."

Both the pastoral image and the emblem of conquest are rooted first in a personal past and then linked by allusions to golden-age literature and history to a collective past. Childhood, though irretrievably ruined by the decadent sophistication of the upper classes or by the loss of innocence (Ana) or idealism (Fermín), is envisioned as a bucolic paradise. Both Ana and Fermín fill in the contours of this earthly Eden with dreams of heroic deeds and grandeur. But adulthood not only spoils the illusions; it attempts to retain the childhood vision too long. Adult characters not only imitate their own individual past but the youthful days of their collective history. Clarín's clever device of telescoping Fermín's past and Vetusta's into one image expresses the inseparability of the individual and the collective pasts in *La Regenta*.

---

cotomías en los personajes de Leopoldo Alas," *Boletín del Instituto de Estudios Asturianos*, XXIX (1975), 65–75.

The excessive reliance upon past modes of existence results in a curious phenomenon: there is no sense of future in *La Regenta*. For Ana, in particular, what is to be already exists in her past. Her final status of social pariah (the adulterous woman) is predicted by her English governess, who sees in the young Ana's behavior the first seeds of the supposedly dissolute character of her mother, an Italian seamstress whose social origins already damned her in Vetustan eyes. Ana also sees her future enacted in the local stage production of Zorrilla's *Don Juan Tenorio* (Chapter 16). She emotionally identifies herself with Inés and Don Álvaro with Don Juan and wonders whether the fourth act of Part I, in which Inés falls into Don Juan's arms and the hero slays the comendador in a duel, presages her own future and Don Víctor's (identified with the father of Inés). Once again, an individual (Ana) is modeling her life on a vanished collective style of life and literature, in this case, a curious, often anachronistic, blend of romanticism, medievalism, and golden age. Thus, for Ana, not only the individual but the aggregate past *are* her future.

The lack of future also characterizes Vetustan society as a whole. Very little change occurs because most behavior reverts to past manners and fashions; and the most contemporary attitudes are notable only for their crass imitativeness of Parisian *moeurs* (Don Álvaro and his clique especially). The impression that life scarcely evolves in Vetusta is not contradicted by the implications of social and industrial change visible in the altered physical structure of the city (Chapter 1). First, Alas does not develop the idea beyond the initial description of Vetusta and its environs. Second, and most important, the change in social structure does not affect the fundamental nucleus of Vetustan existence. That unchanging core paradoxically consists of an inauthenticity which itself is derived from lack of values and beliefs. The very real stasis of Vetustan society, then, is based on an inner instability. How is this possible? The very absence of beliefs—of a moral center—turns in upon itself and creates a static flurry of activity which never moves from its original spot, a stationary whirlwind. It is this deep sense of stagnation which partially accounts for the aura of decadence in the novel. Life declines and fragments as the core of non-belief slips lower and lower but the center itself remains the same. Like the inner life of the mind (Ana's), internal tensions and removal of restraints bring into being divisiveness and decay, but within the flux the mind is fixed.

I do not mean to suggest that the Vetustan universe is stable—it is not—but it is stagnant because in its decay it revolves constantly around the same things, the same attitudes, and behavior. The only end which is offered to such a conception of existence is death. And death, both physical and metaphysical, oppresses the actual and mental landscape of the Vetustan world. It oozes into the stagnating mud of the land, infiltrates the desperate and wavering spirits of its characters (Ana, Víctor), and finally invades the body proper (Santos Barinaga, Pompeyo, Víctor).

One of the causes for this static universe which falls in upon itself can be attributed to the lack of an ordering principle, as seen visibly for example, in the dinner scenes. The physical disarray of the banquet represents the moral and spiritual chaos of Vetustan society. The discord and confusion point to the absence of authority which would organize and control such inner anarchy. The lack of a father figure, and, consequently, of the internalization of authority (radical self-control) in Ana parallels the want of a governing principle in the collective body.

Sham authority is much in evidence in Vetusta. Early in the novel, the fortunes of Ana's father are compared to the destiny of Spain herself. The meaning is clear. Like Don Carlos, Spain is spent and directionless and so, to provide some measure of order, she grasps hold of the false front of Restoration politics, but the imposition of a particular form of government does not by itself establish real order. There only exists an apparent degree of order in Vetustan society because the essential lack of harmony lies deep within the Vetustans themselves. With no inner steering device, all attempts to thrust an external order upon society become false, as the *turno pacífico* was in reality.

The fragmented, Darwinian society which results from the Vetustans' inner anarchy and absence of a governing principle will parallel the divisive, warring spirit found in Ana's psyche. Clarín describes Ana's sensations during an hysterical attack as follows: "Se tomó el pulso, se miró las manos; no veía bien los dedos, el pulso latía con violencia; en los párpados le estallaban estrellitas, como chispas de fuego artificiales, sí, sí, estaba mala, iba a darle el ataque" (p. 138). The symptoms—reduced vision, violent pulse beat, visual hallucinations—form part of that loosely defined malady of the nineteenth century, hysteria.

The incidence of hysteria in women reached its peak in the second half of the nineteenth century perhaps, as Ilza Veith suggests, because by then the malady was associated with emotional vulnerability.[47] "Feminine weakness" lent itself to the suggestibility of hysteria, for a major characteristic of the malady is its protean forms. Prior to the great Charcot and his student Pierre Janet, hysteria was considered to be an essentially physiological disturbance, but the research undertaken at the Salpêtrière in the 1870s and 1880s indicated that hysteria was a mental malady. Janet, however, did not attribute the origins of the disease to a sexual obsession; indeed, he believed that hysterical patients had no more of an erotic disposition than normal persons. He thought that ideas rather than emotions were the underlying determining condition of the malady. Yet, even though Janet largely discounted sexual motivations in hysteria, his definition and description of hysterical symptoms conform to a great degree to Alas' brilliant analysis of Ana's sickly soul.

Janet conceived of the hysterical state as a lowering of the mental level which takes the special form of the retraction of the field of consciousness and the dissociation of personality:

> What is dissolved is personality, the system of grouping of the different functions around the same personality . . . if hysteria is a mental malady, it is not a mental malady like any other, impairing the social sentiments or destroying the constitution of ideas. It is a malady of personal synthesis. . . . Hysteria is a form of mental de-

47. Ilza Veith, *Hysteria: The History of a Disease* (orig. pub. 1965: Chicago: University of Chicago Press, 1970), 18.

pression characterized by the retraction of the field of personal consciousness and a tendency to the dissociation and emancipation of
the systems of ideas and functions that constitute personality.[48]

In Ana, the contracted field of consciousness is evident first of
all in the narrowed sense of vision she experiences during her attacks. According to Charcot and Janet, reduced vision is an extremely significant symptom of hysteria; but Ana's restricted perception is more than a matter of temporary blurred vision during
brief fits. Ana views the world from the position of an outsider.
She retreats into herself and an inner world of dreams and illusion
to protect her personality from the hostilities of external reality. Her
solitude is constant and grows in intensity as her inner tensions
work havoc on her:

> Una tarde de color de plomo . . . La Regenta, incorporada en el
> lecho, entre murallas de almohadas, sola, oscuro ya el fondo de la
> alcoba . . . tuvo de repente, como un amargor del cerebro, esta idea:
> "Estoy sola en el mundo." Y el mundo era plomizo, amarillento o
> negro, según las horas, según los días; el mundo era un rumor
> triste, lejano, apagado, donde había canciones de niñas, monótonas,
> sin sentido; estrépito de ruedas que hacen temblar los cristales, re-
> chinar las piedras y que se pierde a lo lejos como el gruñir de las
> olas rencorosas; el mundo era una contradanza del sol dando vueltas
> más rápidas alrededor de la tierra, y esto eran los días; nada. Las
> gentes entraban y salían en su alcoba como en el escenario de un
> teatro, hablaban allí con afectado interés y pensaban en lo de fuera:
> su realidad era otra, aquello la máscara. "Nadie amaba a nadie. Así
> era el mundo y ella estaba sola." Miró a su cuerpo y le pareció tie-
> rra. "Era cómplice de los otros, también se escapaba en cuanto po-
> día; se parecía más al mundo que a ella, era más del mundo que de
> ella." (pp. 574-75)

This extremely subjective view of external reality colors the
world with the very hues of Ana's emotions: the world is black,
gray, or yellow, according to her moods. Her auditory perception
of the outside is dim and distant. Sounds outside her own mind

---

48. Pierre Janet, *The Major Symptoms of Hysteria* (2nd ed.; New York:
Hafner Publishing Co., 1965), 332.

make no sense, like the monotonous, meaningless songs of children. Irritating noises enter her sphere of consciousness only to vanish in the distance. Ana's distorted vision interprets the universe as a nonsensical, absurd place, a "contradanza del sol," which signifies nothing. Ana's feelings of separateness are so acute that even her body seems cut off from her spirit and joined with external reality. Her inner world has become solipsistic, as she murmurs to herself: "Yo soy mi alma."

Janet calls this reduced consciousness a kind of decay since it involves an enduring though usually not very deep depression, or mental laziness as he terms it.[49] Ana suffers continually from such an inner exhaustion of the psyche, which she manifests in a variety of mental states. Her overwhelming sense of ennui or "hastío" originates in this special kind of mental depression. Her dissatisfaction with herself and the world and her constant boredom are tinged with a pervasive melancholy. Sometimes abulia attacks the *regenta* in moments of acute distress when, for example, she feels her personality is beginning to fissure into fragments or when, during illness, her mental depression has reached its nadir as in the following example:

> Con toda el alma había creído Ana que iba a volverse loca. A una exaltación sentimental sucedía un marasmo del espíritu que causaba atonía moral; la horrorizaba pensar que en tales días eran indiferentes para ella virtud y crimen, pena y gloria, bien y mal. "Dios, como decía ella, se le hacía migajas en el cerebro" y entonces sentía un abandono ambiente y una flaqueza de la voluntad que la atormentaban y producían pánico. (pp. 797–98)

The terror this state of atony produces is evident in the panic-stricken confession Ana makes to de Pas when she implores his guidance and authority: "Haré todo lo que usted manda; no ya por sumisión, por egoísmo, porque está visto que no sé disponer de mí; prefiero que me mande usted. . . . Yo quiero volver a ser una niña, empezar mi educación, ser algo de una vez, seguir siempre un impulso, no ir y venir como ahora" (p. 562).

49. *Ibid.*, xx.

In her attempts to protect herself both from the world's aggressiveness and from her own inner frailty Ana fails utterly. Her fiasco results in an awareness of the increasing tendency of her psyche to fragment within itself, an illustration of Janet's hysterical dissociation. Her crisis of personality is thus depicted in the following passages:

1. El extremo de la tortura era . . . por último el desvanecimiento de la conciencia de su unidad; creía la Regenta que sus facultades morales se separaban, que dentro de ella ya no había nadie que fuese ella, Ana, principal y genuinamente . . . y tras esto el vértigo, el terror, que traía la reacción con gritos y pasmos periféricos. (p. 798)

2. Estoy enferma; a veces se me figura que soy por dentro un montón de arena que se desmorona. . . . No sé cómo explicarlo . . . siento grietas en la vida . . . me divido dentro de mí . . . me achico, me anulo. (p. 561)

3. Aquella mañana, al sentir en el lecho la misma flaqueza, aquel desgajarse de las entrañas, que parecían pulverizarse allá dentro, aquel desvanecerse la vida en el delirio . . . la conciencia había visto, como a la luz de un fogonazo, horrores de vergüenza, de castigo, el espejo de la propia miseria. . . . Yo . . . todo, todos desaparecíamos. ¡Todo era polvo allá dentro! (pp. 741–42)

The emphasis on the state of ill-health in *La Regenta* creates the oppressive atmosphere of the sickroom, the setting in which much of Ana's mental agony takes place. The sickroom image is simply the hospital image on a much smaller scale. Nineteenth-century literary history reveals a number of examples of the hospital taken as a symbol of a closed-in, unhealthy existence. The Goncourts had used the hospital setting in the 1861 *Soeur Philomène*. In 1863, Mallarmé took up the image in his early poem "Les fenêtres," which contains the memorable opening phrase, "Las du triste hôpital." Baudelaire developed the image in his prose poem "Any Where Out of the World" ("N'importe où hors du monde") which begins with the line, "Cette vie est un hôpital où chaque malade est possédé du désir de changer de lit."[50]

50. Anthony Hartley (ed.), *Mallarmé* (Baltimore, Md.: Penguin Books,

Although both Mallarmé and Baudelaire discovered their personal salvation in art, Alas does not suggest this alternative solution in *La Regenta*. Instead, the confining image of the sickroom offers no issue at all. There appears to be no escape from the oppressive, asphyxiating space which constitutes Ana's life. The feeling of suffocation which Ana continually experiences is also characteristic of an hysterical patient. In the nightmare which she dreams during one of her frequent illnesses, Ana imagines herself caught in a narrow aperture, a predicament which causes unspeakable anguish. Etymologically, anguish is derived from the Latin *angustus* which means narrow or tight. Thus, the *regenta*'s feeling of suffocating in a narrow, enclosed space is, in a very real sense, anguish.

The suffocating anguish Ana experiences in her nightmare leads to the conclusion that the imprisoning space is, in reality, her mind. Ana's fears, fatigue, and ennui are mental tortures from which she tries to flee through daydreams which reconstruct life in romantic, idealized terms. She wishes to escape not only the "cárcel" of Vetustan society but her own fragmented, tormented soul. Ana is imprisoned by the limitations of the self, and it is this inner crisis, rather than any external pressure, which induces her eventual fall.

The attempt to transcend self first manifests itself in Ana's pseudomysticism. The *regenta*'s state of chronic asphyxiation is also indicative of the spiritual level of her soul. Aldous Huxley has noted in Father Surin, who figured in the scandalous Loudun witchcraft case, that the priest in his mystical aspirations felt his soul cramped and contracted when he failed to attain the mystical way of spiritual oneness with God. Words expressing this suffocating restriction—*serré, bandé, rétréci*—appear repeatedly in Surin's writings; but when his soul soared mystically to meet and fuse with God, he felt released, *dilaté*.[51]

The mystic seeks that freedom from the narrowness of self in order to become part of a greater Being beyond mere self. One of

1965), 17; Baudelaire, *Petits poèmes en prose* (Paris: Garnier-Flammarion, 1967), 161.

51. Aldous Huxley, *The Devils of Loudun* (orig. pub. 1952; New York: Harper and Row, 1971), 326.

the Christian works which Ana fervidly studies is *The Imitation of Christ* by Thomas à Kempis, who teaches that one must die to self before one can approach God. In order to accomplish this, writes the German monk, "there is no lesson so profound or so useful as this lesson of self-knowledge and of self-contempt." Thomas emphasizes the nothingness of the individual soul, stating "Lord, I am nothing, can do nothing; I have no goodness of my own, in nothing do I reach perfection, but have a constant tendency toward nothingness."[52] When Ana's efforts at mysticism fail, they do so precisely because of the lesson of self-knowledge and self-contempt. First, it is self-knowledge which Ana lacks and never attains in *La Regenta*: she maintains a confused perception of her feelings and motivations throughout the novel. Second, in Ana the sense of nothingness of the soul which Thomas à Kempis shares with Santa Teresa and other mystics merely serves to reinforce her own feelings of inferiority and tendency toward self-dissolution.

Mysticism then becomes perverted through Ana's vague understanding and misuse of the religious practice. In her imitative attempts to follow the path of Santa Teresa, whose life has influenced her since childhood and adolescence, she is unable to shed her sensual nature, which consistently corrupts the *regenta*'s spiritual experiences. Mystical phrases such as "las moradas," the concept of God as a "brasa metida en el corazón," "oscuridad del alma," and "aridez de alma" alternate with feelings of voluptuousness and the dryness of hard desire. Ana devours Santa Teresa's writings as though they were sweets ("iba a él [*Su vida*] como un niño a una golosina," p. 590). Significantly, Ana's need for mystical experiences occurs most often when she is still in the early stages of convalescence. The *regenta*, writes Clarín, "tenía un ídolo [Santa Teresa] y era feliz entre sobresaltos nerviosos, punzadas de la carne enferma, miserias del barro humano. . . . A veces leyendo se mareaba; no veía las letras, tenía que cerrar los ojos, inclinar la cabeza sobre las almohadas y *dejarse desvanecer*. Pero recobraba el sentido, y a riesgo de nuevo pasmo volvía a la lectura, a devorar aquellas

52. Thomas à Kempis, *The Imitation of Christ*, trans. Ronald Knox and Michael Oakley (New York: Sheed and Ward, 1962), 19, 142.

páginas. . . . La debilidad había aguzado y exaltado sus facultades"
(pp. 631–32).

In other words, Ana's mysticism is clearly associated with sickness. It is curious how Alas' description of Ana's mystical tendencies coincides with the views of a writer whom Alas detested in his
criticism: Max Nordau. In his book *Degeneration*, he writes that "a
cardinal mark of degeneration . . . is mysticism." As A. E. Carter
points out, Nordau's work is a late manifestation of earlier medical
theories which enjoyed a vogue till the end of the century.[53] The
identification of mysticism with nervous disease had already been
made by Cesare Lombroso in *Genio e follia* (1863). Though Alas
was criticizing false mysticism, to be sure, his interpretation of it in
La Regenta does tend also to reflect popularly held views on the
subject.

As Ana regains her health, her adherence to the mystical path
weakens and desires of the flesh make their claims. But when Ana,
in her emotional confusion, tries to deny her carnality, she again
enters a critical zone in her soul's travails. The splitting of her consciousness leads her to believe she is dissolving into nothingness,
that she is, in effect, losing her personality. The fear of self-annihi-
lation points to an exaltation of self in Ana which would seem to
be a complete contradiction of the mystic denial of self. Yet the
contradiction is only apparent, for in both cases Ana is so preoccu-
pied with self that it excludes all other concerns. Nordau observes
that "the hysterical person's own 'I' towers up before his inner
vision, and so completely fills his mental horizon that it conceals
the whole of the remaining universe."[54] This is largely true of Ana
who, because she centers her life in an inner world, suffers from a
contracted field of consciousness.

The exaltation of self, in my view, conceals a very real though
latent suicidal urge which would partially account for Ana's continual agonies over the dissolution of her personality. The existence
of this self-destructive impulse is implied in Chapter 25 when Ana

53. Max Nordau, *Degeneration* (New York: D. Appleton and Company, 1895), 22; Carter, *Idea of Decadence*, 68.
54. Nordau, *Degeneration*, 26.

seeks Fermín de Pas's help in her spiritual and mental difficulties only to discover the priest's very carnal passion for her. In the succeeding days, as the constant rain gives the impression that the entire universe is in the process of liquidation, Ana's sense of abandonment becomes so acute that her faith wavers. She runs to the cathedral to calm her fears and doubts, wishing that she could submerge herself in the collective wave of piety that permeates the church. When she hears the sublime music of Rossini's "Stabat Mater," she becomes romantically carried away and resolves to execute some sacrifice on the grand scale (we later learn that it is the role of the Nazarene in the religious procession). Clarín then writes:

> Aquella exaltación era lo que necesitaba para poder vivir. . . . Haría lo que había resuelto. Y tranquila, segura de sí misma, volvió su pensamiento a la Madre Dolorosa, y se arrojó a las olas de la música triste con un arranque de suicida. . . . Sí, quería matar dentro de ella la duda, la pena, la frialdad, la influencia del mundo necio, circunspecto, *mirado* . . . quería volver al fuego de la pasión, que era su ambiente. (p. 757)

If we keep in mind Ana's inner landscape—which is threatened by the rumblings of a mental earthquake—the desire to throw herself into the anonymous wave of devotion, or into the grandiose accents of Rossini's music, and finally into a scheme of idealized sacrifice, becomes significant. She is fleeing the ominous sensation of inner dissolution by hurling herself into the flux and reflux of life itself. Passion, whether of a religious or profane nature, makes her feel alive and partially smothers her inner desperation, she thinks. There is in Ana's actions a headlong and frantic drive to justify her existence. Thus, Alas with his profound knowledge of the human heart, shrewdly calls her gesture "un arranque de suicida" because her behavior will, in actuality, bring her closer to the brink of self-destruction.

The suicidal impulse resurfaces in the final chapter of *La Regenta* when Ana, haunted by guilt and remorse for her betrayal of Don Víctor, which led to his death, feels that nothing but suffering exists. She is enclosed in a private world of mental agonies, a "caos doloroso" of her own making which shuts out the external world of apparent order and logic. A. Alvarez notes that "first and most important, suicide is a closed world with its own irresistible logic." When Ana's physician asks her if she wants to kill herself, she vehemently denies the question. The idea of suicide is, on the conscious level, utterly repugnant to Ana. But, comments Alvarez, there are "people who will do everything to destroy themselves except admit that that is what they are after; they will, that is, do everything except take the final responsibility for their actions."[55] Ana's apparent struggles for survival draw her deeper into the maelstrom of permanent loss of personality. Each step she takes to rescue herself from that threatened loss—her religious fervor, her sexual experiences—propels her precarious human dignity to descend further into degradation.

It is interesting to see what happens to Ana when she finally succumbs to the physical charms of Don Álvaro (the long wait makes her seduction almost anticlimactic). It is characteristic of her temperament to throw herself frenetically into her first love affair and to regard her lover with the same passionate intensity with which she embraced the way of Christ. Behind her fervor lies the fear of being abandoned, of losing this external support which now appears to be the only defense left against "los fantasmas negros que ella a veces sentía rebullir allá en el fondo de su cabeza, como si asomaran en un horizonte muy lejano, cual primeras sombras de una noche eterna, vacía, espantosa" (p. 853). She plunges into sheer sensuous enjoyment with "una especie de furor que groseramente llamaba Mesía, para sí, hambre atrasada" (p. 853). This physical hunger for sexual gratification is so intense that it makes Álvaro very uneasy. He is flattered, but he begins to notice in his physique a certain deterioration, a waning robustness which upsets the aging Lothario. The implication is clear: Ana's passion is draining away Don Álvaro's virility. Like a vampiress, she is drawing off his *élan vital*.

55. A. Alvarez, *The Savage God: A Study of Suicide* (New York: Bantam Books, 1973), 115, 127.

In this moment, Ana resembles a literary type which had become quite popular in the second half of the nineteenth century. Baudelaire, for example, displays the type in "Le Vampire" and "Les Métamorphoses du vampire." Zola's Nana feeds on the depraved desires of the aristocracy. The type proliferates in decadent literature of the 1880s and 1890s, from Huysmans to Octave Mirbeau. Although Alas does not go into great detail over Ana's decline into vampirish lovemaking, the conclusion is unmistakable: Ana has sunk to the level of animal sensuality which characterizes the rest of the Vetustan population. From *supravetustense* she has dropped into the ordinary *vetustense* category. Her actual physical fall into a state of unconsciousness in the darkened church visually represents her descent into the lower orders of humankind while Celedonio's toadlike, viscous kiss puts the finishing touches to Ana's degraded association with human animality.

The picture of Ana's sickly soul is now complete. How does Ana's psychological state correspond to the collective sphere of the novel? First, the morbid and oppressive enclosed space which represents Ana's mind and her daily existence is paralleled in the lives of other characters and in the general Vetustan ambience. The prison image of Vetustan life—"era como encerrarse en un cuarto estrecho con un brasero. Era el suicidio por asfixia," (p. 645)—is also felt, for example, by Fermín de Pas. He frequently experiences the same sensation of asphyxia and incarceration. Although it is usually the more sensitive characters who imagine themselves prisoners, ordinary Vetustans are not exempt either from the feeling of confinement, especially when the interminable rainy season inundates both the urban and rural landscapes. Then Vetustans can be compared to "náufragos," shipwrecked survivors of a watery catastrophe. Circumscribed by a sea of mud and slippery wetness, the people seek diversions to distract themselves from the eternal monotony of Vetustan life.

Second, Ana's retreat into an inner citadel also bears resemblance to the conduct of the Vetustans who are completely absorbed in their own egotism. Each character is engrossed in his own tight circle of self-interest. This supreme self-containment is most effectively expressed in the degree of self-concealment which occurs regularly in native Vetustans. That is, characters wear masks to hide their true personality; they assume roles like actors on a whirling stage to adapt to the changing circumstances.[56] De Pas's deceptive smile and undulating, priestly walk camouflage his totally unclerical and extremely aggressive nature and, like a stalking animal, allow him to hunt his enemy without appearing to do so. Sometimes, characters act out parts because the inner reality is shallow or even vacuous. Víctor's Calderonian gestures and the Vegallana dinner guests' childish games illustrate to what degree artificiality covers up defective or near nonexistent personalities. The concealment of one's true character establishes a thick, sticky crust of hypocrisy which lies oppressively upon the Vetustan milieu.

The advantage of hypocrisy rests in its usefulness as a tool for spying when one does not wish to appear too inquisitive. The sly and sordid gesture of secret observation of others is symbolic of the Vetustan world of duplicity and inner recesses. The wearing of masks then is most appropriate to the layers of deceit and secrecy which constitute Restoration society in La Regenta. Everyone spies on everyone else. The impression of spying manifests itself even when characters seem to be looking directly and unabashedly at something as, during Ana's martyred walk through the narrow streets of Vetusta, they murmur from their balconies while trying to get a glimpse of the regenta's bare, white feet.

Characters are very loath to reveal themselves in the way that Ana inadvertently does during the religious procession. Indeed, Ana probably comes closest to baring the depths of her being before the reader in inner monologues and daydreams. She also seeks the confessional when the need to unburden her soul becomes acute, but even Ana will conceal in front of de Pas some of her most pri-

---

56. Clifford R. Thompson, Jr., "Egoism and Alienation in the Works of Leopoldo Alas," *Romanische Forschungen*, LXXXI (1969), 193–203; Roberto G. Sánchez, "The Presence of the Theater and 'the Consciousness of Theater' in Clarín's *La Regenta*," *Hispanic Review*, XXXVII (1969), 491–509. Nimetz in "Eros and Ecclesia in Clarín's Vetusta" observes that "espionage is one of the many unexplored themes in *La Regenta*" (p. 249).

vate feelings such as her infatuation with Don Álvaro. Confession represents the means by which a character may relieve his inner tensions and guilt, but, on the whole, it is only Ana who runs to the confessional for spiritual and emotional support. Confession is sometimes parodied. Don Álvaro, for example, makes full "confession" of his many amorous exploits after quaffing wine and breaking bread at Don Pompeyo's banquet; but Álvaro never willingly reveals himself for what he is: a shallow peacock of a man. Thus, the confessional, its true purposes perverted or ignored, recedes into the dark background of inner recesses and false façades.

And finally, we see that Ana's retreat into herself, which leads to mental and spiritual fragmentation and threatening dissolution, finds its parallel in the native Vetustans' tight little islands of self-interest which cause them to shatter their society into knife-like shards and thus rip asunder collective cohesiveness. As individual and society become more and more fragmented, they slide closer to dissolution, following the vague and indifferent drift of the "dejarse ir."

Thus, the individual and the collective strands in *La Regenta* meet by means of the common denominator of degeneration. And the sickly soul finds its parallel in the diseased social body shot through with morbidity, corruption, and perversion. The psychological explanation and the social analysis therefore run in parallel lines which eventually converge upon the larger meaning of universal degeneration—"todo parecía que iba a disolverse."

Using a neurotic as the central protagonist in order to manifest not only the individual's physiological-mental decline but, indirectly, the degeneration of a society is a frequent device in European literature of the last half of the nineteenth century. But Clarín's parallel development of individual and collective decadence differs considerably from the naturalist's pattern in two significant aspects. First, in contrast to the Zolaesque emphasis on the physiological etiology of the neurotic and of degeneration in general, Alas' view looks forward to the Freudian conception of neurosis and, specifically, of hysteria as a mental malady. But second and more important, Clarín's psychological analysis of a dissolving, fragmented soul in torment attains far more complexity and depth than previous naturalistic novels. And this sensitive exploration of the individual psyche, which seems far more Baudelairean than naturalistic, is intimately and profoundly tied to an adept realistic analysis of the social body.

By moving away from the physiological explanation of decadence in personality, Alas approaches the later decadent sensibility of the aesthetic movement of the 1880s which rejected the naturalists' emphasis on the physical causes of degeneracy. In addition, both Alas and writers in the decadent movement share the common link of the special Baudelairean metaphysical decadence. I have also noted that Clarín's morbid fascination with decadent types and motifs and with the decadent characteristics of unnaturalness, artificiality, and degeneration approaches to a certain degree the decadent's sense of complicity in his subject matter. But, as already seen, Clarín's moral stance, which views Vetustan existence from the vantage point of a metaphorical tower in order to point out more clearly the depths of degradation below, functions as an ethical controlling principle in the morass of animalized and perverted Vetustan behavior. In *La Regenta*, Alas is still too deeply imbued with the realist-naturalist view of reality to do more than hesitantly ripple the surface of the *fin de siècle* decadent sensibility, but in *Su único hijo* the Asturian novelist will come much closer to this aesthetic.

III *Su único hijo*

Critics of the two novels of Leopoldo Alas have concentrated their attention on the Asturian's first novelistic effort, *La Regenta*, almost to the exclusion of his second, *Su único hijo* (1891). In the 1960s and 1970s, however, several articles on *Su único hijo* appeared, attesting to the mounting interest in Clarín's work, even in his supposedly inferior second novel which, in the past, was considered a "novela más endeble de composición y de factura que *La Regenta*."[1]

Traditionally, *Su único hijo* has been a somewhat unclassifiable work for the critics. As early as 1891 we find this unfavorable opinion of León Máinez: "Y, ¿a qué género de novelas pertenece *Su único hijo*? ¿ Se puede saber? ¿ Es novela histórica, de costumbres, picaresca, idealista, novelesca, naturalista, psicológica, experimental, o trascendental y docente? Tarea ardua sería averiguarlo, cuanto más el sostenerlo." In a glowing article, Azorín states that "no sabemos cómo clasificar *Su único hijo*; no acertamos con la escuela." Baquero Goyanes believes that Alas in his second novel spills over

1. Andrés González Blanco, *Historia de la novela en España desde el romanticismo a nuestros días* (Madrid: Sáenz de Jubera, 1909), 503. Azorín (José Martínez Ruiz), in his *Páginas escogidas de Leopoldo Alas* (Madrid: Calleja, 1917) and other works, proved an exception to the general rule of condemnation and neglect of *Su único hijo*. Mariano Baquero Goyanes, in *Prosistas españoles contemporáneos* (Madrid: Rialp, 1956), 33–125, also paid serious attention to Clarín's second novel; subsequent studies are indebted to this fundamental work on *Su único hijo*. For more recent articles, see the bibliography. Recently published is the first annotated edition of *Su único hijo*, with a substantial introduction by Carolyn Richmond (Madrid: Espasa-Calpe, 1979). It is Professor Richmond's well-argued contention that *Su único hijo* was actually published in 1891 and not 1890, a point to which I subscribe.

the demarcation between the nineteenth and the present century,[2] while the title of Eduard Gramberg's article, "*Su único hijo*, novela incomprendida de Leopoldo Alas," explains itself.

The frustration over the pigeon-holing of *Su único hijo* apparently is due in part to the overwhelming impression which *La Regenta* made on the informed reading public. After Alas' ambitious first effort, reviewers evidently expected the second novel to resemble its predecessor by adhering to the *detallista*, realist-naturalist bent of the first book. But by 1891, the date of publication of *Su único hijo*, Zolaism was on the decline and the psychological novel in the forefront. In response to contemporary idealistic aspirations, novelists shed much of the heavy, detailed framework of the earlier realist-naturalist generation and concentrated more on inner realities than on the visible outer world, as is evident not only in the psychological, idealistic novel but in the works of the decadent movement and of the closely related symbolist group.

Some critics insisted that *Su único hijo* was indeed a naturalist novel—witness the rabid opinion of Father Francisco Blanco García.[3] The presence of physiological needs and morbid eroticism convinced early reviewers of *Su único hijo*'s Zolaism. But it quickly became apparent to subsequent readers that at least two elements weakened this position: the greater attention which Clarín pays to the psychological situation of the characters in lieu of a heavy emphasis on externality; and the strong comic vein, which is inconsistent with the humorless and serious objectivism of Zolaesque naturalism.

If one favored the classification of *Su único hijo* as a psychological novel, however, one still had to contend with the ferocious and

2. José María Martínez Cachero, "Un ataque a 'Clarín': Seis artículos de Ramón León Máinez," *Revista de la Universidad de Oviedo* (Letras), XI (1950), 266; José Martínez Ruiz, " 'Una novela': *Su único hijo*," *ABC* (February 1, 1950); Baquero Goyanes, *Prosistas españoles*, 51.

3. Francisco Blanco García, *La literatura española en el siglo XIX*, II (3rd ed.; Madrid: Saénz de Jubera, 1910), 546–47. See also: Ramón Esquer Torres, "Las luchas del siglo XIX: El P. Blanco García y Leopoldo Alas 'Clarín,' " *Boletín de la Sociedad Castellonense de Cultura*, XXXVIII (1962), 241–55.

merciless authorial voice which seemed bent on deflating and coldly deriding its own creations. In this connection, Baquero Goyanes has called *Su único hijo* "la novela más fríamente narrada de todo nuestro siglo XIX."[4] How did one reconcile the idealism of the hero Bonifacio Reyes' paternal quest with the pitiless realistic satire and irony which succeeds in leaving one with a bitter aftertaste?

The two strains of the satirical/ironical and the psychological, in my view, do not blend very well in *Su único hijo*; indeed, they set up a jarring effect on the reader because each tendency is heading in a different direction. The humorous vein debouches into the traditional current of Spanish realism which, since Cervantes, has characteristically been leavened with the agent of satire and/or irony. But the psychological treatment in *Su único hijo* points to a different form of novel writing, a form which has more in common with the contemporary decadents, symbolists, and psychological idealists than with traditional realism or naturalism.

Clarín's inner unrest was finely attuned to the same uneasiness which had spread throughout Europe. He too sought more profound realities through the exploration of the psyche and the dream and the intriguing relationship between the arts—in particular music—and life. These preoccupations which are manifest in *Su único hijo* lead Clarín to neglect to a certain extent the external in order to concentrate on and enhance the internal.

But Alas' psychological bent in his second novel cannot be satisfactorily described as the same psychological realism which exists in *La Regenta*. If it had been, the characteristically Clarinian humor would, I believe, have harmonized more easily with it. On the contrary, the psychological reality of *Su único hijo* possesses a curiously abstract quality about it which is difficult to grasp and to explain because Clarín seems somewhat indecisive about the formal approach he should take in relation to his characters. Baquero Goyanes appears to have sensed this abstract quality when he wrote that "lo que Alas ofrece en su novela es casi un esqueleto."[5] This skeletal characteristic in *Su único hijo* persists not only in the characters but

4. Baquero Goyanes, *Prosistas españoles*, 50.
5. *Ibid.*, 124.

in the situation and the ambience. I hasten to add that the unfleshed appearance of the novel does not give the impression of incompleteness but, combined with Alas' realistic irony, it does suggest perhaps that the author may not have consciously formulated a lucid and consistent formal structure.

The Clarinian psychology of *Su único hijo* may be called archetypal psychology because the characters and the situation respond to a somewhat abstract design which, in turn, is based on a number of universal patterns. Moreover, these Clarinian archetypes approach to a great extent the decadent typology of the 1880s and 90s, which is itself largely derived from universal molds adapted to contemporary needs and expression. The question of a decadent influence on Clarín's second novel appears not to have occurred to his critics, although his great friend Menéndez y Pelayo unintentionally pointed the way to such a possibility when he wrote to Clarín that the novel was "excesivamente saturada de tristeza *decadentista*." [6]

The approximation to decadent archetypes is also enhanced by the creation of a quasi-archetypal ambience. The sketchiness and indefiniteness of both time and space in *Su único hijo* have been noted and argued over by a number of critics. In their attempts to pinpoint a chronological frame, the critics have reached conflicting answers. Azorín believes that the action of the novel takes place between 1830 and 1840, although he admits that the temporal scheme is vague. Baquero Goyanes, however, advances the date to shortly after 1850, while Küpper opts for the year 1860. [7]

One may readily discard the Azorín thesis on the basis of internal evidence. In Chapter 4 the author writes that "por la tienda de

6. Marcelino Menéndez y Pelayo, *Epistolario de Menéndez y Pelayo y Clarín* (Madrid: Escorial, 1943), 53. See Carlos Feal Deibe, "La anunciación a Bonis: Análisis de *Su único hijo*," *Bulletin of Hispanic Studies*, LI (1974), 255–71, in which an archetypal and psychological analysis is applied to Clarín's second novel.

7. Martínez Ruiz, " 'Una novela': *Su único hijo*;" Baquero Goyanes, *Prosistas españoles*, 55; Werner Küpper, "Leopoldo Alas 'Clarín' und der französische Naturalismus in Spanien" (Ph.D. dissertation, University of Cologne, 1958), 167. Carolyn Richmond, in the introduction to her edition of Leopoldo Alas' second novel, gives an excellent analysis of the problem of time in *Su único hijo* (pp. xxxv–xli).

Cascos había pasado todo el romanticismo provinciano de los años cuarenta al cincuenta."[8] The reference in the last chapter to Verdi's *La Traviata*, which was first performed in 1853, also weakens the argument for a romantic ambience (1830–1840) in *Su único hijo*.

Baquero Goyanes bases his thesis mostly on the information given in Chapter 4, which describes a group of postromantic *tertulianos* whose memories hark back to the epoch of full-blown Spanish romanticism. Indeed, the whole of *Su único hijo* is infused with a postromantic aura which, one hastens to add, is continually punctured by Alas' ironical point of view. It is fairly accurate to state that Clarín's novel does take place sometime after 1850, although the allusion to *La Traviata*, which did not attain European popularity until 1854 (the first Venetian performance in 1853 was a failure),[9] advances the date beyond Baquero Goyanes' contention of 1850 or thereabouts.

There are other references, however, which make one reasonably unsure about the 1850–1860 hypothesis. A glance at two types of allusions—medical and musical—reveals certain inconsistencies. The medical allusions to homeopathy, spiritualism, vitalism, and hysteria seem to point to the decade 1850–1860 when, Baquero Goyanes writes, there was a vogue and interest in such things. The physician Don Basilio declares, however, that he is not only a homeopath but a vitalist and an "espiritualista, aunque no es esa la moda reinante" (p. 138), a statement which seems to contradict Baquero Goyanes' contention. But interest in homeopathy, vitalism, and spiritualism extends from the end of the eighteenth century to the final years of the last, which would suggest a certain difficulty in

8. Leopoldo Alas, *Su único hijo*, ed. Carolyn Richmond (Madrid: Espasa-Calpe, 1979), 29. All subsequent quotations are drawn from this edition and are cited in the text.

9. I have been unable to ascertain when *La Traviata* was first performed in Spain although Luis Coloma's *Pequeñeces* (1891), which takes place in 1872, contains this allusion: "*La Traviata*, ópera a la sazón muy en boga y escogida por Miss Jesup para presentarse por primera vez en la escena madrileña" (*Pequeñeces*, México City: Porrúa, 1968, p. 62). If this is so, then the date for *Su único hijo* may be considerably later than the decade 1850–1860.

finding an accurate date for the action in *Su único hijo*. In particular, the medical controversy between materialists and idealists, or fluidists versus animists (vitalists) as it is sometimes called, continued unabated throughout the nineteenth century. As late as 1901 a book entitled *De L'Influence de l'esprit sur le corps*[10] would appear and go through several editions, attesting to the uninterrupted curiosity in the subject.

Hysteria was not just a malady of young ladies of the romantic era; it persisted with startling frequency throughout the last quarter of the nineteenth century. Indeed, the most publicized cases were those which Charcot exhibited and experimented upon at the Salpêtrière in the 1870s and 80s. It is also interesting to note in *Su único hijo* the definition of hysteria as a Proteus ("El histerismo es un Proteo," p. 138). This particular statement would appear to refer to the well-known medical description of hysteria which the great clinician Thomas Sydenham (1624-1689) formulated in the seventeenth century.[11] The effect of alluding to such chronologically far-flung medical terms as Sydenham's Protean hysteria (1600s) or Stahl's vitalism and Hahnemann's homeopathic medicine (1700s) is to reduce the sense of time felt as a concrete, definite phenomenon in the novel. One is disoriented, unable to state with complete assurance that *Su único hijo* occurs at a particular moment in Spanish history.

The frequent allusions to music, especially Italian opera—Rossini, Bellini, Donizetti, Verdi—seem to deposit one securely in the midst of the Spanish romantic era. But here again, we are encountering something with a long history reaching back into the eighteenth century and extending into the final years of the Restoration, and the influence of Italian music in Spain was still quite potent in 1885, when the eminent musicologist Peña y Goñi was able to say that "la ópera española no existe, la ópera española no ha exis-

10. Baquero Goyanes, *Prosistas españoles*, 59; Dr. Paul Dubois, *De L'Influence de l'esprit sur le corps* (9th ed.; Berne: A. Francke, Ed., 1910). Dubois' thesis is similar to Don Basilio's belief "en la influencia de lo *moral sobre lo orgánico*" (p. 133).

11. Pierre Janet, *The Major Symptoms of Hysteria* (2nd ed.; New York: Hafner Publishing Co., 1965), 18.

Gift

Title The Decadent Vision

_____

Author _____

Check for defects _____
Break in book _____
Check against invoice _____
Check in on computer BH
Write legend in book BH
Barcode book BH
Stamp book JW
Put in security strip _____
Catalog _____
Check call number against
      shelf list _____
Print labels _____
Print card set _____
Label spine _____
Attach needed stickers _____
Cover jacket/book _____
Final check _____
Change status _____

Allegany College of Maryland   6/3/9

tido nunca." Although the majority of Alas' references to Italian opera masters are the early romantic composers of the first third of the century, he also includes the second Italian generation in his allusions to Giuseppe Verdi. It is possible that the scene in which Bonis declares his love for Serafina may have been inspired by Verdi's *Otello* (1887). When Serafina Gorgheggi murmurs passionately, "*un bacio, un bacio*," she seems to be echoing the famous love duet between Otello and Desdemona in which the musical phrase is repeated in the last scene of the opera: "Un bacio, un bacio ancora, un altro bacio." [12]

There are also some other references, mainly historical, which tend to range chronologically far and wide throughout the nineteenth century. Pastness in *Su único hijo* is referred to as taking place "en tiempo de Istúriz" (p. 34), which could possibly mean the years 1836, 1846, or 1858 when Francisco Javier Istúriz held high position in the Spanish government. The mention of "el mal ejercicio del régimen constitucional" (p. 184) might refer to 1820, 1837, or 1869. One of the book's minor characters, Lobato, is an "ex cabecilla carlista" (p. 304), of either the first or second Carlist Wars (1833–40, or 1872–76). The most specific and least ambiguous historical allusion is this: "Así como, si a Sagasta o a Cánovas, caídos, los llamase la Reina al amanecer, poco más para formar Ministerio" (p. 136). This is a clear reference to the Regency of María Cristina (1885–1902), which, of course, places the novel's possible temporal scheme as much later than the critics have believed it to be. Is this an anachronism or simply an obfuscation on Clarín's part? [13]

12. Antonio Peña y Goñi, *España desde la ópera a la zarzuela* (Madrid: Alianza, 1967), 18; Verdi, *Otello*, in David G. Legerman (ed.), *A Treasury of Opera Librettos* (Garden City, N.Y.: Doubleday and Company, 1962), 752. The earlier Rossini version of *Otello* (1816) does not contain the same leitmotif.

13. Some other references include, for example: a Spanish translation of a Thiers book by Miñano (d. 1845), 82; the existence of the Guardia Civil (established 1844), 121; "comer a la *francesa*, gran novedad en el pueblo," 141 (does this mean the 1840s, the 1850s, or possibly later?); the phrase, "un siglo positivo," 226 (in Tamayo y Baus's play, *Lo positivo* [1862], one finds expressed the notion that *lo positivo* was equivalent to *lo materialista*).

What can one conclude from this miscellaneous information? Although it is certain that *Su único hijo* does not take place during the Spanish romantic era, despite the many references to romantic music, literature, and attitudes, it is not equally certain that one can state with assurance the exact period in which the action of the novel occurs since too many contradictory and unclear allusions abound. In this conclusion, I concur with Eduard Gramberg, who states that "para mí la vaguedad temporal sigue siendo un hecho."[14] I also believe, however, that though the author appears to have sought a deliberately indefinite, uncircumscribed temporal scheme, it is possible to assign a much later date to the novel's chronological framework (that is, the late 1880s) simply because a clear allusion to that era exists and other references could be fitted to that scheme. These citations are not plentiful, however, and seem rather fortuitous in their very existence within *Su único hijo*.

What conclusion may be reached about the setting for Alas' second novel? No particular city is named except to state that it is "una melancólica y aburrida capital de tercer orden" (p. 5). From the sparse description of the surrounding countryside and of the hamlets Cabruñana and Raíces, one assumes that Alas is describing his beloved Asturian landscape. The reference to the chemical plant and the gunpowder factory in which the Valcárcels have sunk their money is an example of the beginnings of the growth of industry in the Asturias.[15] But Alas never specifies the locality; he merely suggests the bare outlines of a third-rate city in a rural province.

The apparent vague temporality and uncertain setting will become the framework in which characters drawn with a few, fairly simple strokes of the pen will walk through an uncomplicated plot. In reality, the plot, like the elements of time and place, loses its importance as the situation and the mental state it provokes in Bonis and, to a lesser extent, in Serafina and Emma, quickly pre-

14. Eduard J. Gramberg, "*Su único hijo*, novela incomprendida de Leopoldo Alas," *Hispania*, XLV (1962), 196.

15. Juan Antonio Cabezas, *Asturias: Biografía de una región* (Madrid: Espasa-Calpe, 1956), 159; Raymond Carr, *Spain, 1801–1939* (London: Clarendon Press, 1966), 202, 264, 390.

dominate. The plot gives way to a mood which is essentially deceptive for the reader because it possesses two edges, the soft side of
reverie (Bonis' voice, which sometimes merges with the authorial)
and the cutting underside of satire and irony (the authorial voice).
One of the most significant devices which Alas utilizes in order to
establish this double-edged mood is the pervasive presence of music,
a major element of *Su único hijo*, which also functions as an appropriate frame for the archetypicality of the characters and their
situation.

Music and Melodrama in Su único hijo

Music is inescapably tied to romanticism in *Su único hijo*; and romanticism forms the backdrop against which the novel is set. The
romantic mode functions in two major ways: as a historical period
which is both remembered with warm nostalgia and copied in a
vain endeavor to perpetuate the past; and as a state of mind in
which reverie and idealization predominate. The characters are
rarely able to perceive reality other than from within the romantic
attitude, whether it be a false or an authentic posture, but the authorial point of view is ambivalent. Clarín wavers between a mock-
ingly ironic position and a sympathetic understanding of the need
to daydream and to experience tender, honest emotions. This last
point of view sifts indirectly through the hazy and emotional mind
of Bonifacio Reyes, undoubtedly the pivotal character of the novel.

The musical element operates on this dual level of positive and
negative evaluations of the romantic *modus vivendi* in *Su único
hijo*. As already mentioned, Italian opera predominates.[16] The sin-

16. References to Italian opera are frequent in other contemporary Spanish novels, though none, with the possible exception of the much earlier
and unsuccessful *El final de Norma* (1861) by Alarcón, incorporates opera
into the very structure of the work as does Alas. See especially Coloma's
Pequeñeces (1891), in which allusions to opera are scattered throughout
(pp. 4, 10, 28, 41, 49, 62, 63, 117, 214, etc.). Matías Montes Huidobro is
the first to have recognized the importance of the musical element in *Su
único hijo* ("*Su único hijo*: Sinfónico avatar de Clarín," *Archivum*, XXII,
1972, pp. 149–209). Also of interest: Vernon A. Chamberlin analyzes the

gle most important principle of this musical form is the stress on the solo voice which expresses the melody. What Alas does with Italian opera in his novel is very similar structurally to the actual operatic presentation. One notes, first of all, an unusual emphasis on human voices in Clarín's second novel. Much of Bonis' perception of the two main female characters, Emma and Serafina (la Gorgheggi), is based on the quality of their voices. Emma is a veritable fury, her voice shrill and strident ("la voz chillona, estridente," p. 24). Serafina's singing voice possesses strong maternal overtones for Bonis, and it is her voice which first captivates him: "Y la voz es una voz . . . maternal; canta con la coquetería que podría emplear una madre para dormir a su hijo en sus brazos" (p. 39). There is yet a third voice which characterizes not only Serafina, who as we shall see is conceived as a dual personality, but later Emma Valcárcel. This last voice sounds the note of passion and lust: it is characteristically "una voz ronca, gutural" (pp. 91, 128).

These three voices—the strident, the maternal (which frequently merges with the paternal), and the erotic—operate as a series of leitmotifs which weave in and out of the structure of Alas' work. The characters Serafina and Emma have their individual scenes of novelistic "aria and recitative" which sustain the "melody" or inner harmonies of the book. Clarín does not actually orchestrate his novel in the sense that a Wagnerian opera is orchestrated, but he does permit a flexible, somewhat loose structure to center around melodramatic scenes of one or two principal actors whose voices, *i.e.*, personalities, carry the leitmotif of the moment in question.

In these scenes, one quality strikes the reader quite readily: the tone of exaggeration. The technique of exaggeration has been noted in Clarín's use of caricatures and hyperbole,[17] but here exaggeration is innate to the musical-dramatic mode employed. The characters

---

symphonic structure of Galdós' *Fortunata y Jacinta* in his book *Galdós and Beethoven: Fortunata y Jacinta, A Symphonic Novel* (London: Támesis Books, Ltd., 1977).

17. For a discussion of Clarín's humoristic techniques, see Eduard J. Gramberg, *Fondo y forma del humorismo de Leopoldo Alas, Clarín* (Oviedo: Instituto de Estudios Asturianos, 1958).

behave as though they were operatic figures on a stage, mouthing melodramatic lines and gesticulating with frenetic activity. Exaggeration in *Su único hijo* is translated into the melodrama of opera. The characters act passionately, vengefully, or hysterically on cue, but the conductor (Alas) directs the farrago of cheap emotionalism and sentimentality with a gesture of knowing and perhaps a trifle weary irony. This operatic melodrama of *Su único hijo* can be seen in such scenes as Serafina's and Bonis' love-making, the Valcárcels' conjugal *crises d'amour*, Emma's moments of hysteria and her temper tantrums, the discovery of her pregnancy, her exaggerated fears of a late miscarriage and, later, of labor pains, and finally, the last scene of the novel, in which Bonis and Serafina confront one another in the church. A descriptive analysis of these scenes should suffice to demonstrate not only their operatic quality but the adroit manner in which Alas exploits them.

The first time that Bonis makes a declaration of love to Serafina occurs after the *diva* and the tenor Mochi have cleverly maneuvered Bonis into a situation propitious to a love scene. Bonis plunges into his confession of love. Serafina looks around to make sure there are no witnesses, and then:

> Le brillaron los ojos con el fuego de una lujuria espiritual, alambicada, y, cogiendo entre sus manos finas y muy blancas la cabeza hermosa de aquel Apolo bonachón y romántico, algo envejecido por los dolores de una vida prosaica, de tormentos humillantes, le hizo apoyar la frente sobre el propio seno, contra el cual apretó con vehemencia al pobre enamorado; después, le buscó los labios con los suyos temblorosos. . . .
>
> –*Un bacio, un bacio*–murmuraba ella *gritando* con voz baja, apasionada. Y entre los sueños de una voluptuosidad ciega y loca, la veía Bonifacio casi desvanecido; después no oyó ni sintió nada, porque cayó redondo, entre convulsiones. (pp. 64–65)

Serafina's operatics—the quasi-maternal embrace, the passionate, trembling kiss—contrast ironically with the good-natured and guileless posture of Bonis. Her exclamation of *"un bacio, un bacio"* derives strictly from an operatic situation, possibly as I have noted before (although there is no concrete evidence, merely the suggestion) from Verdi's *Otello*, which is well known for its leitmotif of the kiss. Using a characteristic technique of his, Alas deliberately italicizes not only the Italian phrase but the singer's vocal quality, "gritando," in order to underline ironically the exaggerated and probably false passion which Serafina assumes. Her melodramatic acting, however, is shown up for what it is by the contrastive and humorous shock of Bonis' convulsive fainting fit. This is a typical comic resource of Alas: deflation of a scene which begins on a high key (here, melodramatic) by ending on an incongruous low note. Although the exaggerated mode is mocked by authorial, comic manipulation, the point is that the scene revolves around a nucleus of operatic melodrama.

Hyperbolical gesture and language play a dominant role in the love scenes between Bonis and his wife Emma. A good example is the final scene of Chapter 10, in which the conjugal pair enact the roles that Minghetti the baritone (soon to be Emma's lover) and Serafina have just performed on stage. Bonis activates the scene when, in a capricious fit of lust for his wife, he falls on his knees, embraces Emma, and murmurs words of encouraging lasciviousness to her. Her response is a physical one: she bends down until her mouth reaches his, and "con ambas manos le agarró las barbas, le echó hacia atrás la cabeza, y, como si los labios del otro fuesen oído, arrimando a ellos los dientes, dijo como quien hablando bajo quisiera dar voces: —¡Júrame que no me la pegas!" (p. 161). The moment, which is vocally captured in Emma's repressed *sotto voce*, is eminently theatrical and melodramatic.

It also becomes ludicrous a minute later when the henpecked Bonis meekly complains: "Pero, mira, me vas a desnucar, se me rompe el cogote" (p. 161). Once again, Alas reduces melodrama to comedy—the move is habitual and probably irrepressible in Clarín, the great debunker of the pretentious and the inauthentic. After Bonis' mild protestation, there follows a moment of pregnant silence and mutual enjoyment of Bonifacio's physical pain. Then, Emma suggests that they play an erotic game of make-believe. She will be the Princess Micomicona, Serafina's operatic role, and he will be Minghetti, "señor matamoros" in the opera. What follows then is an exchange of roles, a curious and quasi-prophetic criss-crossing of couples. The illusion is both the anticipation and the realization of a mutual desire, as erotic daydreaming is vicariously fulfilled with a substitute lover. Despite the Clarinian irony, the entire scene, like the love scene between Serafina and Bonis, is infused with an aura of melodramatic corruption, the taint of theatrical posturing and sensual morbidity.

Emma Valcárcel's talent for melodramatic gesture and effect is magnified in her frequent explosions of temper and hysterical fits. She becomes a fury, a demonic whirlwind for the unfortunate Bonis, who is invariably her victim. Emma's usual procedure is to slam her bedroom door noisily and then tear into her husband unmercifully. Clarín writes that one could hear continuously the termagant's "voz chillona, estridente, que gastaba las pocas fuerzas de la anémica en una catilinaria de cuya elocuencia y facundia no era posible dudar" (p. 24). Emma's rage against the supposed culpability of her husband sometimes even materializes into aggressive acts of actually striking her husband. Thus, voice and gesture combine to present a melodramatic, sometimes ridiculous picture of Emma's character.

Emma's reaction to the news of her pregnancy is extreme. Bonis hears a rush of hurrying footsteps; he sees confusion everywhere; trembling, he enters her room to find Emma, "pálida, desencajada, desgreñada, con diez años, de los que había sabido quitarse de encima, otra vez sobre las fatigadas facciones, [who] abrió los ojos, y lo primero que hizo con ellos fue lanzar un rayo de odio y otro de espanto sobre el atribulado esposo" (p. 243). Emma has, first of all, artificially manufactured a melodramatic situation—she has not taken the news calmly. Her verbal reaction is completely out of proportion to the actual situation: "¡Calle usted, Aguado! ¡No se burle de mí! ¡No estoy para bromas! ¡Dios mío! !Qué va a ser de mí! ¡Qué atrocidad! ¡Qué barbaridad! ¡Qué va a ser de mí . . . ! ¡Dios de Dios! Y a estas horas . . . yo me voy a morir . . . de fijo . . . de fijo . . . me lo da el corazón. ¡Yo no paro, no paro, no paro!" (p. 244). The plethora of exclamation marks is an indication of how Emma magnifies all events which affect her personally. Emma's "aria" is absurd, of course, but it is melodramatically absurd.

Emma's resistance to her physical condition becomes so extreme that she ardently desires to put an end to it by deliberately taking a rough coach ride to the seashore. But when she discovers her little jaunt could have been equally dangerous for her, she immediately puts on a tremendous show of melodramatic histrionics: "Emma chilló, cogió el cielo con las manos, insultó a Bonis, y a Minghetti, y a D. Basilio, ausentes. ¡Elle que creía engañar a la naturaleza! ¡Huía de un peligro y buscaba otro mayor! Pero, ¿por qué no me lo han dicho en casa?" (p. 272). Once again, along with her shrill voice, Emma uses large, theatrical gestures to express her sentiments. In Emma's actions, as in Serafina's, many of the movements seem deliberately performed for the benefit of an audience. Her gestures, writ large, are stylized movements which visually reflect not only the words but the tonal quality of her voice.

Two points of view operate in these scenes: Emma's and the author's. Living almost entirely in a world of exaggeration and pose, Emma takes herself and anything that directly affects her most seriously. The author perceives reality skeptically, however, and exposes Emma's innate fraudulence by focusing on her sense of exaggeration and melodrama. This double point of view prevails in most of *Su único hijo*: the characters perceive themselves as personages to be taken seriously while the author diminishes their human dignity by reducing them to comedy and sometimes even farce.

Occasionally, however, Alas treats his characters with more gravity. When, for example, Emma begins to feel her first labor pains, her response is physically overdone: "Horrorizada, con cara de condenado del infierno, Emma se retorcía agarrada con uñas de hierro a los hombros y al cuello de Minghetti" (p. 283). When Bonis arrives, she transfers her vampirish gesture to him. Her facial expression is grotesque:

Encontró una expresión como la de Melpómene en las portadas de la *Galería dramática*. Los ojos espantados, con cierto estrabismo, de la parturiente, no expresaban ternura de ningún género; de fijo ella no pensaba en el hijo; pensaba en que sufría nada más, y en que se podía morir, y en que era una atrocidad morirse ella y quedar acá los demás. Padecía y estaba furiosa. . . . Hubo un momento en que Bonis creyó sentir los afiliados dientes de su mujer en la carne del cuello. (p. 284)

Despite the horrendous, Medusan quality of her visage, one senses here that Alas is as appalled as Bonifacio at Emma's obsessive egotism and unnaturalness. In this example, which is by no means unique, melodramatic extravagance is no longer a comic device but an aspect of reality to be taken quite seriously. It is then that the authorial serio-comic vision is modified enough to approach his characters' own intensified view of reality. *They* perceive life on the grand operatic scale, and in this example and others, Alas appears to also.

This close approximation of the usually divergent viewpoints of author and characters appears again in the final scene of the novel. Here, though, it is not unmixed with a strong sense of Clarinian irony to form a somewhat uneasy blend of the sympathetic and the critical in the authorial vision. The ambivalence of viewpoint which results creates uncertainty of judgment in the reader. How does one properly appraise characters who are at one and the same time the butt of authorial satire and irony and yet manage to preserve a modicum of dignity and gravity in the midst of their simple melodramatics?

A look at the last scene of *Su único hijo* enables us to appreciate this Clarinian ambivalence, which is partially expressed through the background music of *La Traviata*. After his son's baptism, Bonis is left standing alone in the shadows of the church while the baritone Minghetti supplies music from Verdi's opera on the organ. Serafina then returns to plead for assistance from Bonis, who is both unable and unwilling to help her. The *diva* reveals that she has utterly lost her singing voice. This fact becomes significant upon recalling that Bonis has always associated her voice with the maternal urge, goodness, and tenderness. Our suspicions are borne out a moment later when we read the description of Serafina's face after she has heard Bonifacio's refusal of aid:

> Mas el rostro de Serafina volvió a asustarle. Aquella mujer tan hermosa, que era la belleza con cara de bondad para Bonis . . . le pareció de repente una culebra. . . . La vio mirarle con ojos de acero, con miradas puntiagudas; le vio arrugar las comisuras de la boca de un modo que era símbolo de crueldad infinita; le vio pasar por los labios rojos la punta finísima de una lengua jugosa y muy aguda. . . . , y con el presentimiento de una herida envenenada, esperó las palabras pausadas de la mujer que le había hecho feliz hasta la locura.
>
> La Gorgheggi dijo:
> —Bonis, siempre fuiste un imbécil. Tu hijo . . . no es tu hijo. (p. 323)

The maternal sweetness that Bonis characterized as Serafina's essential personality has turned to the vinegar of revenge and cruelty. Serafina's voice, which carried the pure lyricism of the maternal dream, has metamorphosed into the melodramatic hiss of the serpent.

The scene is played in deadly earnest because the object of the dialogue—the disputed paternity of Bonis' son—is of critical importance to the unfortunate Reyes. Bonifacio's vehement denial of Serafina's assertions that Minghetti is the real father[18] is acted in grand operatic style. It is a pathetically bravura performance in which Bonis assumes the stance and expression of the martyred Saint Sebastian. In a magnificent gesture of self-sacrifice, he forgives Serafina's outrageous statement, but he repeats in an exaggeratedly declamatory style that Antonio Reyes is in name and fact his own (and only) son:

> Serafina . . . , te lo perdono . . . , porque a ti debo perdonártelo todo . . . Mi hijo es mi hijo. Eso que tú no tienes y buscas, lo tengo

18. One wonders whether Alas was thinking of a real-life situation in this instance. The disputed paternity of the illegitimate child of Verdi's future mistress (and, later, wife), La Strepponi, was a well-known affair of the 1840s. For details, see George Martin, *Verdi: His Music, Life and Times* (New York: Dodd, Mead and Co., 1963), 580–81.

yo: tengo fe, tengo fe en mi hijo. Sin esa fe no podría vivir. Estoy seguro, Serafina; mi hijo . . . es mi hijo. ¡Oh, sí! ¡Dios mío! ¡Es mi hijo! . . . Pero . . . ¡como puñalada, es buena! Si me lo dijera otro . . . ni lo creería, ni lo sentiría. Me lo has dicho tú . . . y tampoco lo creo . . . Yo no he tenido tiempo de explicarte lo que ahora pasa por mí: lo que es esto de ser padre. . . . Te perdono, pero me has hecho mucho daño. Cuando mañana te arrepientas de tus palabras, acuérdate de esto que te digo: Bonifacio Reyes cree firmemente que Antonio Reyes y Valcárcel es hijo suyo. Es su único hijo. ¿Lo entiendes? ¡Su único hijo! (p. 324)

There are two kinds of irony at work here. The first is a rather heavy-handed sort: the revelation of Minghetti as the real father, which comes as a shock to Bonis, has been expected for quite some time by the reader. It could be argued, of course, that Alas presents no clear-cut evidence that Minghetti and Emma were ever lovers and that, therefore, the baritone fathered the child. After all, much of the proof lies in innuendo and malicious gossip.[19] But in keeping with the other ambiguities of place, time, and viewpoint, the problem of the child's paternity can probably never be adequately explained or resolved. The heavy doses of irony injected into *Su único hijo* lead one to expect that Bonis should not be taken as the actual father, although he undoubtedly is in spirit. If Alas meant to imply, as Cesáreo Bandera asserts, that Minghetti never could have been the father, then a clever and subtle joke has been played on the reader, and not on the scapegoat Bonis.

The irony of the situation, which can be partially ascribed to the difficulty in selecting its proper target, is made more complex by means of the background music of *La Traviata*, which is offered as a mocking counterpoint to the Serafina-Bonifacio duo. Bonis interprets the *Traviata* variations negatively and positively. At first, it seems to him that the music is a species of "desafío burlón un tanto irónico" (p. 318) to the uncertain future of his son, to life's pur-

---

19. It is Cesáreo Bandera's contention that Bonis is really Antonio's father because Emma's only infidelity is a mental betrayal of her husband (pp. 217–23). Carlos Feal Deibe believes, however, that "el padre puede ser tanto Minghetti como Bonis" ("La anunciación a Bonis," 270).

pose, to reality itself. He also remembers that the hero of *La Dame aux camélias* becomes so involved in his passion for the demimondaine, Marguerite, that he completely neglects his own father, and he wonders whether his son Antonio will be equally ungrateful. But then Bonis' incorrigible idealizing begins to sway his imagination so that he is now able to extract the romantic message of passion, suffering, and death from *La Traviata*. The *Traviata* themes of romantic love and the courtesan's noble sacrifice play in complete contrast, however, to the scene being enacted center stage. The love affair of Bonis and Serafina has completely wilted and displays no signs of miraculous regeneration. And Serafina's nature has so turned that, rather than sacrifice herself, she is demanding that Bonifacio offer himself up as the romantic scapegoat for her benefit. Thus, Minghetti's capricious organ playing subtly comments in ironic counterpoint not only on the deceptive question of paternity but on the travesty of romantic love which has prevailed in frequently melodramatic style through *Su único hijo*. The characters in this scene are inverted versions of the operatic figures of *La Traviata*.

Operatic melodrama as expressed through voice and gesture thus establishes a major mood of *Su único hijo*. Sometimes the tension of melodrama is accepted on its own terms; more frequently, though, it is subjected to Clarín's penetrating irony. But there is also a nonoperatic kind of music which creates another mood basic to the novel: the lyricism of reverie. For this leitmotif Alas introduces a male voice in the dreaming and weak character of Bonifacio Reyes. Music and Bonis are inseparable, a point which the author makes in the very first chapter. There, we find that Bonis is a devoted player of the flute, which with its ambivalent symbolism of a masculine shape and an inner feminine feeling or tone, is most appropriate in the hands of a daydreaming, ineffectual male protagonist. The flute is Bonis' voice, since the protagonist's own vocal instrument is frequently drowned out by the harping, screaming voice of his wife or by other dominating characters.

The mood of reverie is frequently evoked through Serafina's maternal-sounding singing voice which allows Bonis to daydream of his long-lost mother and then to slide gently in and reach back to the enchanting dimness of childhood. The music, then, allows him to experience the poignant feelings of nostalgia for the lost paradise, childhood. Bonis does not reconstruct precise narratives of his early years as Ana does in *La Regenta*; rather, his recollections remain misty because he is experiencing once more the emotion of past things and not the event itself. For example, he reflects that Serafina's mellifluous voice "me recuerda la de mi madre . . . que no cantaba nunca. ¡Qué disparates! Sí, disparates para dichos, pero no para pensados" (p. 40). The fact that his mother never sang to him as a child is unimportant, but that she was there brooding over him as a maternal presence is the inner reality which the irrationality of daydreaming re-creates. Thus, for Bonifacio, music is feeling because it plays delicately on the sensitive zones of his being and causes them to react emotionally.

Bonifacio is an untutored admirer of all the arts, but he loves music best because "le llegaba más al alma, con una vagueded que le encantaba y que no le exigía a él previo estudio de multitud de ideas concretas" (p. 163). The key word is *vaguedad*. The delightful vagueness of music is another way of stating its extreme suggestiveness. It not only prompts the memory in the pursuit of the past, but it provokes in Bonifacio wishful daydreams of a heroic future.

The opening scene of Chapter 7 is a good example of the temporary influence which music exercises on Bonifacio's Walter Mitty personality. As he sits in a quiet café and listens to the March of Louis XVI being played on a guitar, gradually "su espíritu se fue identificando con la guitarra" (p. 82). The guitar, for Bonis, caresses his soul with the softness of a cat's fur. Accompanying this sentimentalism is the pressing need within Reyes to gather up his inner resources and confront the enemy, *i.e.*, his wife and her allies. The martial air of the music makes him realize he must act instead of remaining a passive witness to events and to life itself: "La música le daba energía y la energía le sugería ideas de rebelión, deseo ardiente de emanciparse. . . . ¿De qué? ¿De quién? De todo, de todos" (p. 84). In a brief burst of activity, he spurts out of the café and into the street only to discover that without the sound of the music enveloping him, his will begins to weaken and all his resolves turn to water. The music, then, has provided a temporary impetus to be something that he is incapable of being; namely, an active character or, in his own conception, a hero.

Between the sweet nostalgia for the past and the naïve, wishful anticipation of future heroic deeds lies another mood that music creates within Bonis and thus in the novel itself. It is the indeterminate and melancholy inner melody of approaching middle age, the confession of swept-away illusions, and the bitter-sweetness of vague regrets. Clarín feelingly describes this autumnal stage of life which, in reality, dominates the whole of *Su único hijo*:

> A tener allí la flauta y no estar dormida Serafina, [B.] hubiera acompañado con el dulce instrumento aquellas melodías interiores, lánguidas, vaporosas, llenas de una tristeza suave, crepuscular, mitad resignación, mitad esperanzas ultratelúricas y que no puede conocer la juventud; tristeza peculiar de la edad madura que aún siente en los labios el dejo de las ilusiones y como que saborea su recuerdo. (pp. 165–66)

This resigned, yet hopeful attitude toward the loss of youth is, however, not accepted by anyone else in the novel. No one is young in *Su único hijo*. By that I mean that no one possesses the spirit of youthfulness and youth's innocent insouciance. With the exception of Marta Körner, everyone is also in number of years close to middle-age or older; but all, including Marta, are jaded. With the loss of freshness comes a desperate and sometimes frenetic quest after vanished youth (one somehow feels, however, that none of these people, with the possible exception of Bonis, was ever young). Bonis' "melodías interiores" are the romanticized and idealized version of the rotting decay which has taken over the other characters' lives and personalities. In effect, what the music of the flute, the guitar, or Serafina's voice actually creates is this inner melody, a music of interiorities, of secret feelings and vague yearnings too difficult and profound to express verbally or concretely. Clarín's use of music in the context of daydreaming illuminates an elusive state of mind. More simply stated, it *is* a state of mind.

The mental and spiritual pleasure which Bonifacio obtains from music is sometimes mixed with a strong dose of sensualism. Stendhal declared that that which makes music the most seductive and superior of the soul's delights is the extreme physical pleasure one derives from it.[20] Bonifacio's relationship with Serafina Gorgheggi is in the beginning primarily a physical one. Yet he never forgets that Serafina is, above all, an artist. He sees his love affair with the singer in an idealized light, conceiving of himself and Serafina as the torchbearers of the sacred flame of poetry. "¡Besos con música!" he exclaims to himself, as he ingenuously combines the spiritual and the physical aspects of music into the delightful package of a musical romance.

Sensuality is the nether side of the daydreaming music-lover Bonifacio. It is this sensual aspect of music which most commonly appeals to the great majority of music fanciers in *Su único hijo*. The insubstantialities of reverie come tumbling down in the face of such physical realities as a firm and plump *prima donna*. Memories of the romantic decade revolve around an Italian soprano called la Tiplona or la Merlatti. "La *Tiplona*, la *Merlatti*," writes Alas, "había sido el microcosmos del romanticismo músico del pueblo. . . . No concedían aquellos señores formales que en este mundo se hubiera oído cosa mejor que la *Merlatti*. . . . ¡Y qué carnes! ¡Y qué trato!" (p. 35). Even Bonis has to confess that at least part of his early devotion to opera grew out of the appearance of la Tiplona, "aquella real moza, que enseñaba aquella blanquísima pechuga, un pie pequeño, primorosamente calzado, y unos dientes de perlas" (p. 36).

The stress in certain passages on the sensual element of music, or more specifically of its interpreters, results in the recession of the novel's mood from the intemporal inner melody of reverie to the historical definiteness of the romantic era. When music begins to lose its transcendental significance in the novel, it then approaches the very concrete realities of mass appreciation or indifference to it. Music becomes mere entertainment, a fixture of a set period in a society's cultural patterns. Then, of course, the traditional approach

20. Henri Beyle (Stendhal), *Vie de Rossini* (orig. pub. 1823; Paris: Le Divan, 1929), I, 18.

of satirical or ironic realism lends itself very well to an analysis of the influence of music (or lack of it) on a society. A good example of this is Alas' description of a provincial orchestra found in the initial paragraph to Chapter 12. Both good and bad musicians make up the ensemble, but the orchestra, in Alas' words, always sounds "como los tornillos de una máquina sin aceite." Then Clarín lets loose his penchant for hyperbolic satire: "Los instrumentos de cuerda estaban asmáticos, sonaban a la madera, como sabe la sidra al barril; los de bronce eran estridentes sin compasión; bastaba uno de aquellos serpentones para derribar todas las fortificaciones de cinco Jericós. Afortunadamente el público filarmónico oía la orquesta como quien oye llover" (p. 179). Attending a concert is a social affair, devoid of artistic significance for the greater proportion of music patrons.

We have now reached the nadir in the sphere of influence which music exerts over a society. It offers a strong contrast both to the interpenetration of operatic melodrama and life and the intimate relationship between music and Bonifacio Reyes, but it does not prevail. In contrast to the dense concreteness of detail in *La Regenta*, Alas is extremely economical in his use of realistic touches in *Su único hijo*. As a result, realistic scenes like the provincial orchestra and dance are infrequent, while the close yet intemporal relationship between music and the characters' lives predominates and manages to establish a mood unlike that of the traditional realistic-naturalistic novel.

I stated earlier that the musical configurations of the novel's structure present an appropriate frame for the archetypicality of the characters. Before beginning the discussion of the precise archetypes which define the personalities of the main characters, I will briefly explain what I mean by the word *archetype* and its relationship to the musical element in *Su único hijo*. Archetype, first of all, refers to "a pattern from which copies are made." An archetypal character is, therefore, one which repeats itself over and over again in the history of literature and which manifests itself in a variety of forms, conforming in large part to the cultural and societal framework of the historical and literary period. The archetypal conception of not only characters but situations and symbols as interpreted in contemporary myth criticism is based on Carl Jung's conception of the "collective unconscious," or an unconscious mental record of universal human experiences. The archetype, then, is the concrete, whether it be visual or verbal, form of the Jungian collective unconscious. It is a universal phenomenon.

There is also a secondary definition of the term archetype which is closely related to its universality. An archetype is an abstract conception of a type. During the analysis of archetypicality of the characters and situations in Clarín's novel, these two points—universality particularized by the historical period, and the abstract quality of the archetype—should be kept in mind. The concreteness of the personages does not contradict their abstract characteristic. It merely signifies that one may extract from the particular the universal and the abstract.

In what way is the archetypal conception related to the operatic atmosphere in *Su único hijo*? First, the characters in Italian romantic opera are, to understate the case, not complex. They are fundamentally stock characters. Such *dramatis personae* usually do not develop or grow in the course of the action. Figures of few characteristics lend themselves fairly easily to an abstract treatment. The abstractness of operatic and melodramatic characters is a highly appropriate instrument to express a universally repeated pattern of human experience.

Closely related to the abstract simplicity of operatic figures is the quality of historical indefiniteness which characterizes most Italian operas of the nineteenth century. True to the romantic spirit, most operas were set in a period sufficiently distant from the present with the result that a kind of space-time exoticism was created. The titles of these works give a clear indication of their lack of historical immediacy: *Semiramide, Nabucodonosor, Atila, Il Crociato,* etc. Not only was historical distance deemed necessary for an acceptable opera, but historical inaccuracies and vagueness as well. Bonifacio is quite aware of the historical vagaries of Italian opera: "¡La historia! ¡Oh! la historia en las óperas era una cosa muy divertida" (p. 37). The result of such romantic capriciousness was to negate the sense of history in Italian opera. History *qua* history was irrelevant. Only the universality of sentiment as embodied in melodramatic characters counted.

The uncomplicated and unhistorical character of Italian operatic figures becomes especially significant in relation to Clarín's novel because not only do many of the characters in *Su único hijo* behave in operatic fashion but sometimes they even consciously imagine themselves in the roles of characters of specific Italian operas. On one occasion, Bonis imagines Emma in the role of Rossini's Otello: "Al acercarse a su mujer se le ocurrió recordar al moro de Venecia, de cuya historia sabía por la ópera de Rossini; sí, él era Otello y su mujer Desdémona . . . sólo que al revés, es decir, él venía a ser un *Desdémono* y su esposa podía muy bien ser una *Otela*, que genio para ello no le faltaba" (p. 108).

Another illustration of the interpenetration of opera and life is found in the use to which Bonis puts the Bellini work *Norma* (1831). Bonis conceives of his amorous predicament, the triangle created by himself, Serafina, and his wife, in operatic terms: " 'En las óperas podemos decir que también hay catástrofes'; y se acordó de la *Norma*, que era su mujer; y de *Adalgisa*, que era la tiple; y de Polión, que era él; y del sacerdote, que era Nepomuceno, encargado sin duda de degollarle a él, a Polión" (p. 144). In this moment, the constant operatic attitudinizing of the characters consciously surfaces in the open and direct parallels Bonis makes between Bellini's *opus* and the fictional life of the characters. One layer of fiction is thus pressed upon another. The operatic make-believe of *Norma* takes place in the vague mistiness of the decline of Druidic civilization; the plot centers upon a romantic triangle, Norma, the high priestess, her lover Pollione, and Adalgisa, a temple virgin; and the dramatic tension resides in the conflict between Norma's uncontrolled, wild passion and the dictates of conscience, duty, and maternal love. Bonis is evidently enamored of the two themes of passion and maternal tenderness in the opera, two leitmotifs which also run through the pages of *Su único hijo*. In Bellini's work, one voice (Norma's) carries the dual themes; Alas, however, distributes them across two roles, Emma's and Serafina's.

The parallels between the two works are by no means strict and consistent, since Bonis chooses to see only those elements that coincide with his own situation. Thus, while Norma's character is a combination of the devoted mother and the passionate, vengeful Medea type, Bonis extracts only her terrible aspects and transfers them to his wife Emma. Likewise, the initially deceptive Serafina assumes the sweet and modest qualities of Adalgisa, who is no match for the domineering Norma. Bonis envisions himself as the heroic pawn, Pollione, who is caught between the two women. Interestingly enough, in *Norma* the two women become fast friends, a development which anticipates Serafina's and Emma's eventual friendship. Romantic spontaneity and effusions play no part, however, in the Emma-Serafina alliance, which is based on mutual distrust and self-interest.

The identification made with the opera *Norma* furthers the vagueness of the temporal scheme in *Su único hijo*. Bellini chose the Druidic period because it appealed to his love of exoticism. It was exotic precisely because the period was locked in mystery and vagueness, lacking a clear sense of historicity. For Bonis, however, the significance of *Norma* lies in its archetypal situation, and not in the particular historical trappings—vague or not—through which the situation is manifested.

One should not be misled into believing that the characters in Clarín's novel are being presented solely on this one level of operatic melodrama. Part of the difficulty in judging *Su único hijo* lies in the fact that while the characters usually conduct themselves on one plane of characterization, namely the archetypal operatic line, the author more often than not views them from another plane, that of the ironical realist. Further ambiguity is created, as I have noted before, when the author slides from the viewpoint of ironic distance to sympathetic identification with his own creations (mostly with Bonis, though occasionally with Serafina and almost never with Emma).

In the case of Bonifacio's association of his situation with that of the opera *Norma*, it would be hazardous to state whether or not the author himself concurs with Reyes' romantic identification, particularly if one recalls that *Norma* plays an important role in the history of Spanish romanticism. I refer specifically to Pedro Antonio de Alarcón's early effort, *El final de Norma* (1861), a thoroughly silly novel which, perhaps for its very absurdities, has enjoyed great popularity for many decades. The title alludes to the last scene of Bellini's opera in which Alarcón's heroine (the "Hija del Cielo" or Brunilda) sings the part of Norma. The hero, Serafín Arellano, falls wildly in love with the mysterious *prima donna* as she is performing the title role. In Alarcón's highly improbable and melodramatic work, Bellini's *opus* is tied to the workings-out of the fantastic plot. It seems quite possible that Alas' use of *Norma* might convey to a Spanish reading public thoroughly familiar with Alarcón's fiction a mixed sentiment of nostalgia and mockery. Bonifacio's naïve identification with the characters of *Norma* would then be colored by the more sophisticated authorial viewpoint.

Before proceeding to an analysis of the characters and their situation in relation to the archetypal conception, I will conclude this discussion of the importance of music in Clarín's work with the observation that Alas' novelistic treatment of the art coincides to a great extent with the *fin de siècle* idea of music. First, in the Spanish novelist's use of operatic melodrama as a serio-comic device it is possible to see a reflection of both the aesthetics' and the symbolists' interest in the intermingling of the arts. It was Richard Wagner who largely spurred artists and writers to conceive of the loosening of strict genres in order to encourage a greater interpenetration of the arts. Wagner's idea of "total art" had been championed in 1861 by the alert Baudelaire, but the German musician did not come into his own until the 1880s. The symbolists and decadents saw in the Wagnerian conception a means of penetrating broader and deeper strata of reality. The disintegration of the norm of the genre signified liberation from the restrictiveness of genres which seemed to have gone stale from overdevelopment.

One novelist, Élémir Bourges, even went so far as to incorporate the Wagnerian "twilight of the gods" theme into the structure of his novel, *Le Crépuscule des dieux* (1884), which recounts the family history of the Duke Charles of Blankenbourg and his children in the Paris of the Second Empire. Bourges apparently decided to approach the story through a series of operatic devices and conceptions. Most obvious of all is the title, which refers to the fourth part of the tetralogy, *The Ring of the Nibelung*. More important, the characters, who move through a sumptuous, operatic decor, behave as though they were Wagnerian figures replete with the motifs of incest, murder, and frenetic emotionalism.

Clarín, of course, was not a devotee of Wagnerian opera but of the Italian mode of musical drama. Yet, despite this difference, he participates in the basic idea of combining one art form with another. *Su único hijo* often gives the impression of being constructed along operatic lines as though Alas were trying to enlarge the scope of the traditional realistic novel by infusing into it a musical strain. But Clarín only partially approaches the high seriousness of operatic melodrama which prevails in *Le Crépuscule des dieux* (this humorlessness does not, however, prevent the novel from unintentionally burlesquing itself). The Spanish writer inclines more to a parodistic treatment of operatic characters and devices, an approach which is appropriate to the theme of decadence. If Alas' characters often seem like a degenerate travesty of romantic operatic *personae*, it is because decadent characters, like the decadent sensibility itself, ultimately derive from romanticism. Thus, it is fitting that Italian opera, a highly romantic genre, be the means through which Alas may demonstrate his characters' moral decay.

A second aspect of music in *Su único hijo*, namely its vagueness and suggestiveness, links Alas to another segment of the *fin de siècle* sensibility, the symbolist aesthetic and its interpretation of music. The best known example of the symbolists' attitude toward music is Verlaine's "Art poétique,"[21] in which he declares that poetry should be a kind of music which would be both vague ("l'Indécis") and suggestive ("la Nuance"). His poems, which are redolent of a dreamlike ambience, are musical in the sense that the words and special associations of words convey a musicality of sound.

21. Paul Verlaine, *Jadis et naguère* (orig. pub. 1885; Paris: Livre de Poche, 1967), 25.

Verlaine's conception of music in poetry, which, as Anna Balakian points out,[22] ultimately prevailed in later symbolists because his approach was simple and lyrical, differs from Baudelaire's and Mallarmé's. In a more intellectual vein, the symbolist precursor Baudelaire saw that words, like music, could suggest feeling without specifying a particular meaning, but Baudelaire also conceived of the sensual use of music in poetry to stimulate oneiric sensations. Mallarmé used the very structure of music—theme and variations, orchestration and pauses—to compose his verse. All three poets believed that the suggestiveness of music and poetry enables one to penetrate and appreciate the mystery and depths of reality.

In what way does Alas approach the symbolists' use of music in literature? A passage from the last chapter of *Su único hijo* contains a clue to Clarín's interpretation of music: "Era que la música le ayudaba a entender, a penetrar el significado hondo de las cosas. El órgano, el órgano, le decía lo que él no acababa de explicarse" (p. 317). Music, then, although Alas does not state it directly, is like poetry in that it expresses the ineffable, the mystery, and sacredness of life, all of which Bonis is incapable of verbalizing because he possesses too limited an intellect. Rather, he is a tender soul who feels the inexpressible. Here, Alas' concept of music bears a likeness to the Baudelairean identification of music with feeling. Clarín never seems to have stressed the musicality of words in themselves as Verlaine does—he was not enough of a poet to manipulate words for their suggestive auditory values.[23] But he does appear to concur with Mallarmé's employment of musical structure. We have seen that, in accordance with the concept of the voice and the singer in Italian opera, Clarín alternates, though in no consistent, orchestrated pattern, different voices to create frequently melodramatic, sometimes purely lyrical effects in the composition of his work. It is improbable that the idea of using musical devices was suggested to

22. Anna Balakian, *El movimiento simbolista* (Madrid: Guadarrama, 1969), 85.
23. For an example of Alas' early efforts at poetry, see José María Martínez Cachero, "Los versos de Leopoldo Alas," *Archivum*, II (1952), 89–111.

Alas by Mallarmé since he apparently was not sufficiently familiar with the French poet's work; but his use of both operatic characterization and devices and reverie-producing musical accompaniment reflects not only his profound love of music but an absorption of the contemporary literary trend to utilize other art forms, especially music.

Romanticism, Decadence, and Archetypal Characters

If romanticism functions as the underlying motivating force for the presence of music in *Su único hijo*, it is equally certain that the romantic mode provides the key to an understanding of the characters. By that I do not mean to imply that we are dealing with the phenomenon of neoromanticism. It would be more accurate to state that Clarín's characters are not so much pseudoromantics as degenerate romantics. They share with the decadent characters of the 1880s and 1890s a common heritage and origin in romantic literature. As the title of his book, *The Romantic Agony*, indicates, Mario Praz believes that the decadent movement is essentially the final stage of romanticism. Even A. E. Carter, who sharply disagrees with Praz by insisting that the decadent stress on the unnatural in love and nature is in entire opposition to the spirit of romanticism, must admit that the decadent sensibility germinates in a particularly morbid strain of romanticism.[24]

He notes, as Praz before him had observed, that decadent types begin to act more and more like the fatal men and women of the earlier literary movement.[25] Less reliance is placed on physiological explanations of character which, one should add, are never completely rejected in later decadent literature, while more emphasis is given to the idea of innate qualities of wickedness and weakness in character. A decadent type of the 1880s and 1890s is degenerate

24. A. E. Carter, *The Idea of Decadence in French Literature, 1830–1900* (Toronto: University of Toronto Press, 1958), 25.

25. *Ibid.*, 90. I am referring to Carter's third phase in the evolution of the idea of decadence, the period from 1884 to the end of the century which begins with *A Rebours* and ends with *Le Jardin des supplices, i.e.*, the decadent movement proper.

less because it is his destiny to be so inclined (that would be too romantic) than because either weakness or viciousness, or both for that matter, is essential to his personality.

In this way, the later decadent types that follow the creations of Huysmans and Bourges become, to a large degree, less and less naturalistic in conception. They partially return to a prenaturalistic, romantic typology by which characters may be drawn with a simpler line. Romantic characters are, by and large, not very complex.[26] And, despite the façade of neurosis and depravity, neither are decadent types. As in the romantics, decadent characters rely more on the gesture than on inner motivation. That is, they are conceived more externally, frequently even theatrically, than internally. Even when they are represented as dreamers, a condition which would supposedly encourage the technique of psychological analysis, it is the state of reverie rather than the dreamer himself which interests such writers. The extra ingredients of the unnatural, the perverse, and the neurotic—all of which can be traced back to their embryonic stage in romantic creations—make decadent characters inverted romantics.

One of the major romantic inversions in decadent typology consists in the reversal of roles in males and females. Praz observes that, from approximately the middle of the nineteenth century on, the usual relationship of the active, dominating male and the ineffectual maiden-victim is upset when females begin to emerge as fatal sexual goddesses who exercise frequently sadistic powers over more passive and weak males. No longer the persecuted maiden (Mrs. Radcliffe's Emily in *The Mysteries of Udolpho*, 1794; Hugo's Esmeralda in *Notre-Dame de Paris*, 1832), female protagonists take on almost diabolical dimensions, immerse themselves in evil and sexual corruption, and drag the passive male into the maelstrom of decadent experience. The type is found in Zola (Renée in *La*

26. There are exceptions of course. Stendhal's characters, which are in part derived from romantic notions, are complex; so is Sainte-Beuve's Amaury (*Volupté*, 1834). But both these writers display a profound skill for analysis, a talent which simultaneously approximates them to the eighteenth-century novelists and to the later realists.

Curée, 1872), Barbey d'Aurevilly (Alberte in "Le Rideau cramoisi" or Mlle Hauteclair in "Le Bonheur dans le crime," *Les Diaboliques*, 1874), Huysmans (Miss Urania in *A Rebours*, 1884), and Élémir Bourges (Giulia Belcredi in *Le Crépuscule des dieux*, 1884), to name but a few examples.

George Ross Ridge develops Praz's observations on the dominating woman to their logical conclusion. He notes that by the 1880s it is not just the vampirish *femme fatale* who overwhelms males but women in general. Modern women in decadent literature incline to be destructive of their sexual opposite. The neurotic housewife could be as viciously domineering over the male as any Salammbô or Cléopâtre of the romantic era:

> Modern woman is malevolent and has a malignant effect upon men. Although this is baldly the decadent thesis, there are nonetheless different categories of the modern woman. They are not all "evil" in the same way. The most salient strain, noted by Praz and other commentators, is the *femme fatale*, or the fatal woman. . . . Yet there are more domestic types who are none the less "fatal," i.e., malevolent, and more attenuated, though no less devastating passions motivate them. The effect, however, is the same: the man always withers and dies.[27]

It is this relationship between the sexes, abnormal as the nineteenth century sees it,[28] which predominates in *Su único hijo*. Bonis is weak, passive to the point of abulia, and continually manipulated and abused by stronger feminine characters.

It is my aim to explore the decadent characteristics of Emma Valcárcel, Serafina Gorgheggi, and Bonifacio Reyes and then indicate how, as decadent personalities, they are also archetypal creations. I view the characters first as decadent types of the *fin de siècle* and,

27. George Ross Ridge, *The Hero in French Decadent Literature* (Athens, Georgia: University of Georgia Press, 1961), 34, 144.

28. Clarín is no feminist in this matter. For Alas' traditionalist views on women, see his play *Teresa* (1895); Fernando Ibarra's "Clarín y Azorín: El matrimonio y el papel de la mujer española," *Hispania*, LV (1972), 45–54; and Pierre L. Ullman, "The Antifeminist Premises of Clarín's *Su único hijo*," *Estudos Ibero-Americanos*, I (1975), 57–91.

then, uncover beneath the particularized elements of their personalities—*i.e.*, their specific decadent traits—their archetypal significance. Thus, Emma Valcárcel, a decadent *femme fatale* and hysterical neurotic is, in archetypal terms, an example of the negative
feminine principle or the Terrible Mother. Serafina's initial bacchantic nature is a case of the decadent, overpowering sexual goddess. But Bonifacio's idealizing imagination transforms what is an
instance of the negative feminine archetype into the nondecadent,
positive image of the Good Mother. And, finally, Bonifacio is not
only a decadent type by virtue of his abulic, dreaming nature but an
archetypal expression of the weak individual's need to strengthen
his inner being through the journey of self-discovery. This quest of
Self is manifested, in archetypal terms, as a kind of heroic experience. The dream of heroism and heroic transformation ironically
points to the disparity between the heroic illusion and the pathetic
reality of Bonifacio's passive scapegoat personality.

To begin with, there are the decadent and archetypal traits found
in the two women who rule Bonifacio Reyes' life. First, and above
all, there is Emma. A characteristic device of Clarín is the selection
of names which comment ironically or satirically on the characters'
personality.[29] As a twisted and neurotic "romantic" type, Emma's
name inescapably recalls Flaubert's Emma Bovary—but there the resemblance ends. Her corrupted nature effectively extinguishes any
trace of the authentic romantic spirit. Her surname, Valcárcel, is an
interesting combination of *val*, meaning valley or an open sewer,
and *cárcel* or prison. The first alludes to the depths of corruption
and malevolence into which she is capable of plunging. The reference to Emma as a prison is a sly comment on Alas' part with regard to the authoritarian posture which she assumes in front of her
husband. For Bonis, marriage with Emma is a life sentence.

Emma's character is delineated in clear, concise lines in the very
first chapter of *Su único hijo*, indeed, in the very first sentence
which reads: "Emma Valcárcel fue una hija única mimada" (p. 3).

29. John Kronik, "The Function of Names in the Stories of Alas," *Modern Language Notes*, LXXX (1965), 260–65.

From a spoiled child, she proceeds to become a spoiled, capricious, and arrogant young woman who is used to having her own way in everything. How does Alas explain her character? Other than mentioning her pampered childhood in one line and devoting a few paragraphs to the familial degeneration of the Valcárcels, Alas does not really endeavor to put the onus of Emma's tyrannical and neurotic nature on the deterministic causes of milieu and family. He duly notes these factors, but there is no attempt to carry the matter any further.

Just as Huysmans introduces the image of a line of ancestral portraits into *A Rebours* to demonstrate the physical and mental degeneration of the des Esseintes family, Alas also has Emma restore a number of old family portraits. She cannot help noticing that the present generation of Valcárcels is less robust and handsome than the painting of her ancestor, Don Antonio Diego Valcárcel Meras, the founder of the house and a distinguished soldier in the Alpujarras War (1569–1571). In fact, this sturdy race of individuals which originated in the Asturian mountains, one of the Christian strongholds of Reconquest Spain, is retrogressing morally and socially to the point of becoming once more a horde of primitive mountain people: "Por el camino de retroceso que llevaba aquella raza se volvía a la horda; era aquél el atavismo de todo un linaje" (p. 18). Here, Alas' explanation of the Valcárcel degeneration is couched in purely naturalistic terms. Zola would have been in full agreement.

The idea that the human race was in the process of deviating from a primitive type was extremely popular in the 1860s and 1870s. Carter notes that Zola borrowed this concept from such medical treatises as B. H. Morel's *Traité des dégénérescences physiques, intellectuelles et morales de l'espèce humaine* (1857) and his sequel, *De la Formation du type dans les variétés dégénérées* (1864).[30] It would be otiose to deny Alas' reliance on naturalistic doctrines here, for he never severed his connections with Zolaism. Physiological cause and effect will, moreover, reappear in the expla-

30. Carter, *Idea of Decadence*, 66.

nation given of Emma's hysteria and her subsequent renewal of good health.

It would, however, be erroneous to conclude from these passages that Alas has once more constructed a realist-naturalist novel similar to his earlier creative effort. One could be equally misled from a cursory reading of the first two or three pages of *A Rebours* into believing that Huysmans, once a devoted disciple of Zola, was again following the well-trod path of naturalism. But, after a naturalistic beginning, Huysmans' character, des Esseintes, gradually inches away from a purely deterministic universe in order to lead a life based solely on his own insatiable needs for sensation. His self-created isolated world of refined depravation is cut off from its naturalistic roots by Huysmans' stress on aesthetic motivation.

The eventual exclusion of physiological motivation, after having been introduced in the beginning, also occurs in Élémir Bourges' *Le Crépuscule des dieux*. Bourges attributes the sexual perversity and moral degeneration of the Duke of Blankenbourg and his children to an ancient, tainted family tree but, as Carter points out, their decadence is "presented in such feudal and almost legendary terms that . . . it is more like diabolic possession than a pathological state."[31] No writers of the decadent movement proper failed to include neuroses, sexual depravation, and other physical and mental defects which could originate as much in physiological causes as in a deliberate will to assume the decadent posture. Although most of these writers liked to think they had moved quite far from Zola's position by promoting the aesthetic doctrine, it is evident that some borrowing and intermingling occurred between naturalists and decadents. Their mutual preoccupation with decadence and their common heritage of romanticism brought them together.

A similar interpenetration of the naturalist and the decadent may be found in Alas. As in Huysmans and Bourges, Clarín's characters move away from a naturalistic presentation into another dimension which the operatic posture has already revealed as something non-

31. *Ibid.*, 95.

realistic. Indeed, with the exception of Emma, Alas makes little attempt to present any other character in naturalistic terms. And, in Emma's case, we soon learn that two factors, of a non-naturalistic nature, influence her behavior: her self-conscious ability to pretend sickness, love, or anything else; and her innate propensity to do evil.

Emma's histrionic talents come to the fore with great ease during her periods of hysteria. It is revealing to compare the difference between Alas' attitude toward the afflicted Ana and the hysterical Emma. Ana's hysteria originates in deep-seated fears, inadequacies, and a paternal-maternal obsession. A pre-Freudian, semideterministic analysis is given to explain her neurosis; but no such solution is provided in Emma's personal history. No childhood trauma is mentioned or even implied; her father's personality is discussed briefly but bears no relation to Emma's hysteria, and her mother does not even appear in the novel. Other than the possibility of her family background, which is never brought in to explain her hysteria, Alas makes no attempt to propose the past as a key to Emma's neurotic condition. We are forced to conclude that something antipathetical in Emma's nature is responsible for her malevolent and twisted personality.

Ana's hysteria is founded on a dissociated self which leads to a diminished consciousness, but Emma's neurotic condition is characterized by sham. Her hysteria is the medical expression and symbol of her inauthenticity. The falsity and pretense with which she is imbued spill over from her sickroom and invade the rest of the house. Emma's soul is as unhealthy as Ana's, but her illness is of a different nature: in Emma, the cancer of unnaturalness has eaten away at her soul until there is no soul left in the spiritual sense of the word. The moral and spiritual crisis which divides Ana's inner being does not exist in Emma. She is not only a complete atheist but a wholehearted materialist, a seeker of new sensations to replace the old and tired ones. The insatiable quest for fresh thrills makes her cancerous sickness a contagious one, infecting other characters. It would be unfair, however, to impute the growing corruption in *Su único hijo* solely to Emma Valcárcel. Decadence spreads from one person to another, but only after individuals' actions and personalities have intermingled and thus provided a mutual harmful influence: "Y a unos y a otros los seducía, los corrompía, y los juntaba en una especie de solidaridad del vicio la vida que hacían" (pp. 221–22). No one person, then, is responsible for the aura of corruption which pervades *Su único hijo*, but Emma's sickroom atmosphere, like Ana's in *La Regenta*, supplies an apt metaphor for the degenerate environment in Clarín's novel.

I have noted that much of Emma's unpleasantness derives from her unnaturalness. Every aspect of her personality and life somehow becomes perverted so that even the roles of wife and mother are transformed respectively into concubine and frustrated childkiller. Clarín attributes her unnatural qualities to an "espontánea perversión del espíritu, prurito de enferma" (p. 8). On another occasion, he declares that Emma's moral aberrations had nothing to do with the influence of the decadent romantic literature of her generation but that she was "original por su temperamento" (p. 157). Both authorial comments lead to the conclusion that Emma's malevolence and perverted spirit are innate characteristics which would have surfaced in any environment and family. There exists in Emma a willful determination to behave contrary to conventional norms, to go against the grain, as the decadents would have it:

> Este afán de separarse de la corriente, de romper toda regla, de desafiar murmuraciones y vencer imposibles y provocar escándalos, no era en ella alarde frío, pedantesca vanidad de mujer extraviada por lecturas disparatadas; era espontánea perversión del espíritu, prurito de enferma. (pp. 7–8)

Emma believes she is a superior being, exempt from the rules and patterns of behavior that govern most individuals.

This same sense of superiority forms the basis of another character's personality, Marta Körner's. Not surprisingly, the two women —in essence vulgar, insensitive creatures—find themselves attracted to one another, the depravity of one responding to the other. Marta is described as a "bacante de pensamiento," whose soul is rotted away by a "depravación ideal que llevaba dentro de sí" (p. 189).

Unlike Emma, the German girl has been profoundly influenced by bad literature, or what Alas terms "la lascivia letrada." But like Emma, she is also adept at pretending to a sincerity and modesty the depths of which, writes Alas, no man could ever penetrate. Marta's physical appearance reflects her inner corruption: she is "llena de grasa barnizada de morbidez y suavidad" (p. 180). But the most interesting aspect of Marta's personality is her insistence that she is a superior soul. She explains to Emma that there are two classes of human beings, "los escogidos y los no escogidos, las almas superiores y las vulgares. El toque estaba en ser alma escogida, superior" (p. 191). Marta believes that she is a very complicated personality, hence misunderstood by ordinary people. In reality, she is an affected *poseur* and a unidimensional pseudointellectual.

It is no mere coincidence that the holder of these opinions should be a German. Although the philosophy of Nietzsche was not very well known in Spain at the time, Clarín was one of the few who had read a considerable amount of the German writer. He particularly disliked the superficial and snobbish popularity which Nietzsche had acquired in shallow souls such as Marta Körner's. The Nietzschean ideal of the superman also appealed very much to the decadents and aesthetics of the 1880s and 1890s, who saw in the conception a reflection of their own insistence on individuality at all costs. It is not surprising, therefore, that many critics considered Nietzsche as decadent as the decadents themselves. Max Nordau's view, for example, is typical of the times.[32]

It is evident that in Marta's Nietzscheanism Alas finds a suitable target for his irrepressible satiric bent. Yet the fact that Marta's attitudes are mere pose should not conceal from us her deep-seated inner depravity. Emma's friend is, in fact, a sybarite, who justifies

32. Max Nordau, *Degeneration* (New York: D. Appleton, 1895), p. 416: "From the first to the last page of Nietzsche's writings the careful reader seems to hear a madman, with flashing eyes, wild gestures, and foaming mouth." The chapter on Nietzsche is subsumed under the general title "Ego-mania." See also Lisa E. Davis, "Max Nordau, *Degeneración* y la decadencia de España," *Cuadernos Hispanoamericanos*, Nos. 326-27 (1977), 307-23; and Gonzalo Sobejano, *Nietzsche en España* (Madrid: Gredos, 1967), 175-78, for a discussion of Clarín's views of Nietzsche.

her desires to taste the fruits of evil with a façade of philosophic Kultur. Both she and Emma in their discussions place an extremely high value on love and art. Their ideal is presumably an artistic one: to experience love in aesthetic terms. What all this aestheticizing and philosophizing boils down to in actuality is that both women would like to have an affair with an artist. So much for the aesthetic ideal. In Emma and Marta, Alas has satirized the decadent image of the superior individual who, following the spirit of anarchy, indulges his sensuous needs by justifying them as aesthetic experiences.

By viewing these two women in ironic and satirical terms Alas does not, however, imply that these are characters of little consequence. In passages where the critical realist dominates, Alas has devalued the glamor of decadence by demonstrating that corruption as manifested in the souls of two insensitive and affected women is a vulgar affair. Nevertheless, he is aware that the nasty commonness of corruption makes it no less deadly. Had Alas adhered to this one viewpoint, it would have been a relatively easy matter to judge *Su único hijo*, but a further examination of his characters indicates that he more than occasionally wavers between the deflating view of the critical realist and the more alluring, hence less critical, view of one who sees in decadence a fascinating subject.

Further investigation of the various perversions of Emma Valcárcel's personality demonstrates Clarín's oscillating viewpoint. It is characteristic of a decadent character—whether presented from a naturalist or an aesthetic angle—to be intensely interested in the sensuous side of existence. Emma's bedroom becomes the setting for a series of erotic experiences. One such scene, often repeated in the married couple's life, is the massage in which Bonifacio, acting in a characteristically subordinate capacity of nursemaid to his wife, applies creams and unguents to Emma's body. Bonifacio's efforts to soothe and improve his wife's physical condition stimulate erotic sensations in Emma:

Un día Emma, a gatas sobre su lecho, se recreaba sintiendo pasar la mano suave y solícita de su marido sobre la espalda untada y frotada, como si se tratase de restaurar aquel torso miserable sacándole barniz. "¡Más, más!," gritaba ella, frunciendo las cejas y apretando los labios, gozando, aunque fingía dolores, una extraña voluptuosidad que ella sola podía comprender. (p. 95)

One also notes, in passing, Bonifacio's opinion of his wife's physical status. He believes that, since her disastrous miscarriage, she has become nothing but a physical ruin, "aquel mísero conjunto de huesos y pellejo y de importunas turgencias, edificio ruinoso que el dueño defiende contra la piqueta municipal a fuerza de revoques de cal y manos de pintura y recomposición de tejas" (p. 94). But, unknown to the naïve Bonis, Emma's withdrawal to her bedroom heralds a regeneration of the flesh. To the picture of physical decadence Clarín attaches an explanation of her ill-health and subsequent recrudescence couched in purely naturalistic terms (pp. 117–18). But then Alas goes on to compare Emma to a delicate hothouse plant: "Pensaba Emma, al verse renacer en aquellos pálidos verdores, que era ella una delicada planta de invernadero" (p. 118). One is reminded of the plant image applied to Fermín de Pas in La Regenta. In both cases, recollection of the "flowers of evil" is inescapable. By likening Emma to a plant, particularly one which requires artificial conditions in order to survive, Alas moves from a naturalistic view of his character to a decadent approach. This transition to another aesthetic occurs a number of times in his treatment of character.

Certainly Emma's morbid sensuality is a decadent characteristic. Ventura Agudiez had noted this aspect of the decadent sensibility in Ana's enjoyment of the tiger skin. But the pleasure taken in not only tactile but olfactory and gustatory sensations is intensified in Emma's personality because, unlike the originally uncorrupt Ana, Emma is a thoroughly degenerate character. In addition to the touch of creams and ointments, she derives a secretly erotic gratification from her batiste sheets, her warm bed, feathers, the closed-in air of the chamber, the carpeted floor, the cracks of the hermetically sealed doors, the mattress stuffing, the perfumed odors of her clothing, and the camphor and lavender smells of the medicine chest. All this morbidity is viewed critically and negatively by the author, who observes that "con las nuevas fuerzas habían venido nuevos deseos de una voluptuosidad recóndita y retorcida, enfermiza, extraviada, que procuraba satisfacerse en seres inanimados, en contactos, olores y sabores" (p. 118). Yet the effect of dwelling so long on Emma's unnatural feelings is to create in the reader a degree of fascination with the refined perversion of Emma's spirit that no amount of irony is able to dispel. Clarín's use of exaggerated terms in his description of Emma's sensuality—a practice which he criticizes in Bonifacio's natural inclination toward hyperbole—manufactures the same glamorous aura of decadence which prevails in such writers as Huysmans and Verlaine.

Emma's erotic sensibility grows increasingly perverse when she decides to abandon her pretense of ill-health and her cocoonlike existence of secret and solitary voluptuousness in favor of a more public form of no less egotistical behavior. Her physical recovery spurs on an interest in the opposite sex and culminates in the seduction of her husband (one is forced to label their amorous experiences as such because her bizarrely aggressive behavior amounts to a sexual conquest over the weak but willing Bonis). The seduction scene is permeated with an aura of sickly perversion as Emma corrupts the natural feelings of the conjugal relationship. At first, however, Bonis misinterprets Emma's intentions, thinking she has discovered his carousing with the opera company by detecting the scent of rice powder on his clothing. His fear elicits a comically exaggerated verbal response in the abused romantic cliché, "un rayo que hubiera caído a sus pies no le hubiera causado mayor espanto" and in its variant, "mal rayo me parta!" (pp. 109–10).

But the humorous touches begin to disappear when Alas settles down to a serious description of Emma's aberrant sexuality. The viewpoint has moved from comic irony to serious melodrama. Bonis initially imagines Emma's encirclement of his neck and her inhalation of his scent to be a prelude to a vampirish act: "Emma entonces olfateó muy de cerca sobre el cuello de Reyes, y éste llegó a creer que ya no le olía con la nariz, sino con los dientes. Temió una traición de aquella gata; temió, así Dios le salvase, un tremendo mordisco sobre la yugular, una sangría suelta" (p. 110). In *La Regenta*,

Clarín has already implied in Ana's growing eroticism a certain vampirish cast, but here the image is forthrightly expressed. The vampiress is a decadent offshoot of the *femme fatale* and usually implies a topsy-turvy relationship of an overpowering female and a weak, ineffectual male.

Emma's desire to savor the excesses of sexual experience causes her to imitate the very gestures and intimate language which Serafina has used in her relationship with Bonis. The result, Bonis is well aware, is akin to having caught a contagious disease: "y vio en ella [Emma] especies de caricias serafinescas; todo ello era un contagio; le había pegado a su mujer, a su *esposa ante Dios y los hombres*, el amor de la italiana, como una lepra" (pp. 112–13). Because she copies the frenetic and bacchic gestures of a paramour (and an opera singer in addition), Emma eventually assumes the role of a concubine, "una odalisca loca," in the eyes of Bonifacio. Indeed, Alas effects an almost complete reversal of couples and roles in the changes which occur in Emma and Serafina. The *diva* who originally represents the sexual goddess for Bonis gradually metamorphoses into a motherly and somewhat passionless companion in misfortune, while Emma, though no morally upright individual at any time in her life, erupts from her self-imposed egotistical isolation to embrace a kind of moral leprosy in both her sexual and nonsexual relationships with other individuals.

Emma's insatiable curiosity leads her to develop other unpleasant aspects of her personality. Bonis continually affixes the epithet of tyrant or "tirana," and on one occasion, a variant, "sultana caprichosa" to Emma. Emma's innate store of energy has never been properly directed because her basic personality is distorted. Bonis comments on her active nature (as opposed to his passive character), thinking she might have made a magnificent man of action, a statesman, or a captain had her moral fiber been otherwise constructed. George Ross Ridge makes a similar, more generalized statement on the neurotic and domineering decadent female: "They also have a great reservoir of energy. Their activity, however, is often abortive because their energy remains untapped or becomes warped. In this role the modern woman becomes a neurotic who cannot control herself." [33]

This tyrannizing side of Emma's character reveals a strong sadomasochistic bent which she exploits to the utmost: "Mortificar a los demás y divertirse ella, de mil maneras desconocidas, todo lo posible, éstas eran las dos fuentes de placer que quería agotar a grandes tragos; dos fuentes que venían a ser una misma" (p. 128). The author attributes her perverted qualities to Emma's "comezón de lo raro, original e inesperado" (p. 127), her itch for rare, original, and unexpected sensations. Clarín makes it quite clear to the reader that underneath her sadomasochism lies Emma's insatiable desire for new thrills, "su sed de emociones extrañas," which finds itself dissatisfied with the arcane chrysalid world of the voluptuary and ventures into the public domain in search of fresh jolts to her jaded spirit.

There is only one short step from delighting in others' misfortunes to taking pleasure in their wickedness. The urge to go against the grain of conventional behavior evidences itself in Emma's sanctioning of immoral, even criminal activities. For Emma, writes Clarín, "el descubrimiento de la maldad ajena la embelesaba, la enorgullecía y la animaba a abandonarse a sus perversiones caprichosas" (pp. 124–25). Unlike Ana Ozores, who is horrified when evil invades the citadel of her inner being, Emma welcomes evil into her soul. She wholeheartedly approves of illicit love affairs and daring sexual feats on the part of women. She finds herself, for example, so much attracted to the image of the courtesan in Serafina that she even envies the opportunity of the male to win such a prize. Standing next to the *diva*, Bonis' wife is enchanted with the sensation of manly protection which Serafina's superior height induces. The scene is infused with the tint of latent lesbianism.

But Emma particularly admires the criminal whom she exalts as her heroic ideal. She devours popular serialized novels in which the *pícaro* or a Luis Candelas is idealized. Her love of the criminal type is a far cry from her original, romantic caprice in which she became

33. Ridge, *Hero in French Decadent Literature,* 155.

infatuated with the portrait of one of her ancestors. Although mild-
ly incestuous by implication, her early whimsy was at least partially
justified by the fact that her ancestor had been a genuinely heroic
individual. But, true to her essentially insatiable nature, she is incapable of sustaining such a relatively harmless infatuation. Each
new sensation must be more daring than the previous one. Consequently, the criminal replaces the hero in her twisted imagination.
Both idealizations hark back to romantic attitudes. The idealization
of the criminal, in particular, is a well-known motif in romantic
literature—witness Byron's Corsair, Espronceda's Pirata, or Hugo's
Hernani. But while the romantic writer perceived in the criminal
the spirit of anarchy and independence, the supreme symbol of
the natural, decadent writers saw in the criminal that which went
against the grain, the rebellion against the normal.[34] It is evidently
this last aspect of the criminal which Emma favors.

Another aspect of Emma's unnatural instincts is her rejection of
motherhood. Her twisted view of the maternal reaches the extreme
of ardently desiring an abortion to terminate her pregnancy:

> Se quedó adormecida, y medio soñando, medio imaginando volun-
> tariamente, sentía que una criatura deforme, ridícula, un vejete
> arrugadillo, que parecía un niño Jesús, lleno de pellejos flojos, con
> pelusa de melocotón invernizo, se la desprendía de las entrañas, iba
> cayendo poco a poco en un abismo de una niebla húmeda, bru-
> mosa, y se despedía haciendo muecas, diciendo adiós con una mano,
> que era lo único hermoso que tenía. . . . Y ella le cogía aquella
> mano, y le daba un beso en ella; y decía . . . a la mano que se aga-
> rraba a las suyas: "Adiós . . . no puede ser . . . no sirvo yo para eso.
> Adiós . . . mira, las leyes de la naturaleza son las que te hacen caer,
> desprenderte de mi seno. . . ." Y la figurilla, que por lo visto era
> de cera, se desvanecía, se derretía en aquella bruma caliginosa, que
> envolvía a la criaturita y a ella también, a Emma, y la sofocaba, la
> asfixiaba. (p. 271).

34. One need only recall Oscar Wilde's admiration of the infamous
Thomas Griffiths Wainewright, writer, forger, and poisoner. See Wilde,
"Pen, Pencil and Poison: A Study in Green," *Complete Works* (London:
Collins, 1966).

By rejecting motherhood, Emma embraces its opposite, sterility. Praz observes that the decadent aesthetic ultimately leads to a vision of sterility which is frequently symbolized not only in the androgyne but in the cold and isolated virgin such as we see in Mallarmé's Hérodiade.[35] Although Emma is certainly no maiden of unblemished purity, her deliberate encapsulation in a cold egotism of solitary pleasures is similar to the Parnassian and later aesthetic conception of the powerful yet infecund goddess. Emma remains essentially untouched by her sexual experiences. She does not love and she is probably incapable of loving. True, she bears a child, but she herself remains a cold and sterile creature who would never willingly create anything.

Thus far we have seen that Emma Valcárcel by and large conforms to the decadent typology of the depraved, neurotic, and overwhelming female; and that by use of exaggerated description and scenes, her character—as well as Serafina's and Bonifacio's—emerges as an operatic and melodramatic type. Clarín also makes use of a number of well-chosen epithets to emphasize, again, a certain exaggerated, nonrealistic quality in Emma's character. These epithets are a device to express the archetypicality of Emma's character. All these epithets are offered by her husband: a Fury or a Eumenide, a witch, a dragon, the muse of tragedy (Melpomene) and, already mentioned, a vampiress. Each of these terms is of a legendary or mythological nature and each (even Melpomene) stresses the demonic aspect of Emma's personality. The most characteristic of them is the term *furia*. Bonifacio believes, for example, that he is a captive "en poder de su Emma, una furia, sí, una furia, no había para qué negárselo a sí mismo" (p. 37). On another occasion, Emma is described as a Eumenide (a Fury) : "No faltaba fibra al cuerpo eléctrico de aquella Euménide" (p. 118). The first allusion to the witch image is rather humorous:

Sólo cuando oyó aquello de anhelar salir volando por el balcón, pensó, sin querer, en las brujas que van los sábados a Sevilla por

35. Mario Praz, *The Romantic Agony* (New York: World Publishing Co., 1968), Ch. 5 ("Byzantium").

los aires, montadas en escobas; y tuvo cierto miedo supersticioso de esta inclinación, que ofrecía relativa y sospechosa novedad. Se puso colorado, avergonzándose de su mal pensar. Ni en idea se atrevía a ofender a Emma, por temor de que le adivinase el pensamiento. (p. 137)

Bonis employs the term on at least two other occasions. He not only conceives of his wife as a witch, but of his marriage as a "valpurgis matrimonial."

The dragon image is implied in an imagined picture which the frightened Bonis summons up when he thinks Emma has discovered his growing debts: "La imaginación, *la loca de la casa*, le ponía delante el cuadro aterrador: 'Emma saltaba de la cama con su gorro de dormir, pálida, huesuda, echando fuego por los ojos' " (p. 73). The portrait is without doubt exaggeratedly humorous, but it does not lessen the effect of consistently stressing Emma's monstrous side. Bonis finds her expression of rage and horror similar to that of Melpomene, the muse of tragedy: "Los ojos espantados, con cierto estrabismo, de la parturiente, no expresaban ternura de ningún género. . . . Padecía y estaba furiosa" (p. 284). This bizarrely "tragic" visage so impresses Bonis that for a moment he imagines Emma has vampirishly sunk her sharp teeth into his neck. Melpomene has been metamorphosed into that fantastic creature the vampire.

Clearly, by attributing to Emma the traits of mythological and chimerical creatures Alas creates another dimension to her already demonstrable vileness, a dimension which can be called archetypal. Jung writes that "the archetype is essentially an unconscious content that is altered by becoming conscious and by being perceived, and it takes its colour from the individual consciousness in which it happens to appear." When the archetype becomes recognizable, it usually takes the form of symbolic images. The archetypal image may also be "experienced indirectly through individuals upon whom it is projected." [36] It is this latter aspect of the archetype as

36. C. G. Jung, *Four Archetypes* (Princeton, N.J.: Princeton University Press, 1971), 5; Erich Neumann, *The Great Mother: An Analysis of the Archetype* (Princeton, N.J.: Princeton University Press, 1972), 22.

particularized in concrete characters which most concerns us in this essay. For the moment, let it suffice to mention that the projector of these archetypal images is Bonifacio Reyes who, in some instances, blends indistinguishably with the authorial voice.

In Emma Valcárcel we have an example of one aspect of the archetypal female: the *femme fatale*. This side of the feminine is what Jung would call the negative aspect: "All these symbols can have a positive, favourable meaning or a negative, evil meaning."[37] But Emma is not merely a sadomasochistic and neurotic female: she is also a mother, the role which she most detests and for which Bonis fervently yearns. The maternal factor places a somewhat different interpretation on Emma, the Fury, the witch, and the dragon-vampire. The maternal archetype, a more specific manifestation of the archetypal female, may be divided into the Good Mother, the Terrible Mother, and the Great Mother (a combination of good and bad), although in theory the three form a cohesive archetypal group.

The Terrible Mother mainly draws its images from fantastical and chimerical motifs, terrifying monsters such as the witch, dragon, vampire, and Fury,[38] all of which have been identified at one time or another with Emma. In addition, Bonifacio compares her, in more general terms, to a "bestia hembra," and wonders whether some modern Orpheus might domesticate her—another instance of the half humorous, half serious use of mythological beasts and characters. The Terrible Mother is so described because this negative elementary character of the feminine represents the dark and fearful side of the nether reaches of the unconscious. In contrast to the Good Mother, who brings forth the fruits of the earth, the Terrible Mother represents sterility, death, and destruction. The womb has become the maw of the abyss as the mother becomes, instead of a warm protectress, a devouring monster.

Is it mere hyperbole to suggest that Emma Valcárcel represents that terrible devouring mother? It is no mere coincidence that Emma

37. Jung, *Four Archetypes*, 15.
38. Neumann, *The Great Mother*, 148–49.

is identified with Bellini's Norma, a Medean type who almost succeeds in murdering her children. The use of epithets functions in a similar fashion: they suggest that we are dealing with intemporal universals. Just so. Emma is a particularized conception—seen through Bonifacio's eyes—of that abstract, the Terrible Mother.

That Emma is a rotten mother (lower case) is indisputable; but that she is also that dark creature, the Terrible Mother, becomes evident in a pair of revealing dreams. Dreams, of course, express sometimes tritely, sometimes most imaginatively, the unconscious. An instance of an almost vulgar dream is this one of Bonifacio: "Tomó dos huevos pasados por agua, y acabó por acostarse. Tardó mucho en dormirse; y soñó, llorando, con Serafina, que se había muerto y le llamaba desde el seno de la tierra, con un frasco entre los brazos. El frasco contenía un feto humano en espíritu de vino" (pp. 260–61). The least significant aspect of this dream is the fact that it is precipitated by the ingestion of food just before retiring. But, having disposed of that element, we may then proceed to analyze the principal components of Bonis' dream: a maternal image; death; the depths; and a symbol of fertility or life. Reyes' dream occurs after having heard the news of his wife's pregnancy. Consciously, he welcomes her condition; unconsciously, he wishes the real mother were Serafina Gorgheggi, who represents for him the Good Mother. The dream is a curious mixture of the traits of both Good and Terrible Mother because Bonis has been unable to separate properly the two women in his mind. His intense fear of losing "su único hijo" manifests itself in the image of the contained fetus. The flask ("frasco") is an example of the womb image; but the child is dead in this womb because, unconsciously, Bonis has anticipated Emma's daydreams of abortion. He is quite aware of her negative attitudes toward childbearing. Her child-killer instincts (not Serafina's) are symbolized not only by the flask-fetus but by the mention of the depths ("el seno de la tierra"). The Terrible Mother is characteristically associated with the Stygian underworld. Here, it is suggested that Emma—wishfully replaced by Serafina—has devoured the image of life and borne it away with her to the abyss below.

This dream, which ends Chapter 14, is followed by another in the next chapter, Emma's fantasizing over an abortion. In it, there is an allusion to the abyss which, of course, represents annihilation. This chasm, which is described as "un abismo de una niebla húmeda, brumosa," is an archetypal manifestation of the Terrible Mother's dark underworld which sucks in life's victims (the unborn child) and destroys them.

Some of the *femme fatale* characteristics applied to Emma Valcárcel also fit Serafina Gorgheggi's personality, but Serafina possesses a dual nature. Her name is indicative of this double-sided personality. Serafina inescapably calls to mind those celestial beings, the seraphs. Gorgheggi, however, suggests both a negative and a positive meaning. On the one hand, a "gorgheggio" is a trill, an unsurprising term since Serafina is an opera singer and, for Bonis, has the voice of a nightingale. But the word also is etymologically related to *gorgo*, meaning vortex, whirlpool, or abyss. And, although there appears to be no etymological connection, *gorgo* and the "*gorgh*" sound itself also suggest the noun *gorgone*, the mythological Gorgon which has come to stand for the Medusan female. La Gorgheggi, then, would appear to be a seraphic-gorgonian figure, according to her name.

One could almost say that even her double nationality supports the notion of her dual personality. She is originally English. As an English nightingale whose description recalls the ethereally serene and sweet faces of the Pre-Raphaelite models, the singer possesses a voice which melodically materializes the spirituality of the maternal ideal. But, in addition, Serafina is now very much an Italian. This aspect of her character calls forth literary and historical reminiscences of dark and passionate Italian females, Lucrezia Borgias and Vittoria Accorambonis. The association, opera singer and Italian nationality, is a natural one since Italian *prima donnas* enjoyed enormous prestige in the nineteenth century and also frequently toured Spanish cities at that time. In contemporary literature, an immediate example emerges in the case of Giulia Belcredi, the manipulative and passionate Italian singer of *Le Crépuscule des dieux*. The motif of revenge is also common to both Serafina and to the Italian female characters. It is even possible that revenge (against Mochi) as a refined form of sadomasochism, might be considered, from a nineteenth-century standpoint, an English characteristic. Traditionally, writers on the continent associated sadomasochism with the English. Thus, in Serafina Gorgheggi, one notes a light (positive) and a dark (negative) side in her personality.

Serafina's actions in *Su único hijo* bear out the veracity of her two-sided name and nationality. Her initial relationship with Bonifacio Reyes is, in his view, akin to a volcanic eruption. She appears as a bacchante, a *femme fatale* exuding frenetic ecstasy and an irresistible erotic depravity. In effect, her sexuality overwhelms the passive Bonifacio. Melodramatically, the singer exclaims that "le estoy matando de placer y que va a morir entre delicias!" (p. 92). Thus, Serafina conceives of herself as the decadent, vampiric fatal woman who will destroy her weaker lover in an excess of corrupt passion.

It is revealing to see how Alas himself appears to be carried away with the decadent image of Serafina:

> Eso hacía [Serafina], sin darse cuenta de que tomaba parte en aquellos furores de lubricidad con aires de pasión, la lascivia, la corrupción de su temperamento fuerte, extremoso y de un vigor insano en los extravíos voluptuosos. Se entregaba a sus amantes con una desfachatez ardiente que, después, pronto, se transformaba en iniciativa de bacanal, es más, en un furor infernal que inventaba delirios de fiebre, sueños del haschís realizados entre las brumas caliginosas de las horribles horas de arrebato enfermizo, casi epiléptico. (p. 90)

In this passage, Alas has dropped the critical voice of the ironic realist and has, instead, immersed himself in a bacchanalian stream of decadent eroticism. Even the structure of this paragraph betrays the temporary abandonment of the lucid, critical vision. The two sentences are constructions of almost hyperbolic length. The first, in addition, suggests a certain grammatical looseness, a lessening of Alas' usual verbal coherence. The second builds, in a combination of dependent clauses and prepositional phrases, to a melodramatic crescendo of decadent imagery. Serafina is described first as a bacchanalian and then as an infernal Fury whose erotic sensibility is capable of creating feverish deliriums, hashish dreams played out in the dark mistiness of sickly, almost epileptic passion. Decadent terminology and exaggeration have entirely replaced the more sensible realistic prose. The decadent sexual goddess which is, one recalls, ultimately derived from the romantic fatal woman, is characteristically a demonic figure whose passion is perceived as unnatural. Here, the unnaturalness of Serafina's eroticism is translated into images of fevers, epileptic fits, and drug-inspired dreams. The suggestion of disease and artificiality (narcotics) hangs over this gorgon of voluptuousness.

And yet, in moments of tranquillity and silence, this diabolical female assumes the posture and air of a young matron:

> Las últimas caricias de aquellas horas de transportes báquicos, las caricias que ella hacía soñolienta, parecían arrullos inocentes del cariño santo, suave, que une al que engendra con el engendrado. Entonces *la diabla* se convertía en la mujer de la voz de *madre*, y las lágrimas de voluptuosidad de Bonis dejaban la corriente a otras de enternecimiento anafrodítico; se le llenaba el espíritu de recuerdos de la niñez, de nostalgias del regazo materno. (pp. 91–92)

Clarín stresses Serafina's conversion from the negative side of the feminine archetype to the positive side by italicizing the dual conception Bonis invents for Serafina's personality. Why "invent"? It becomes evident that Alas has decided to delve only into the bare outlines of Serafina's life and psyche. If we know little about her life, we know even less about her psychological makeup. Other than the feelings of revenge against Mochi, we know only that, as a result of her association with the middle-class Bonis, she grows tired of the wandering and erratic singer's life and wants to settle down to become a wife and mother.

But what do we know of her real character, of her real motivations which must exist behind the façade of operatic melodrama? Very little. We perceive Serafina Gorgheggi mainly through the romanticizing and hyperbolic imagination of Bonifacio Reyes, who sees her only in the elementary positive and negative aspects of the feminine archetype. In the end, we are left with a vague sense of dissatisfaction over the gaps in our knowledge of her character. We can only conjecture over her personality after we have stripped away Bonifacio's projected dual façade of the voluptuary and the serene madonna. And even so the authorial voice sometimes coincides with Bonifacio's vision of Serafina and thus effectively obscures an accurate perception of her character.

One senses that we the readers are not expected to be particularly interested in the psychological (and other) backgrounds of the three main characters. Rather, we are to look for their essences, their fundamental typology. In order to define their characters we need not inquire how they came to be as they are—we would in any event get no answer from Alas on that score. The formation of their personalities is, then, irrelevant because what we see are not so much realistically developed characters as embodiments of archetypal conceptions. That the two principal female roles, Serafina's and Emma's, are essentially archetypal projections of Bonifacio's psyche is graphically illustrated in the curious drawing the dreamer Reyes makes in Chapter 11, an imaginative working out of the unconscious levels of his inner being. In this scene, feeling the need to express in aesthetic terms his state of reverie, Bonis takes up his pen and begins to draw capricious and fantastic arabesques in lieu of his usual flute playing. Gradually, the lines and curves begin to take shape as "la música del alma"—the inner melody—descends into the allegory or symbolic drawing he has fashioned.

Clarín carefully distinguishes in this passage between Bonis' voice or mode of expression and the authorial view, which he calls the "historian" of Bonis' life. He explains that the drawing and the thoughts that it evokes in the flautist are both conscious and unconscious manifestations of Bonis' mind ("palabras interiores, y en parte aun sin palabras") and that the character is evidently of too limited an intellect and too poorly educated to express himself (at least verbally) as well as he appears to be doing in this passage. Clarín, then, in his roundabout way here, is endeavoring to make clear that obviously the words are the historian's (the author's), while the thoughts and feelings are the character's.

What, then, does the drawing reveal? The description goes as follows:

> Y al fin brotó, como si naciera de la cópula de lo blanco y de lo negro, brotó en un cielo gris la imagen de la luna, en cuarto menguante, rodeada de nubes, siniestras, mitad diablos o brujas montados en escobas, mitad colmenas de formas fantásticas, pero colmenas bien claras, de las que salían multitud de bichos, puntos unidos a otros puntos que tenían cuerpos de abejas, con patas, rabos y uñas de furias infernales. Aquellas abejas o avispas del diablo, volaban en torno de la luna, y algunas llenaban su rostro, el cual era, visto de perfil, el del mismísimo Satanás, que tenía las cejas en ángulo y echaba fuego de ojos y boca. Por encima de esta confusión de formas disparatadas, Bonis dibujó rayas simétricas que imitaban muy bien la superficie del mar en calma, y sobre la línea más alta, la del horizonte, volvió a trazar una imagen de la noche, pero de noche serena, en mitad de cuyo cielo, atravesando cinco hileras de neblina tenue, las líneas del pentagrama, se elevaba suave, majestuosa y poética, la dulce luna llena: en su disco, elegantes curvas sinuosas decían: Serafina. (pp. 166–67)

The drawing is, as Alas says, a symbolic manifestation, a blend of abstract and chimerical forms, of geometric shapes—spheres, symmetrical lines, pentagrams—and irrational sinuosities—queer clouds of witches and devils, monstrous beehives inhabited by hellish creatures. It is, in effect, a drawing split into two parts, one rational and one irrational. What Bonis is expressing is not really a thought, not a fragment of the logical processes of the mind, but a feeling, or to be more exact, a projection of his sentiments which is visualized in this drawing. In contrast to the serenity of the night and full moon of the upper half, the bottom half of the sketch is fraught with dark and fearsome disturbances, monstrous transformations of natural objects. Clouds are not clouds but fiends arising out of Avernal beehives. The moon is not a moon but a satanical profile heaving flames from eyes and lips. This lower half of the drawing is another sky, another heaven, the photographic negative of the upper, serene, and spiritually illuminating heaven.

These two heavens are images of the two women in Bonifacio's life:

La alegoría, que le había salido sin querer de la pluma, estaba bien clara, era la *síntesis* de su vida presente. En el cielo de sus amores, en la región serena, sobre el océano de sus pasiones en calma, brillaba la luna llena, el amor satisfecho, poético, ideal, de su Serafina. Ya no eran aquéllos los días de las borrascas sensuales, en que el amor *físico*, mezclándose al *platónico*, se entregaba al *arabesco* de la pasión disparatada y caótica; el alma ya se había sobrepuesto y daba el tono al cariño, que, al arraigarse y convertirse en costumbre, se había hecho espiritual. Y de repente, de poco tiempo a aquella parte, debajo del océano, en las regiones misteriosas del abismo en las que habitaba el enemigo, de las que venían voces subterráneas de amenaza y castigo, aparecía como on reflejo infiel, otro cielo con otra luna, un cielo borrascoso con espíritus infernales vestidos de nubarrones, con el mismísimo demonio disfrazado de cuarto menguante . . . de la luna de miel satánica, de Valpurgis, que su mujer, Emma Valcárcel, había decretado que brillara en las profundidades de aquellas noches de amores inauditos, inesperados y como desesperados. (p. 167)

This analysis, coming as it does from the authorial voice, leads one to believe that Clarín, like Bonifacio, identifies the two women, Serafina and Emma, as respectively an angelic, serene figure of maternal perfection and a repulsive human monster of demonic proportions. Here, then, the distance between creator and creation, between author and character, arising out of Clarín's sense of irony and satire, is diminished to the point of closing the gap and ending the jarring effect of two disparate points of view in relation to the characters. Emma is no mere neurotic and tyrannical housewife, Serafina no frustrated and mediocre artiste; instead, they have become in Bonifacio's creative imagination two aspects of the eternal and elementary feminine archetype. The images which Bonifacio ascribes to the two women are the visualized expression of the protagonist's inner experience. They are conscious articulations of unconscious sentiments.

The neurotic, hateful Emma has become a witch, a devil who inhabits a Walpurgian universe of imaginary witches' sabbaths and arcane underground reaches. Emma is represented in the drawing by the ocean, the mysterious regions of the abyss: the enemy below. Emma's surname, Valcárcel, now takes on added significance: she is in truth a horrifying gulf of seemingly endless depths. Bonifacio, or rather the author, expresses the sense of being swept into the nether world of the feminine in this witches'-sabbath image:

> Sus caricias [Emma's] . . . se me contagian y me llevan consigo al aquelarre tenebroso, donde entre sueños y ayes de amor que acaban por suspiros de vejez, por chirridos del cuerpo que se desmorona, vivo de no sé qué negras locuras sabrosas y sofocantes, llenas de pavor y de atractivo. Yo soy el amante de una loca lasciva . . . de una enferma que tiene derecho a mis caricias. (p. 168)

The mouth—one recalls how stridently and continually Emma uses hers in her tirades—of the negative female devours her victim, the weak and ineffectual male.

If Emma represents the negative side of the feminine, Serafina, whose earlier bacchic fatal-woman image has faded by this time, symbolizes the positive side. Although no direct mention is made of her maternal significance in the sketch, Neumann again offers us a useful instrument for interpretation of Bonifacio's allegorical description of the singer. The Jungian observes that "the favored spiritual symbol of the matriarchal sphere is the moon in its relation to the night and the Great Mother of the night sky. The moon, as the luminous aspect of the night belongs to her; it is by her fruit, her sublimation as light, as expression of her essential spirit."[39] By "matriarchal sphere" Neumann alludes to the concept of the "Great Round" in the feminine archetype. This sense of roundness can be represented in a variety of forms, such as the night sky, the earth, the underworld, and the primordial ocean. These examples are meant to suggest the womb, the belly, the center of fecundity which contains and protects its fruit.

The feminine as containing vessel originally is conceived as dark:

39. *Ibid.*, 55–56.

"Whether, as in countless myths, the source of all life is the primordial ocean or whether it is earth or heaven, these sources have one thing in common: *darkness*. It is this primordial darkness which bears the light as moon, stars, and sun, and almost everywhere these luminaries are looked upon as the offspring of the Nocturnal Mother." [40] In his drawing, Bonifacio imagines Serafina precisely in the role of Nocturnal Mother. Her affection for Reyes is that serene perfection of the full moon. The circular completeness of the image suggests a spiritualized love, its passion spent. The glowing brilliance of the moon furthers the idea of the spiritual in the Serafina archetype. The moon image should not, however, be singled out as the one symbolic object of prime significance. In reality, the dark heavens are inseparable from its light. Thus, both brightness and darkness define Serafina's archetypicality. The material enclosure of the nocturnal womb is perceived in a spiritual light because the act of creation is itself a divine attribute. It is characteristic of the dual interpretation of the feminine archetype to see in the womb image both its negative and its positive aspects. In Emma, the womb is a yawning, destructive abyss. In Serafina, however, the nocturnal heavens are viewed in a positive, glowing light—it is a protective, containing element.

Neither Serafina nor Emma accepts the maternal role. In this connection, Ridge notes that in decadent literature "*the natural woman*—wife, mother, earth-woman—disappears and the *Modern Woman* appears in her stead." [41] It is only Bonifacio who transforms the two women into archetypal symbols by projecting onto them the unconscious workings of his psyche. The drawing clearly illustrates that point. As such, it confirms that Bonifacio is the pivot around which the entire novel turns. Leaving aside for the moment the authorial point of view which succeeds in being disturbingly ambivalent, it is Bonafacio who is obsessed with the idea of birthing "su único hijo." And it is his paternal-maternal quest, which is in reality the quest for the self perceived principally through his daydreaming, which forms the substance of this transitional novel.

40. *Ibid.*, 212.
41. Ridge, *Hero in French Decadent Literature*, 142.

Both the strength and the weakness of the novel derive in part from the pivotal role of Bonifacio Reyes. Reyes' quest provides a unifying structure for *Su único hijo*, but it is in the nature of reverie to possess little sense of dramatic tension or conflict. This lack of dramatic conflict is a constant in the novel. Bonis' daydreaming will reveal to us that there exists a psychological split between the conscious and the unconscious, but this separation is not rendered in dramatic terms. The fact that Bonis is above all a dreamer, a weak-willed man of inaction, more often than not causes the novel to stagnate because it gets stuck in the undefined contours of the world of dream.

Bonifacio's situation is essentially of an archetypal nature, and it is the situation, not the plot, simple as it is, which is of prime importance in *Su único hijo*. Bonifacio's exploration of the Self through an inner journey into his past and his father's nature is envisioned by the protagonist as a heroic adventure. Furthermore, this archetypal experience is closely bound to Bonis' decadent, unheroic character since it is due to his weak and dreaming nature that Reyes undergoes his inner voyage of the psyche. And it is the authorial voice which maintains sufficient distance to point out the gap between Bonifacio's idealized, heroic conception of himself and the miserable, prosaic reality of his insignificant character. In a word, as an archetype, Bonis is a nonhero who wants to be a hero.

Before embarking on this archetypal quest, an analysis of Bonifacio as a decadent type is in order here. Just as both Emma and Serafina are particularized by means of the decadent typology and, then, through Bonis' inner transformative powers, become transcendent archetypal figures, so in the case of Bonifacio Reyes. We must first view the protagonist from the outside by use of the decadent typology and then proceed to strip away the concrete, particularized attributes in order to lay bare the inner being, the archetypal essence of Bonifacio Reyes.

First, there is the name. As usual, the choice of the name is of ironic significance. "Bonifacio" may be divided etymologically into *bonis* = good and *facere* = to do, make. *Bonificare* means to ameliorate. It is true that Bonifacio is good, in the sense that generally he does no evil. That is, he does not actively and malevolently seek to be wicked. In essence, then, Bonis possesses what might be called a negative goodness. His immorality is more the result of weakness and spinelessness than a willful desire to sin. One notes that Alas stresses the shortened form, Bonis, rather than the entire first name. In other words, the ending, -*facio*,[42] is dropped, indicating the basically inactive nature of Bonifacio. He is incapable of making or producing anything. The surname Reyes is equally ironic. Clarín makes vague references to the long-forgotten nobility of Bonifacio's ancient lineage, but the shadow of degeneration—what kind is never indicated—hangs over his family tree and obliterates the vestiges of minor aristocracy (*hidalguismo*). Clarín also compares Reyes to Ulysses, a sovereign dispossessed of his lands and wife. The parallel is significant but also highly ironic. Most important, Bonifacio Reyes, like every other character in *Su único hijo*, is mediocre: there is nothing kingly about him, for this is, as Alas has pointed out in his criticism, the age of "medianías y nulidades," not of kings and heroes.

If there is one term which aptly fits Bonifacio, it is that he is a cipher. His position in his wife's household is subordinate not only economically—he has no money of his own—but in all other ways. Bonis is fully aware that he is an underdog in the social hierarchy, but he is unable to control the situation because he lacks the will to be active. Clarín deliberately stresses the passive voice by means of the verb "dejarse" in referring to Bonis:

Se había dejado querer. . . .
Se dejaba vestir.
Reyes se dejó compadecer, cuidar, mimar podría decirse. . . .
El se dejó agarrar. . . .
Y se dejó caer en una silla. . . .
Y cuando pensaba en esto, fue cuando sintió absoluta
    necesidad de dejarse caer.
Se dejó caer de rodillas delante de su mujer. . . .
(pp. 4, 11, 55, 62, 76, 80, 161)

42. The name may also be connected with "faz" (face) in reference to his pretty face.

The examples could be multiplied: all reveal Bonifacio's low energy level as he lets himself be alternately bullied, dressed, loved, and pitied. He drifts, directionless and abulic in the extreme.

Bonifacio Reyes is, then, a weakling, a fine example of the ineffectual, abulic type. As such, he evidences some similarity to the male protagonist in the rash of decadent literature of the 1880s and 1890s. Huysmans' des Esseintes epitomizes the type with his loss of vitality and spontaneity; but Bonifacio differs considerably from des Esseintes in the reasons given for his weakness. The typical decadent hero, writes Ridge, is "overwhelmed by abulia in the tedium of life" and "must force himself to act." A des Esseintes quickly becomes bored and jaded by the plethora of varying sensations offered as one after the other fades, unable to satisfy the voracious appetite of the sensation seeker. As a result, the decadent male loses interest and ceases to be active. He has thought himself into lethargy and, consequently, can be called a "cerebral hero."[43]

This sort of motivation is largely nonexistent in Bonis' psychological constitution. Reyes is weak because he is essentially a gentle, unassertive male. It is possible, of course, as it is in the case of Emma Valcárcel, to attribute his weakness to the degeneration of his family tree. But here again, we are confronted with the problem of a vague naturalistic insertion which is never developed and only hazily connected to Bonifacio's crisis of will. Clarín drops the subject after barely introducing it. So we seem to return to a prenaturalistic rationalization: Bonis is constructed as he is because it is a given factor in Clarín's analysis.

Bonis is abulic not because he is a thinker, but because he is inclined to daydream at the slightest encouragement. Music, in particular, induces him to wander into states of reverie. This somewhat romantic propensity echoes the characteristic introspective nature of the decadent hero: "He is dreamily languid, reclines on cushions, reads symbolist poetry. He may listen to the delicate strains of subdued music. His abulia has aesthetic overtones certainly."[44] Much of this is true for Bonifacio Reyes. Music, poetry, art, all these creative

43. Ridge, *Hero in French Decadent Literature*, 31, 83.
44. *Ibid.*, 87.

media stimulate a turning in upon himself in Bonis. Thus, his reverie hinges on an aesthetic ambience. One is, therefore, not surprised to learn that Bonis is a passionate enthusiast of the arts. Like the typical decadent male, he is a noncreator who reverences creativity in others. It is partly for that reason that he falls readily in love with Serafina Gorgheggi. In loving her, he is living part of his life in aesthetic terms.

As a dreamer, Bonifacio offers some points of contact with another aesthetic of the time which itself is closely connected to the decadent movement, that of the symbolists. Both decadents and symbolists perceived in the dream a means of escape from the prosaic reality of daily existence. It was better to imagine than to engage actively in the material realization of the dream. In *A Rebours*, des Esseintes makes numerous preparations for a journey to England but discovers that by vicariously living the experience in his mind, he is able to surpass the reality of the trip. This exaltation of the dream over base reality even creeps into the writings of that archnaturalist Emile Zola (see *Le Rêve*, 1888). But it is the symbolists who make most effective use of the dream as the apotheosis of existence (see, for example, Villiers de l'Isle-Adam's symbolist play, *Axël*, 1885–1886). The result of this preference for the dream over reality is the denial of life itself. All these efforts to live within the dream are ultimately sterile as rejection of the outside world leads to an attrition of the will.

A curiously voluptuous cast colors Bonifacio's daydreaming, a good deal of which takes place in his bed. The memories which reverie summons forth are also tinged with what Alas calls "la voluptuosidad de los recuerdos." When we also consider that Bonis the dreamer is, moreover, of an abulic nature, we perceive that there is a relationship between voluptuousness, on the one hand, and reverie and abulia on the other. It is the same connection which Sainte-Beuve made in his *Volupté*. He too saw *volupté* as a kind of daydreaming which is never actualized because the protagonist is too frail of will to change his dreams into realities. Sainte-Beuve's voluptuous dreamer, Amaury, anticipates the decadent male whose dreams are also sensuous memories. Thus, Bonifacio's abulic and dreamy nature with its voluptuous tinge approximates him not only to Sainte-Beuve's character but to the decadent dreamers as well.

It is certainly true that for Bonis daydreaming offers a warm, poetic consolation to the tribulation of his daily, henpecked existence. To dream is to return to a past of poignant nostalgia or to imagine a future of illusory perfection. Both tenses are equally vague in Bonis' reveries, but they nourish a soul deprived of an enduring love and an inner sense of worth. On the other hand, constant daydreaming causes Bonifacio to be supremely inactive. The dream is, then, as in the decadents and symbolists, a convenient refuge in order to escape responsibility and to deny the demands of real life.

But Alas is not content to let Reyes' dreams end in unqualified sterility. It is the peculiar tenor of his reveries that enables us to view them in both a positive and a negative light. The fact that Bonis' reverie is largely centered upon his quest for a son leads one to believe that the dream, if it revolves around an ennobling ideal (heroic, in Reyes' mind), may strike a regenerative chord in the inner man. It would be misleading to imply that Alas' conclusion offers an unqualified affirmation. Indeed, the very ambiguous ending to the novel and the fact that Bonis, after the birth of his son, still fails to assert himself (except to deny Serafina's coarse allegations) weaken the presumably regenerative effect of Bonis' paternity, at least as he perceives it in his daydreaming.

Thus far, we have seen that as a solitary individual Bonifacio shares with the decadents and symbolists three traits: abulia, aestheticism, and dreaming. But Alas' character does not exist in a social vacuum as sometimes appears to be the case in decadent characters. Bonis is inextricably tied to other characters in the novel and, in particular, to his wife. It is their relationship especially which connects Bonifacio (and of course Emma) to the decadent typology. Emma's tyrannical nature is a necessary ingredient in order to understand Bonis' anemic conduct. Without Emma, and to a certain extent Serafina, we would be left with a dreamer whose inner experiences are bereft of any outer conflict. In other words, Emma is the requisite foil to Bonis' weak personality. Emma as the neurotic, vampirish tyrant is the necessary counterpart to Bonifacio as the sapless slave. In their most basic oppositeness they embody the *fin de siècle*, modern, decadent couple in which traditional roles have been reversed.

Clarín frequently displays an ironic attitude toward his character. The author appends epithets to Reyes which reveal a kind of ironic, condescending pity as though Alas could not decide whether to admire Bonis' gentle, dreaming nature or to despise it. "Poor Reyes" is the most typical epithet applied to the protagonist. Taken out of context, it might suggest undiluted compassion for Bonis, but the frequency of the device and the fact that it usually appears whenever Bonis is made to look like a foolish victim indicate it is an ironic technique of Clarín.

This ambivalent way of treating his character is essentially Cervantine. It is, moreover, not surprising that Alas should have viewed Bonis in such a wise because Reyes is, up to a point, a quixotic character. He never approaches the profound dualities of Cervantes' creation, but the very fact that he may be so interpreted reveals to what extent Alas is able to stretch a decadent type into something more significant. On occasion, Clarín even applies the adjective "quijotesco" to some of Bonifacio's actions. He describes, for example, Reyes' patient ministrations to Emma's physical complaints as the romantic exaggeration of a quixotic love:

> Aquel plegarse a todos los oficios íntimos de alcoba, a todas las complicaciones del capricho de la enferma, de las voluptuosidades tristes y tiernas de la convalecencia, parecían en Bonifacio, por lo que toca al aspecto material, no las aptitudes naturales de un hermafrodita beato o cominero, sino la romántica exageración de un amor quijotesco, aplicado a las menudencias de la intimidad conyugal. (p. 26)

Although Bonis is a decadent character because he is weak willed, Alas makes clear in this passage that, unlike Emma or Marta Körner, he possesses no perverted traits. He is no "hermafrodita beato o cominero." In the above quotation, the allusion to an "amor quijotesco" reveals Bonifacio's underlying romanticism and idealism. Even though he is aware of Emma's feelings of contempt for him and the absence of warm affection in her, he still remembers the long-lost, all-too-brief days of their honeymoon. This memory and his own gentle nature color his regard for Emma.

The quixotic element in Bonis' character consists in his capacity to delude himself about the nature of reality. He is the foolish idealist who projects onto the actual the dreams and visions he finds within himself. He convinces himself, for example, that his rather commonplace love affair with Serafina is a grand romantic passion. And yet, as in the case of Don Quixote, cracks begin to appear in the once smooth façade of his illusion. Even as he makes love to his wife, he begins to realize that by so doing he is betraying Serafina and, hence, his great romantic love. He is forced to conclude that his grand passion did not really exist.

Perhaps Bonifacio's greatest delusion is to imagine himself in the guise of a hero. This obsession follows him throughout the novel, taking on a variety of forms as it metamorphoses from the novelesque hero to the image of the father in the final pages. By investigating the problem of heroism in *Su único hijo*, we touch upon the central situation in Bonifacio's life, a situation which can be called archetypal because it reveals the universal pattern of the trials of the hero and his encounters with the cosmic elements of life, death, and rebirth. It is this catholic, archetypal experience of the hero against which Bonifacio's drab existence is played out. The inner experience of heroic adventure which is expressed in the character's reveries represents the standard toward which Bonifacio must strive.

It is obvious that the real Bonis, the middle-class, harassed weakling, is no hero. But neither is he an anti-hero.[45] He is unheroic, but in no way does Bonis stand in opposition to the concept of the hero. He attempts not only in his daydreaming but in his daily activity to emulate the heroic stance, but he lacks the decisiveness to do so. He tries, for example, to set straight the financial accounts of the Valcárcel household by directly confronting the steward Nepomuceno, but he is pathetically confused by the barrage of figures Emma's

45. Cesáreo Bandera, for example, calls Reyes an anti-hero ("La anunciación a Bonis," 205).

uncle throws at him. He then journeys to the hamlet Cabruñana in order to redress the thievery that the local *cacique* Lobato, a rapacious fellow as his name indicates, has perpetrated to the detriment of the Valcárcels. Again, he is made a fool. He is totally incompetent. His behavior there can be interpreted in a quixotic sense, for he has gone to right wrongs, but the results do not measure up to the original dream. Clarín ironically comments on Bonis' quixotic attitude by means of Emma's irritation over her husband's unexpected trip to Cabruñana: "Pero al despertar aquella mañana y saber que Bonis, sin su permiso, dejándola con la calentura, se había marchado a la aldea a enderezar entuertos, que nunca se le había ocurrido enderezar, se había irritado" (p. 312). The Cervantine phrase "enderezar entuertos" is loaded with ironic connotations. If Don Quixote is the heroic model for Bonis' behavior, then the romantic idealist has failed miserably in his heroic endeavors. On the other hand, the failure itself is quixotic.

Bonifacio's conception of the hero is not, however, limited to the Don Quixote pattern. In the beginning, he envisions himself as a hero out of a novel. He entertains no fixed delusions arising from a state of madness and he is sometimes aware that he is a pathetic nonentity, but his dream-making capacity allows him to escape, at least temporarily, that prosaic reality: "Se creía a veces un miserable, el más miserable de todos los maridos ordinariamente dóciles; y, a ratos, se tenía por un héroe, por un hombre digno de figurar en una novela en calidad de protagonista" (p. 56). Clearly, as a result of his romantic readings, Bonis wants to become a romantic hero, the individualistic man of fateful will and passions. Again, while transforming his affair with Serafina into a "gran pasión," he reflects that, although he is unable to create novels, his present life is now so adventurous and romantic that it can be construed as a novel:

> Pero, a pesar de cierto vago temor a ponerse tísico, estaba muy satisfecho de sus hazañas. Se comparaba con los héroes de las novelas que leía al acostarse, y en el cuarto de su mujer, mientras velaba; y veía con gran orgullo que ya podía hombrearse con los autores que inventaban aquellas maravillas. Siempre había en-

vidiado a los seres *privilegiados* que, amén de tener una ardiente imaginación, como él la tenía, saben expresar *sus ideas*, trasladar al papel todos aquellos sueños en palabras propias, pintorescas y en intrigas bien hilvanadas e interesantes. Pues ahora, ya que no sabía escribir novelas, sabía hacerlas, y su existencia era tan novelesca como la primera. (pp. 92–93)

Eventually, Bonis is forced to abandon the novelesque conception of the hero as he begins to notice the widening fissure between the dream and reality; but he does not cease for that reason to believe in the hero. He merely transfers his obsession to another genre of heroism. He is somewhat akin to a Walter Mitty type as he proceeds to imagine himself as a great writer, a brave captain, a brilliant musician, and a splendid artist. All these careers are conceived of in heroic terms.[46]

His penultimate heroic conception is that of the saint:

Entre todas las grandes cosas que se le habían ocurrido ser en este mundo, gran escritor, gran capitán (esto pocas veces, sólo de niño), gran músico, gran artista sobre todo, jamás sus ensueños le habían conducido del lado de la santidad. Si en otro tiempo se había dicho: ya que no puedo inventar grandes pasiones, dramas y novelas, hagamos todo esto, sea yo mismo el *héroe*, ¿por qué no había de aspirar ahora a un heroísmo de otro género? ¿No podía ser santo? (pp. 230–31)

But Bonis realizes that he is too full of doubts, that his disorderly mind is incapable of maintaining a simple faith. Nevertheless, he recognizes in his penchant for self-abnegation and humiliation that he bears some resemblance to the mystical juggler saint, Jacopone da Todi. He dimly perceives that he too is "un clown místico." He will be laughed and jeered at, mocked for his ingenuousness and incompetence in the world of practicalities.

Clarín frequently is unable to resist taking pokes at Bonifacio's belief in himself as a hero. After confessing to the opera company

46. One wonders whether Clarín was making good-humored fun of Carlyle's various heroic divisions in *On Heroes, Hero-Worship and the Heroic in History*, a book which he otherwise admired and for which he wrote a preface in a Spanish translation (1893).

at a provincial banquet his inadequacies and underdog status, the protagonist flops down into a chair, after which Mochi approaches the hero ("se aproxima al héroe") and offers his congratulations on a speech well done. This little vignette is permeated with Clarinian irony. Later, Mochi again mocks Bonifacio's heroics by alluding in a pun to his ability to pay for the meal. "Palabra de rey," he jokes—Bonis will surely do the honors of getting stuck with the bill. In another example, Bonis, trembling for fear that his wife has discovered his liaison with Serafina, is determined to lie, if necessary, like a hero in order to protect his relations with the singer: "Pero estaba dispuesto a disimular, a mentir *como un héroe*, si era preciso" (p. 153). The context is, once more, ironic.

Bonifacio's final conception of the hero is the most significant of the lot. The paternal ideal is related to the heroic idea of sainthood since both possess divine attributes in Bonis' eyes. For that reason, the protagonist thinks of impending fatherhood as "su futuro *sacerdocio* de padre" (p. 281). As in the saint's life, the father must make heroic sacrifices: "Pero ya se sabía que un diligente padre de familia tiene que ser un héroe. Empezaban los sacrificios, y bien que dolían; pero adelante" (p. 297).

Bonifacio has, to a certain extent, already been primed for fatherhood by the strong nostalgia for maternal love which characterizes him from the very beginning. Examples from Chapter 4 indicate that Bonis is susceptible to the maternal to the point of identifying not only Serafina Gorgheggi's voice with "lo maternal" but of unconsciously feeling the warmth of a mother in his customary *tertulia*: "Se sentía bien quisto en la tertulia y se acogía a su seno, tibio como el de una madre" (p. 33). The *tertulia* takes place in a provincial clothing store which with its deepening shadows and mysterious silences suggests the appearance of a dark cave: "Se seguía suspirando, y muchos de aquellos silencios prolongados que solemnizaban la ya imponente oscuridad de la tienda con aspecto de cueva" (p. 32). Significantly this scene of the cavelike *tertulia* which suggests the womb of maternal embrace anticipates a chain of associations to be established in future chapters: the state of reverie which awakens memories of the past, specifically of childhood, is perceived as a return to the origins, to the security of the womb. The reminiscence is frequently bittersweet since it points to things irrevocably lost, to the ruin of a house and a family, to the disappearance of that which was most meaningful to Bonis, but at the same time, through the dream, the individual is able to recapture the dim reaches of the past. He may evoke things forever gone yet withal recurring over and over in the mind's eye. In this way, the receding distance of the past is fixed; and Bonis may feel as secure in that unchangingness as in his mother's lap. The past and the maternal image, then, are tightly associated in Bonis' mind through the device of reverie.

The need for "lo maternal" is, in one scene, transmuted into the need to be the mother. Reyes imagines Serafina's melodic prayer to the Virgin to be the Annunciation of his child's birth. He is bathed in a sweet, warm sentiment of maternalness, experiencing the sensation that the inmost recesses of his body are slowly widening to receive the seeds of conception:

> ¡Pues no se le antojaba a él, a Bonis, que aquella voz le anunciaba a él, por extraordinaria profecía, que iba a ser . . . madre; así como suena, madre, no padre, no; más que eso . . . madre! La verdad era que las entrañas se le abrían; que el sentimiento de ternura ideal, puro, suave, pacífico que le inundaba, se convertía casi en sensación, que le bajaba camino del estómago, por medio del cuerpo. "¡Esto debe de ser, pensaba, en eso que llaman el gran simpático! ¡Y tan *simpático*! Dios mío, ¡qué delicias; pero qué extrañas! Estas parecen las delicias de la concepción." (p. 199)

The suggestiveness of the music, its spirituality leads Bonis to perceive the birth as a species of immaculate conception and himself as a virgin mother: "Pues lloro de amor . . . nuevo; porque la voz de esa mujer, de mi querida, me anuncia que voy a ser una especie de vírgen madre . . . es decir, un padre . . . madre; que voy a tener un hijo, legítimo por supuesto, que aunque me la paras tú, *materialmente*, va a ser *todo* cosa mía" (p. 200).

This great need to experience the most transcendent event of woman is striking because it indicates that we are dealing with a curious variant of the androgyne, a type which proliferates in decadent literature of the *fin de siècle*. The sterility and corruption of the androgynous type for some critics exemplify the decadent sensibility. The androgyne "may be a man with feminine characteristics or a woman with masculine traits. . . . The decadent writers stress the androgyne's biological sterility: it incarnates what is antinatural in its most obvious form."[47]

Clarín's treatment of the inner androgyne that exists in Bonifacio is characteristically ambiguous. Reyes' habitual weakness and indecisiveness are unmanly traits. And yet his very feminineness may be said to be the most creative aspect of the character. There exists in Bonifacio's limited being a strong creative impulse which he is unable to harness and exploit. Part of that urge to create is expressed as the maternal instinct to conceive life; but the end is necessarily sterile, hence the appearance of the immaculate conception image. There is something curiously unnatural and yet delicately refreshing in Bonifacio's maternal expressivity.

In addition to the maternal sentiment as a feminine trait, Bonifacio's continual daydreaming is indicative of a feminine nature. He is happiest when he is daydreaming, but to compare the dream with reality dampens his ingenuousness. He is cognizant of approaching middle age, of impending ruin—moral, physical, financial. The atmosphere is autumnal in *Su único hijo*—*otoño* is, in fact, a key word. That which has not decayed already is on the verge of slipping downward. The smell of rotting leaves is in the air. It is against this background of decline that Bonifacio dreams of his childhood, a past which itself is not exempt from the sense of ruin and disintegration.

The dream not only offers more security and a more beautiful vision of existence than reality but, in the process, idealizes the nature of the dreamer. In short, "it 'poetizes' the dreamer." This power of poetization, this creative faculty, derives from the *anima*, the Jungian term for the personification of all feminine psychological tendencies in a man's psyche. Bachelard concisely sums it up by

47. Ridge, *Hero in French Decadent Literature*, 40.

stating that "it is *Anima* who dreams and sings. Reverie—not the dream (*rêve*)—is the free expansion of all *anima*."[48] Bonis' identification of Serafina's voice with the maternal, then, originates in the psyche's *anima*. Likewise, his daydreaming is a feminine state of the soul.

The gentleness and repose which the eventless nature of reverie inspires allows the dreamer to enter more deeply into the unconscious. It brings him closer not only to the child within himself but to the irrational forces of the depths. There is something truly childlike in Bonifacio's personality, a capacity to see things more rosily than a disillusioned male of the same age would. Because he possesses the naïveté of a child, his ability to interpret the psychological phenomena which reverie reveals to him is necessarily limited. It is left to the author and the reader to comprehend more fully Bonifacio's psychological ramblings. It is by means of reverie that the *anima*, the feminine principle of the psyche, is able to disclose certain psychological truths to Bonifacio Reyes.[49]

When Bonis identifies himself with his father's shadow during his reverie, he is, in reality, exploring not his father's nature, but his own. His further identification with his future son, through which he sees hopes of regeneration, also indicates that it is the renaissance of his own psyche which concerns him, and not the son's birth itself. This exploration of "lo paternal," which becomes a voyage of self-discovery, is expressed in heroic terms because, as Joseph Campbell has pointed out, the hero archetype is a symbolic expression of the experience of self-revelation and inner growth. The hero must undergo a kind of initiation into a dark and mysterious dimension and then return to the world we know. Campbell expresses it in these succinct terms: "The adventure of the hero normally follows the pattern of . . . a separation from the world, a penetration to some source of power, and a life-enhancing re-

48. Gaston Bachelard, *The Poetics of Reverie* (New York: Orion Press, 1969), 16, 67.

49. The *anima* is the " 'woman within,' who conveys vital messages of the Self" (M. -L. von Franz, "The Process of Individuation," *Man and His Symbols*, New York: Dell Publishing Co., 1971, p. 198).

turn."[50] By this means the hero effects a kind of regeneration within himself. Bonifacio's greatest effort at heroism, then, will be of an archetypal nature.

How does Reyes perceive the father-son relationship? First, Bonifacio ardently desires his son to be conceived miraculously, that is, that there should be a virgin birth (Chapter 12). Virgin birth is in myth and legend associated with the birth of a hero. In very primitive thought, the separation between hero (human) and god was nonexistent, hence the frequent explanation of miraculous birth for heroes.[51] This suggests that Bonis regards his son as a hero-god or divine hero. The idea is reinforced by Bonis' acceptance of the notion of his son as an avatar, which he interprets as a reincarnation of himself; "¡Un ser que sea yo mismo, pero empezando de nuevo, fuera de mí, con sangre de mi sangre!" (p. 228). It is clearly implied that the regeneration effected through the divine hero-son will be of a heroic nature for Bonifacio. This process of psychological rebirth, which is, in Jungian terms, the goal of the archetypal situation of the hero, is frequently accompanied at the start by a divine presence whose role is to support the hero in his journey. Upon hearing the news of his wife's pregnancy, Bonifacio is now certain that Providence exists and has been helping him all along (Chapter 14).

When Bonifacio decides to name his son after his father, Pedro, the choice evokes a train of thought which brings him closer to an understanding of his father, hence, indirectly, of himself:

> Aquélla era la fuente; allí estaba el manantial de las verdaderas ternuras. . . . ¡La cadena de los padres y los hijos! . . . Cadena que, remontándose por sus eslabones hacia el pasado, sería toda amor, abnegación, la unidad sincera, real, caritativa, de la pobre raza humana; pero la cadena venía de lo pasado a lo presente, a lo futuro . . . , y era cadena que la muerte rompía en cada eslabón; era el olvido, la indiferencia. Le parecía estar solo en el mundo, sin

50. Joseph Campbell, *The Hero with a Thousand Faces* (Princeton, N.J.: Princeton University Press, 1972), 35.
51. Sir James George Frazer, *The Golden Bough* (abridged ed.; New York: Macmillan Co., 1960), 106.

lazo de amor con algo que fuese un amparo . . . , y comprendía, sin embargo, que él era el producto de la abnegación ajena, del sacrificio amoroso en indefinida serie. ¡Oh infinito consuelo! El origen debía de ser también acto de amor; no había motivo racional para suponer un momento en que los ascendientes amaran menos al hijo que éste al suyo. . . . Bonifacio se había vuelto un poco hacia la pared; la luz, colocada en la mesilla de noche, pintaba el perfil de su rostro en la sombra sobre el estuco blanco. Su sombra, ya lo había notado otras veces con melancólico consuelo, se parecía a la de su padre, tal como la veía en los recuerdos lejanos. Pero aquella noche era mucho más clara y más acentuada la semejanza. "¡Cosa extraña! Yo no me parecía apenas nada a mi padre, y nuestras sombras sí, muchísimo: este bigote, este movimiento de la boca, esta línea de la frente . . . y esta manera de levantar el pecho al dar este suspiro . . . , todo ello es como lo vi mil veces, en el lecho de mi padre, de noche también, mientras él leía o meditaba, y acurrucado junto a él yo soñaba despierto, contento, con voluptuosidad infantil, de aquella protección que tenía a mi lado, que me cobijaba con alas de amor, amparo que yo creía de valor absoluto. ¡Padre del alma! ¡Cuánto me habrás querido!" se gritó por dentro. (pp. 254-55)

The chain of fathers and sons is a great chain of being of universal significance. By feeling himself a part of this chain, Bonifacio discovers the unity of the cosmos: things are not disparate but pull together to form a meaningful whole. The chain of fathers and sons, of past, present, and future draws Bonis to the roots, to the source of all being. The paternal quest has brought him to the nucleus of creation. Out of the comprehension of fatherhood arises the revelation of infinite creation.

Bonifacio then takes notice of the resemblance of his shadow to that of his father. Reflection about his shadow causes a plethora of memories of his childhood to explode in a hallucinatory simultaneity:

Los recuerdos de la infancia se amontonaban en su cerebro, y adquirían una fuerza plástica, un vigor de líneas que tocaban en la alucinación; se sentía desfallecer, y como disuelto, en una especie de plano *geológico* de toda su existencia, tenía la contemplación simultánea de varias épocas de su primera vida; se veía en los brazos de su padre, en los de su madre; sentía en el paladar *sabores* que había gustado en la niñez; renovaba olores que le habían impresionado, como una poesía, en la edad más remota. (p. 256)

The italicized word *geológico* suggests depths and delving deep under the surface of things to reach the hidden meaning. This reverie of the chain of fathers and sons and of the shadow is essentially a psychological revelation to Bonifacio, hence the vigor with which his memories strike him. Temporarily, he no longer exists in the real world; through reverie, he is separated from the world we know and has entered a mysterious dimension of childhood memories in which space and time exist in a simultaneous multiplicity. He feels himself dissolved in this wondrous vision of the past. Like the hero of mythological proportions, he has crossed into the land of adventure and must either be lost or imprisoned there or return to the real world. This fantastical world of memory and past symbolizes the depths of the unconscious from which the grown man has become separated.

Bonifacio's identification with his father and, in more general terms, with the universal chain of fathers and sons is visually represented by the device of the shadow to which the protagonist has been introduced by means of his reverie. What does Bonifacio's "sombra" signify? In primitive thought, the shadow or reflection is regarded as the soul. Cesáreo Bandera believes that Reyes' shadow "es algo así como el frustrado protagonista de una novela que nunca llegó a escribirse." Like his memories which are only a shadow of reality, so too is Bonifacio's present existence a pale reflection of his dreams and illusions. I would suggest, however, that the shadow plays a more positive role in this passage. The shadow is a psychological guide to Bonifacio's past, and it is through the past, through memory, that the protagonist is allowed to approach himself, his inner being. M. -L. von Franz explains that "the shadow is not the whole of the unconscious personality. It represents unknown or little-known attributes and qualities of the ego—aspects that mostly belong to the personal sphere and that could just as well be conscious. In some aspects, the shadow can also consist of collective factors that stem from a source outside the individual's personal life."[52]

In the case of Bonifacio's "sombra," both individual and collective elements enter into its composition. It is first a psychological indicator of the resemblance between Bonis' personality and his father's. But if we penetrate more deeply into its significance, we realize that the identification son-father is really a way for Reyes to reach his past, his childhood and, finally, his unconscious being. Through the father's shadow he discovers himself. And through the chain of fathers and sons he is also linked to a collective existence of cosmic dimensions.

Reflection about "lo paternal" stimulates a latent aggressive impulse to dignify once more the noble name of the Reyes. The Reyes, thinks Bonis, ought not to be underdogs, victims of the domineering and commonplace Valcárcels: "Sintió, con orgullo de raza, una voz de lucha, de resistencia, de apellido a apellido: lo que jamás le había pasado en largos años de resignada cautividad doméstica. *Los Reyes* se sublevaban en él contra *los Valcárcel*" (p. 256). Bonifacio's quest of Self leads him to exalt the noble, hence heroic aspect of his family. They were like kings: he must go in search of his past and re-create the heroic age of his ancestors through his own spiritual regeneration. Thus, his individual psychological growth is intimately related not only to an individual history but to a collective past.

Bonis, in fact, undertakes an actual journey to his ancestral beginnings by returning to Raíces, the coastal town from which the Reyes originated: "Era Raíces un misterioso escondite verde, que inspiraba melancolía, austeridad, un olvido del mundo, poético, resignado" (pp. 306–307). Bonifacio journeys to a remote place, a mysterious and isolated corner of the universe, a town called Roots, in order to dream and meditate on his ancestral past. In a metaphorical sense, then, he is returning to his roots, to his origins.

Surveying the humble and crude village which, nevertheless,

52. Frazer, *Golden Bough*, 220; Bandera, "La anunciación a Bonis," 202; von Franz, "Process of Individuation," 174.

possesses a melancholy aura of poetry, Bonis is reminded of the scene of Ulysses returning to Ithaca, but regards himself as a poor sort of wanderer-king, only "un pobre retoño de remota generación" (p. 307). The Ulysses story is used twice in *Su único hijo*, once in Chapter 4 and again in Chapter 16. The first allusion to the Greek legend takes place within a theatrical context. Observing the silent and wandering actors as they cross the darkened stage at a rehearsal, Bonis imagines them as the errant shades who inhabit the dim recesses of Erebos in Book 11 of *The Odyssey*. Cesáreo Bandera points out that the theater scene is another instance of the reality-illusion theme in *Su único hijo*.[53] The actors seem doubly unreal because not only are they playing fictitious roles, but they themselves seem like mere shadows. But the Homeric reference is also significant for another reason. The recollection of Ulysses' descent into Hell anticipates and thus prepares us for Bonifacio's journey to Raíces. The Greek hero visits the underworld in order to learn of his future from the seer Tiresias. While there, he also speaks with his mother and with a goodly number of other shades. The underground episode or the Nekyia is a classic archetypal experience which must be undertaken by the hero. In passing from life to death and back again, he returns revitalized. Ulysses' trip below acquaints him with his past and enables him to face the future.

We recall that Bonifacio goes to Raíces after meeting with crushing defeat by the wily Lobato. His spirits at an ebb, his inner resources need to be renewed. The ride to Raíces fulfills that function. While there, Reyes observes the resemblance and disparity between Raíces and the Ithaca setting. The pigs and dogs Ulysses encountered upon his return are there, but Eumaios, the swineherd, is not. He sadly reflects that whereas Ulysses returned, the original Reyes— "El Ulises de Raíces"—did not. He wonders what became of that first "Ulysses-Reyes" and why he left. But suddenly he remembers the recognition episode between Ulysses and the nurse Eurycleia. He had had no nurse but his mother, who was dead; his son Antonio, however, would have need of a wet nurse. The inspiration

53. Bandera, "La anunciación a Bonis," 202.

occurs to him to bring back a pair of sturdy, young wet nurses from Raíces itself. It is probably the only decisive act he accomplishes in the entire novel.

The journey to Raíces is a visual representation of the archetypal heroic quest into the dead past and one's origins. As such, it is only fitting that Bonis should see parallels between himself and that archetypal hero, Ulysses. The hills and rough spots through which Bonis must pass resemble the obscure bottom of the sea; and the town itself is hidden on one side by an elevated steep hill. Its peninsular isolation gives it the appearance of being at world's end. Like the bizarre and fantastical time-space of Bonifacio's reverie about childhood, the village represents the land of darkness, the unknown through which the hero must pass before returning home. Raíces is literally and figuratively Bonifacio's origins, his entry into the enigmatic past. He feels immediately drawn to this quiet and melancholy spot of which "nada concreto, nada plástico le hablaba ni podía hablarle de la relación de su raza con aquel pacífico, humilde y poético lugar; y, sin embargo, se veía atado a él por sutiles cadenas espirituales, de esas que se hacen invisibles para el alma misma, desde el momento en que se quiere probar su firmeza" (p. 309).

Bonifacio descends into the ancestral past to bring back upon his return a new vision, a renewal of his inner being. He knows he is a failure, but the son who will represent him will be the glory of the Reyes ("Una medianía" recounts what happens to Antonio). Bonifacio hears the bell for evening prayers, recalls his mother's prayer which begins "El ángel del Señor anunció a María," and associates this with his own paternity and son: "Una ternura infinita le invadió el alma. Hasta el caballo, meditabundo, inmóvil, le pareció que comprendía y respetaba su emoción. ¡Raíces! ¡Su hijo! ¡La fe! Su fe de ahora era su hijo" (p. 310). The message of rebirth through the son has been reinforced by the journey to Raíces, the quest backward into the past and collective memory.

Bonifacio's archetypal experience, pressed in the heroic mold, reveals that "the need for hero symbols arises when the ego needs strengthening."[54] This is certainly the case in Bonifacio's situation

54. Joseph L. Henderson, "Ancient Myths and Modern Man," *Man and His Symbols* (New York: Dell Publishing Co., 1971), 114.

but, significantly, the result of this psychological poetization of archetypal experience, of the heroic quest, is not what one might expect. When Bonis returns home with his two wet nurses, everyone laughs at the sight of Bonis squeezed between the two "buenas vacas de leche de aspecto humano" (p. 309). In quixotic fashion, Bonifacio's intentions are misunderstood. His inner heroic transformation does not emerge, so that he remains externally a pathetic nebbish. It is even highly doubtful if his psychological adventure would ever fundamentally change his weak, abulic nature.

Yet the fact remains that he has undergone this transcendent experience; it colors our appreciation of the character; and as a result, we are left to reflect uneasily on the ambiguous ending to the novel. I have commented elsewhere on this last scene, but a final observation is in order. In Bonis' last speech to Serafina, we are dealing with the strength of an illusion, of an ultimate attempt at faith. As such, it reflects the inner and archetypal passage from underdog to hero. In this respect, it is possible to regard Bonifacio Reyes as a kind of inner hero of the psyche, but the fact that his outer person remains the same, *i.e.*, weak and ineffective, disturbs our final conception of the character. We are unable to make up our minds about him, and we are left with Clarín's final ambiguous tonalities.

Irving Howe has commented on the dilemma of modern man in contemporary literature by observing that "the modern hero discovers that he cannot be a hero. Yet only through his readiness to face the consequences of this discovery can he salvage a portion of the heroic."[55] Something of this is evident in Bonifacio Reyes. By the end of the novel he knows that, despite his inner recognition of the heroic stance, he is unable to be a hero; but his readiness to sacrifice himself for his son's future has emerged as a result of a heroic archetypal experience of the psyche. He is no hero, but in the final scene vestiges of the hero's grandeur cling desperately to his pathetic figure.

Bonifacio's reiteration that Antonio is his son, his only son, is a

55. Irving Howe, *Literary Modernism*, cited by Victor Brombert, "Introduction: The Idea of the Hero," *The Hero in Literature* (New York: Fawcett, 1969), 21.

reaffirmation of the universal value of the family. The family, which is subsumed under the larger collective whole of Vetusta in *La Regenta*, becomes of paramount importance in *Su único hijo*. It implies that regeneration is not forthcoming in the national sense of the word but in the universal application of the term. Because we are dealing with universals—family, roots, self-identity—the author has had recourse to archetypal characters and situations.

What, in the meantime, has become of Spain? The collective element looms large in *La Regenta* but not so in *Su único hijo*. Indeed, the theme of Spanish decadence has become a cliché in the novel. In this connection, the German Körner mouths such banalities as:

> Lo atrasada que estaba España, a pesar de la riqueza del suelo y el subsuelo; en concepto de Körner, tenían la culpa la Inquisición y los Borbones, y después el mal ejercicio del régimen constitucional, que ya de por sí no era bueno. Con este motivo, se lamentaba de la general decadencia española, y hasta llegaba a hablarle a Nepomuceno del probable renacimiento del teatro nacional, si todos hacían lo que a él le aconsejaba: poner en movimiento los capitales, sacar partido de los tesoros de la tierra. (p. 184)

Yet the final solution suggested distinctly moves away from the idea of Spanish regeneration to the theme of universal regeneration through the renewal of self and family. Is it possible to interpret Bonifacio's return to his roots, to the primitive northern hamlet of Raíces, as an indirect comment on the Spanish situation? The Christian strongholds of the north were the nucleus of the Reconquest for many centuries. Is Alas implying that Spain needs to re-establish her identity by returning to her origins? If so, then his suggestion can only be taken in the metaphorical sense that Spain needs to look inside herself, to seek self-knowledge before a renaissance can take place.

It is not likely, however, that Alas intended to draw parallel lines between country and self in *Su único hijo* as he does in *La Regenta*. And, as I have tried to show, the archetypal nature of the setting, time, characters, and situation precludes, in my view, a naturalist-realist pattern of that kind. On the contrary, using the contemporary preoccupation with decadence as expressed in the particular decadent typology (strong woman–weak male) and *fin de siècle* ambience of decay and corruption, Alas transcends that particular literary trend to embrace the universal theme of regeneration. In this way, Alas makes use of the cosmic patterns of birth-decay-death-rebirth. Thus, out of a particular conception of decadence arises the theme of cosmic renewal. Most significant, however, is the fact that the realist in Clarín, by clearly perceiving the distance between this dream of regeneration and the flat, prosaic reality, ironically punctures his own ideal.

The Sequel: "Una medianía"

By itself, the fragment "Una medianía," which constitutes the continuation of the ironically treated, decaying family of Valcárcels and Reyes, furnishes but a modicum of interest to the Clarinian researcher, but taken in its context with *Su único hijo* reveals a little of what Alas intended to do with the next generation of Reyes, in short, with Bonifacio's "único hijo," Antonio Reyes. The sequel has attracted little critical attention except from Sergio Beser, whose article "Sinfonía de dos novelas: Fragmento de una novela de 'Clarín,'" merits reading and, recently, from Carolyn Richmond, who views *Su único hijo* as an introduction to the projected but unfortunately never completed triptych of "Una medianía," "Esperaindeo," and "Juanito Reseco," and who offers a solid explanation of why these novels were never finished. In her view,

> *Su único hijo* represents the search and hope for faith, [while] "Una medianía" is the complete disillusionment. Perhaps the necessity Alas felt to write *Su único hijo* before "Una medianía" reflects a need on his part to understand, and even justify, the negative and rebellious Antonio Reyes. His suicide, however, would symbolize the destruction of Bonifacio's only hope, and we would indeed be left with "el vacío total." Quite possibly this prospect so appalled Leopoldo Alas (who, himself, was going through a period of tremendous pessimism and doubt) that he

could not bring himself to describe it. And without the "center panel" of his "triptych," he may have eventually lost interest in, and a reason to finish, the "panels" on either side.[56]

Beser declares that, besides Clarín's evident concern with composition in the sequel, the fragment is notable for the personality of its protagonist, Antonio Reyes. The Clarinian emphasis on the internal, on the psyche, is also evident in Antonio's character delineation, which will be presented here as an example of the successful blending of both the *fin de siècle* Spanish intellectual and the typical decadent hero.

To begin with, however, we note that the fragment oscillates between two tendencies, the expected Clarinian critical realism and a psychological exploration of personality in relation to its roots or past. Since this alternating treatment, merely suggested in the fragment, is a constant in *Su único hijo*, one might conclude then that Alas had intended to continue in the same vein but for one factor which considerably alters the situation in the sequel. As Beser points out, events in *Su único hijo* take place in a temporal mode of pastness in which there is no sense of the contemporary, of the actual in the novel.[57] In contrast, the main action of the sequel is played out against a contemporary background, with Antonio's memories of childhood contrasting strongly with the predominating rhythm of the present. Against the sharply delineated realistic world of contemporary political and intellectual conflicts, Antonio's dreamworld of illusions and childhood reminiscences appears in fuzzier outlines and, naturally enough, with a less clearly defined temporality attached to it (although it is not so vague as Bonifacio's).

Of these two worlds, past and present, the harshly satirical view of the Madrid intellectual circle seems most familiar to us because

---

56. Sergio Beser, "Sinfonía de dos novelas: Fragmento de una novela de 'Clarín'," *Insula*, No. 167 (1960), 1, 12; Carolyn Richmond, "A 'Peristyle' Without a Roof: Clarín's *Su único hijo* and its Unfinished Trilogy," in Vern G. Williamsen and A. F. Michael Atlee (eds.), *Studies in Honor of Ruth Lee Kennedy* (Chapel Hill, North Carolina: Estudios de Hispanófila, 1977), 102.

57. Beser, "Sinfonía de dos novelas," 12.

it has appeared time and again in Clarín's journalistic and critical endeavors. The Ateneo setting of Chapter 6, especially, is permeated with the characteristic Clarinian use of hyperbole as a satirical technique to crush all those inauthentic, imitative, and generally mediocre or worse *pretendientes* to intellectual superiority. The author lets loose a barrage of satirical insults at the members of the Ateneo whose leftist and rightist positions are made one by their "nativo cretinismo en un gran partido, el partido del *bocio invisible*, del nihilismo intelectual. Sí, todos eran unos, y ellos creían que no; todos eran topos." These "anémicos de alma" mouth "fórmulas de vaciedades históricas o filosóficas" and the result of this "estupidez humana" is "caos intelectual." [58]

Most of the fragment centers upon the problem of Spain's intellectual life with the focal point on one individual, Antonio Reyes.[59] Unlike the Ateneo members, Antonio is no intellectual fraud, but in a larger sense he typifies the *fin de siècle* crisis in Hispanic thought and life because he is a paralyzed intellectual. Because he is unable to exercise his will, to put into practice the desires and illusions he nourishes within himself, he is as anemic as any of his peers, but he is cursed with an awareness of his abulia. Like his father Bonifacio, he prefers daydreaming to activity, but unlike the older Reyes, who is a highly emotional and intellectually untutored fellow, Antonio Reyes is, above all, an intellectual.

Antonio's abulia stems not from a lack of ideas to stimulate him but from the crushing influence of thought itself. He is incapacitated by his own stream of thoughts, a trait most characteristic of the decadent hero who, as George Ross Ridge points out, is above

58. Leopoldo Alas, "Sinfonía de dos novelas: *Su único hijo*—Una medianía," Appendix I in Carolyn Richmond (ed.), *Su único hijo* (Madrid: Espasa-Calpe, 1979), 350. All quotations are taken from this edition and cited in the text. "Una medianía" was originally published in 1889 under the title "Sinfonía de dos novelas: *Su único hijo*—Una medianía," in *La España Moderna*, VIII, and later collected in the posthumous *Doctor Sutilis* (Madrid: Renacimiento, 1916).

59. The name is an interesting combination of the commonplace (Antonio) and the aristocratic (Reyes). This polar meaning of protagonists' names occurs in Unamuno's Augusto Pérez in *Niebla* and in Azorín's *Antonio Azorín*, as well as in Galdós' Pepe Rey in *Doña Perfecta*.

all a cerebral hero. Thought leads him to consider the ways of the world, and the ways of the world disgust him, or as Ridge puts it, "the decadent is cerebral because activity is infantile."[60] Reality never measures up to the dream, so why bother about it? And as the tension between the two saps the decadent's energies, the decadent hero's cerebralism isolates him more and more from the world and immures him in a world of dreams. He turns in upon himself and creates an inner world which emotionally and intellectually satisfies him much more than prosaic reality.

Reyes' high degree of intellectuality favors a private view of himself as a superior being in a world of inferior "topos" and "anémicos de alma," one which is characteristic of the decadent male protagonist of *fin de siècle* literature. The decadent male derives a certain sour satisfaction from knowing he is misunderstood by the philistines. Antonio uses his sense of superiority to encapsulate himself in a near solipsistic universe of egoism and alienation, but underneath this seeming superiority exists a permanent layer of inferiority deriving from a neglected childhood.

Antonio's isolation from the outer world can also be attributed to his status as a *resentido*. The fact that he has failed to establish himself publicly as an exceptional individual creates a well of resentment within; and consequently, his refusal to participate in politics, for example, originates in the self-knowledge that he is ill-suited to be a man of action. He rationalizes his inaction by declaring to himself that "la política ya no es carrera para un hombre como yo; es una humillación, es una calleja inmunda" (p. 346).

This attitude does not prevent him from fantasizing himself into the role of creator of a new political party to be called "el partido zutista,"[61] the members of which, the *zutistas*, would be a species of anarchists whose goal would be to annihilate the government.

60. Ridge, *Hero in French Decadent Literature*, 83.
61. It is quite possible that Alas appropriated the term from one of the many ephemeral decadent groups of young, bohemian poets called *les zutistes*, a name which derived from the interjection, *zut*. Founded in 1883, the Parisian circle of poets was noted for its anarchistic eccentricity. See Noël Richard, *A l'aube du symbolisme* (Paris: Nizet, 1961), Ch. 5.

Here, Clarín indirectly refers to the growing Spanish anarchist movement of the late nineteenth century among whose later members was the young Azorín, who also would write novels about intellectual impotents and who probably found in Alas a seminal source for his work.[62] For Reyes, these quick spurts of mental activity are nothing more than *"relámpagos de calor*, menos, fuegos de artificio a que él no daba ninguna importancia. Dejaba que la fantasía construyera a su antojo aquellos palacios de humo, y después se quedaba tan impasible, decidido a no meterse en nada" (p. 347). He will not take part in the political arena.

This refusal to participate extends to nearly all forms of activity and, in sum, signifies Antonio's removal from life itself. Like many of Alas' characters, he behaves negatively, taking "evasive action," hence, not coming to grips with life and, indeed, defeated by life, he withdraws more and more from it and encloses himself in a world of daydreams. Disrupted out of his reverie (Chapter 4), he wanders aimlessly until he comes to the Ateneo, "sin saber cómo tampoco, sin darse cuenta de que la voluntad interviniese en sus movimientos" (p. 345). His physical ramblings, which are akin to somnambulistic movements, are symbolic of his directionless, anemic soul. Once at the Ateneo, however, his criticism of the intellectual cretinism there—"¡Qué país!," he exclaims in a Larra-like vein—bolsters his sagging ego, and, self-satisfied, he is able to close himself to the external world. He is so egotistically alienated that when he leaves the Ateneo at the end of Chapter 6, he does not even notice the beggar woman approaching him.

His narrow smugness—"Reyes, en el fondo de su alma, se sintió digno de ser estrella" (p. 355)—parallels the similar state of isolation, of encapsulation that is evidenced in the Ateneo, which in a larger sense represents Spain. In Chapter 6, then, we note a close association between country and individual which exists to a certain degree in *La Regenta*, but which is not evident in *Su único hijo*.

62. See *La Voluntad* (1902) and *Antonio Azorín* (1903). Also: Antonio Ramos-Gascón, "Relaciones Clarín-Martínez Ruiz: 1897–1900," *Hispanic Review*, XLII (1974), 413–26.

The decadence in the individual, as evidenced by his abulia, echoes the collective degeneration of the country as seen in the intellectual nullity of the Ateneo; and, of course, this crisis of will in both country and individual will appear as a major preoccupation in the Generation of 1898.[63]

Antonio's introspection in the final chapter of "Una medianía" is an example of the decadent's self-enclosed world of dream and inactivity. The physical setting of this section symbolizes the isolated state of Antonio's mind: it is an ancient, grimy, and somewhat bare berlin in which Reyes is able to meditate and shut himself off from the real world. The rocking rhythm of the carriage's wheels and swaying body encourages Antonio to reminisce about his childhood. Embraced in the maternal lullaby of the coach-cradle and of reverie, he indulges in a bitter-sweet *volupté* of childhood memories, of "recuerdos muy lejanos y vagos." Here, as in *Su único hijo*, the combination of abulia and reverie makes for a voluptuousness similar to that of Sainte-Beuve in *Volupté*.

Beser has observed in this scene the pre-Proustian ambience of physical sensation and mental association, for, in addition to the rocking of the vehicle, a pungent odor—"un olor punzante, indefinible, pero muy conocido (olor de coche de alquiler lo llamaba él para sus adentros)" (p. 356)—brings back forgotten memories.[64] Raindrops splashing and sliding on the windows reflect in a variety of fantastic and capricious shapes the city lights; they establish an aura of irreality propitious to the state of reverie. Antonio suddenly remembers a moment of early childhood when he was sitting on his father's lap in a carriage similar to the present berlin. He compares that world with the actual one: "¡Qué lejos estaba todo aquello! ¡Qué diferente era el mundo que veía entre sueños de una conciencia que nace, aquel niño precoz, del mundo verdadero, el de ahora!" (p. 357). The utter separation between reality and dream in which the decadent wholeheartedly believes and feels is quite

63. Doris King Arjona, "La Voluntad and Abulia in Contemporary Spanish Ideology," *Revue hispanique*, LXXIV (1928), 573–671.
64. Beser, "Sinfonía de dos novelas," 12.

explicit in this quotation. It is a sentiment which Antonio shares with his father but, because Bonis is not an intellectual, he is not crushed by the disparity between the two realities.

Antonio exalts his childhood memories just as his father did: "Reyes atribuía a los recuerdos de su infancia un interés supremo; conservábalos con vigorosa memoria y con una precisión plástica que le encantaba" (p. 357). His reminiscences seem to be sharper and clearer than Bonifacio's, recalling that from the age of six he delighted in the "vida interior" and that reality, "tal como era desde que él tenía recuerdos, le había parecido despreciable; sólo podía valer transformándola, viendo en ella otras cosas; la actividad era lo peor de la realidad; era enojosa, insustancial" (p. 357). None of his father's romantic attitudes is present in this passage to color the purely decadent stance face to face with reality. Reality is distasteful; activity insubstantial. The same attitudes define Huysmans' des Esseintes, the quintessential decadent hero of *A Rebours*.

Antonio's recollection that no one, with the exception of his father, loved or appreciated him, causes a deep sense of injustice over the world's neglect and misunderstanding of his nature, which is, in part, responsible for his rejection of external reality. The resemblance between his father and himself draws them together, but his relationship with his mother is totally unsatisfactory. Bitterly reflecting about her, he abandons himself to the tears of a deep and abiding pain: "Encogió los hombros, cerró los ojos, y sintió en ellos lágrimas. El ruido de los cristales y de las ruedas, más fuerte ahora, le resonaba dentro del cráneo; ya no era como canto de nodriza; tomó un ritmo extraño de coro infernal, parecido al de los demonios en *El Roberto*" (p. 359). The pre-Proustian associations of sensation and memory now become tainted with the diabolical aura of the fatal woman. Even Emma's own son regards her as an infernal being who to be justly described can only be compared to the demons of Giacomo Meyerbeer's lushly spectacular *Robert le Diable* (1831).

In this last chapter, Alas has moved away from the traditional realistic presentation and the close connection between the individual and the group in order to concentrate on the individual psyche and the intangible world of dream. The same movement away from traditional realism toward the psychological universals of dream, childhood, and the past is evident in *Su único hijo*. Whether he intended to construct all of "Una medianía" along the same lines is difficult to determine, but from the fragment that remains it is a reasonable assumption to entertain.

Conclusion

Using A. E. Carter's three-part division of the theme of decadence in nineteenth-century French literature as a rough guideline, one may then place *La Regenta* in the second or naturalist phase and *Su único hijo* in the last or *fin de siècle* phase. *La Regenta*, although it exhibits many characteristics of the realist-naturalist trend, does not, however, conform entirely to the Zolaesque school of thought, for the realistic-naturalistic description of the decadent ambience and characters alternates with the inner realities of the psyche. Yet both the collective and the individual elements of the novel are profoundly unified by the threatening sense of disintegration which informs their character. This downward movement into the depths of degeneration, which at times comes close to the decadent sensibility of the *fin de siècle* phase, characterizes both society and self. As they splinter and begin to crack apart, they demonstrate the traits which define decadent characters and societies: sickliness, perversion, unnaturalness, artificiality. The aura of evil which hangs over the collective being of Vetusta becomes so intense that it assumes near metaphysical dimensions and approaches a Baudelairean universe of evil and corruption.[1]

Decay becomes autumnal in *Su único hijo* not only because the sense of things past is of a nostalgic, pseudoromantic nature, but because it is a product of the tired times of the 1880s and 90s (and of Clarín's own worn-out life). The sense of dramatic conflict in

1. For Alas, Baudelaire represented, I believe, a more profound interpretation of decadence, that of the sickly soul. It is evident that this concept appealed very much to Clarín: his entire analysis of the *regenta*'s psyche can be seen as a novelistic response and parallel to the despairing soul presented in *Les Fleurs du mal*. For a study along these lines, see my article, "The Landscape of the Soul in Clarín and Baudelaire," *Revue de littérature comparée*, LIV (1980), 17–31.

society and self which characterizes *La Regenta* has drained away in this second novel into an external operatic universe of melodramatic contrivance and an inner cushiony world of reverie. The strength of the will has either become misdirected (Emma) or simply nonexistent (Bonis). The sense of inefficacy and of abulia which invades *Su único hijo* was prefigured in parts of *La Regenta* (Ana and Víctor, for example) but nowhere reaches the epidemic proportions of the second novel. Decadence is still a matter of moral and spiritual ill-health in *Su único hijo* as it is in *La Regenta*, but the unnaturalness, artificiality, and corruption of Alas' later creations attain the monstrous quality of the morbid strain of romantic characters. While vestiges of naturalistic interpretation cling to them, by and large they have been patterned after the decadent typology of the times, which centers round the weak male–dominant female relationship.

A major distinguishing mark in *Su único hijo*, as compared to *La Regenta*, is the emergence of the theme of regeneration out of the preoccupation with decadence. The *fin de siècle* decadent sensibility was not lacking in ideals, and a concern with regeneration was the natural outcome of the excessive interest in decay. *Su único hijo*, then, with its middle-aged lassitude and need for renewal, epitomizes in this sense the *fin de siècle* mood. Significantly, Alas' treatment of the theme of regeneration leads him to develop his characters into archetypal creations of symbolic value. A transformation consisting of three steps in the evolution of the characters takes place: they proceed from the original romantic nucleus of characterization to the decadent typology, which itself derives from romanticism and, finally, to the last stage of archetypicality in which their roles function symbolically.

Decay in *Su único hijo* focuses first upon a family, the Valcárcels, and finally on one individual, Bonifacio Reyes. And it is through the dreamer Bonis that regeneration must be effected. His archetypal quest into self-discovery reevaluates in positive terms the past as a signpost to the self's renaissance. The ideal of the family (the son) initiates Bonis on his symbolic quest which, upon his return home in the final chapter, turns full circle back to the universal value of the family. The exaltation of one's roots and the family signifies in Clarín a turning away from the preoccupation with national or societal decay, as seen in *La Regenta*, to a concern with the eternal and cosmic values of rebirth in self and family. The belief in the ideal of the family, a belief which stretches beyond individual, group, or country, does not, however, prevent Clarín the ironic realist from perceiving the disparity between the dream and the reality, especially when the dream comes to naught.

Although Clarín remains a persistent critic of the decadence in Spanish society and individuals, his moralistic approach—symbolized in the tower image from which he surveys the depths of decay below—is often colored by a fascination with, and sometimes even complicity in, his decadent subject matter. This sometimes results in an ambiguous point of view. And it is this intense involvement with decadence in its various manifestations—ambience, character types, motifs, images—which has allowed us to view Clarín, the critical realist, in the light of the French decadent sensibility.

Bibliography *

Major Works by Leopoldo Alas
(Arranged in chronological order by date of publication)

El derecho y la moralidad. Madrid: Casa Editorial de Medina, 1878.

Solos de Clarín. Madrid: Alfredo de Carlos Hierro, 1881.

La literatura en 1881. In collaboration with Armando Palacio Valdés. Madrid: Alfredo de Carlos Hierro, 1882.

Programa de elementos de economía política y estadística. Madrid: Impr. de la Revista de Legislación, 1882.

"Prólogo" to Emilia Pardo Bazán's *La cuestión palpitante.* 4th ed. Madrid: Imprenta de A. Pérez Dubrull, 1891. (first published in 2nd ed., 1883).

La Regenta, 2 vols. Barcelona: Daniel Corteza y Cía., 1884–1885.

Sermón perdido. Madrid: Fernando Fe, n.d. [1885].

Un viaje a Madrid. Folletos literarios, I. Madrid: Fernando Fe, 1886.

Pipá. Madrid: Fernando Fe, 1886.

Alcalá Galiano: El período constitucional de 1820 a 1823. In *Ateneo científico literario y artístico de Madrid. La España del siglo XIX.,* Vol. II. Madrid: Librería de don Antonio San Martín, 1887.

Nueva campaña. Madrid: Fernando Fe, 1887.

Cánovas y su tiempo. Folletos literarios, II. Madrid: Fernando Fe, 1887.

Apolo en Pafos. Folletos literarios, III. Madrid: Fernando Fe, 1887.

Mis plagios. Un discurso de Núñez de Arce. Folletos literarios, IV. Madrid: Fernando Fe, 1888.

Benito Pérez Galdós. Madrid: Ricardo Fe, 1889. Expanded version: *Galdós.* Vol. I of *Obras Completas.* Madrid: Renacimiento, 1912.

Mezclilla. Madrid: Fernando Fe, 1889.

A 0,50 Poeta. Folletos literarios, V. Madrid: Fernando Fe, 1889.

*This bibliography is not intended as an exhaustive compilation of primary and secondary sources. The author has recently completed a book-length, annotated bibliography, emphasizing secondary source material on Clarín.

Rafael Calvo y el teatro español. Folletos literarios, VI. Madrid: Fernando Fe, 1890.

Museum. Folletos literarios, VII. Madrid: Fernando Fe, 1890.

Un discurso. Folletos literarios, VIII. Madrid: Fernando Fe, 1891.

Su único hijo. Madrid: Fernando Fe, 1891.

Doña Berta, Cuervo, Superchería. Madrid: Fernando Fe, 1892.

El Señor y lo demás son cuentos. Madrid: Manuel Fernández y Lasanta, 1892.

Ensayos y Revistas. Madrid: Manuel Fernández y Lasanta, 1892.

Palique. Madrid: Victoriano Suárez, 1893.

Teresa. Madrid: José Rodríguez, 1895.

Cuentos morales. Madrid: Imp. "La España Editorial," 1896.

Crítica popular. Valencia: F. Vives Mora, 1896.

La Regenta, 2 vols. Prólogo de Benito Pérez Galdós. Madrid: Fernando Fe, 1901.

El gallo de Sócrates. Barcelona: Maucci, 1901.

Siglo pasado. Madrid: Antonio R. López, 1901.

Doctor Sutilis. Vol. III of *Obras completas.* Madrid: Renacimiento, 1916.

Páginas escogidas. Ed. "Azorín." Madrid: Calleja, 1917.

Epistolario de Menéndez y Pelayo y Leopoldo Alas. Madrid: Escorial, 1943.

¡Adiós, Cordera! *y otros cuentos.* Madrid: Espasa-Calpe, 1944.

Obras selectas. Edited by Juan Antonio Cabezas. Madrid: Biblioteca Nueva, 1947 (2nd ed., 1966).

Cuentos de Clarín. Edited by Laura de los Ríos de García Lorca. Cambridge, Mass.: Houghton Mifflin, 1954.

La Regenta, 2 vols. Edited by Juan M. Lope and Huberto Batis. México: UNAM Colección "Nuestros Clásicos," 1960.

La Regenta, 1 vol. Edited by José María Martínez Cachero. Barcelona: Clásicos Planeta, 1963.

Cuentos escogidos. Edited by G. G. Brown. Oxford: Dolphin, 1964.

La Regenta, 1 vol. Madrid: Alianza, 1966.

Su único hijo. Madrid: Alianza, 1966.

Superchería, Cuervo, Doña Berta. Madrid: Taurus, 1970.

Solos de Clarín. Madrid: Alianza, 1971.

Preludios de 'Clarín.' Edited by Jean-François Botrel. Oviedo: Instituto de Estudios Asturianos, 1972.

Leopoldo Alas: Teoría y crítica de la novela española. Edited by Sergio Beser. Barcelona: Laia, 1972.

Palique. Edited by José María Martínez Cachero. Barcelona: Labor, 1973.

Cuentos morales. Madrid: Alianza, 1973.

Obra olvidada. Edited by Antonio Ramos-Gascón. Madrid: Júcar, 1973.

Teresa. Avecilla. El hombre de los estrenos. Edited by Leonardo Romero. Madrid: Castalia, 1975.

Pipá. Edited by Antonio Ramos-Gascón. Madrid: Cátedra, 1976.

La Regenta, 1 vol. Edited by Gonzalo Sobejano. Barcelona: Noguer, 1976.

Su único hijo. Edited by Carolyn Richmond. Madrid: Espasa-Calpe, 1979.

Articles and Studies on Alas

Agudiez, Juan Ventura. *Inspiración y estética en La Regenta de "Clarín."* Oviedo: Instituto de Estudios Asturianos, 1970.

————. "La sensibilidad decadentista de Barbey d'Aurevilly y algunos temas de *La Regenta.*" *Revista de Occidente,* XXXIII (1971), 355–65.

Alarcos Llorach, Emilio. "Notas a *La Regenta.*" *Archivum,* II (1952), 141–60. Repr. in *Ensayos y estudios literarios.* Madrid: Júcar, 1976, pp. 99–118.

Alas, Adolfo. *Epistolario a Clarín: Menéndez y Pelayo, Unamuno, Palacio Valdés.* Madrid: Escorial, 1941.

Alonso Cortés, Narciso. " 'Clarín' y el 'Madrid Cómico'." *Archivum,* II (1952), 43–61.

Aponte, Sally Ortiz. *Las mujeres de "Clarín" (Esperpentos y camafeos).* Universidad de Puerto Rico: Universitaria, 1971.

Arroyo de López-Rey, Justa. "*La Regenta* de Clarín: Justicia, verdad, belleza," in *Homenaje a Casalduero (crítica y poesía).* Edited by Rizel Pincus Sigele and Gonzalo Sobejano. Madrid: Gredos, 1972, pp. 325–39.

Asensio, Jaime. "El motivo del 'alarde' en *La Regenta,* de Clarín." *Revista de Archivos, Bibliotecas y Museos,* LXXVII (1974), 597–600.

Avello, Manuel F. "*La Regenta* y la niebla." *Boletín del Instituto de Estudios Asturianos,* XXXI (1977), 17–27.

Avrett, Robert. "The Treatment of Satire in the Novels of Leopoldo Alas (Clarín)." *Hispania,* XXIV (1941), 223–30.

Balseiro, José A. *Novelistas españoles modernos.* New York: Macmillan Co., 1933.

Bandera, Cesáreo. "La sombra de Bonifacio Reyes en *Su único hijo.*" *Bulletin of Hispanic Studies,* XLVI (1969), 201–25.

Baquero Goyanes, Mariano. " 'Clarín,' creador del cuento español." *Cuadernos de Literatura,* V (1949), 145–69.

———. " 'Clarín,' novelista." *Insula,* No. 76 (1952), 1, 9–10.

———. " 'Clarín' y la novela poética." *Boletín de la Biblioteca Menéndez y Pelayo,* XXIII (1947), 96–101.

———. *Prosistas españoles contemporáneos.* Madrid: Rialp, 1956, pp. 33–172.

Barja, César. *Libros y autores modernos.* 2nd ed. rev. New York: Las Américas Publishing Co., 1964, pp. 367–76.

Bécarud, Jean. *La Regenta de "Clarín" y la Restauración.* Madrid: Taurus, 1964. Repr. in *De La Regenta al "Opus Dei."* Madrid: Taurus, 1977, pp. 11–30.

Beser, Sergio. "Documentos clarinianos." *Archivum,* XII (1963), 507–26.

———. *Leopoldo Alas, crítico literario.* Madrid: Gredos, 1968.

———. " 'Sinfonía de dos novelas.' Fragmento de una novela de 'Clarín'." *Insula,* No. 167 (1960), 1, 12.

Blanco García, Francisco P. *La literatura española en el siglo XIX.* Vol. 2. 3rd ed. Madrid: Sáenz de Jubera, 1910, pp. 546–47; 603–604.

Blanquat, Josette. "Clarín et Baudelaire." *Revue de littérature comparée,* XXXIII (1959), 5–25.

———. "L'Hommage de Clarín à un prélat asturien." *Bulletin hispanique,* LXVIII (1966), 216–52.

———. "La Sensibilité religieuse de Clarín. Reflets de Goethe et de Leopardi." *Revue de littérature comparée,* XXXV (1961), 177–96.

Bonafoux, Luis. *Yo y el plagiario Clarín.* Madrid: Administración, 1888.

Bonet, Laureano. "Clarín ante la crisis de 1898." *Revista de Occidente,* XXV (1969), 100–19.

Boring, Phyllis Z. "Some Reflections on Clarín's *Doña Berta.*" *Romance Notes,* IX (1969), 322–25.

Botrel, Jean François. "Últimos ataques de Bonafoux a 'Clarín'." *Archivum,* XVIII (1968), 177–88.

Brent, Albert. *Leopoldo Alas and La Regenta.* Columbia, Missouri: University of Missouri Studies, 1951.

Bull, William, "Clarín and his Critics." *Modern Language Forum,* XXXV (1950), 103–11.

———. "Clarín's Literary Internationalism." *Hispanic Review*, XVI (1948), 321–34.

———. "The Liberalism of Leopoldo Alas." *Hispanic Review*, X (1942), 329–39.

———. "The Naturalistic Theories of Leopoldo Alas." *PMLA*, LVII (1942), 536–51.

Bull, William, and Vernon Chamberlin. *Clarín: The Critic in Action*. Stillwater, Oklahoma: Oklahoma State University Publication, 1963.

Cabezas, Juan Antonio. *"Clarín," el provinciano universal*. Madrid: Espasa-Calpe, 1962.

Carenas, Francisco. "¿Anticlericalismo en *La Regenta* de Clarín?" *Norte*, X (1969), 1–7.

Clavería, Carlos. *Cinco estudios sobre la literatura española moderna*. Salamanca: Consejo Superior de Estudios Científicos, 1945, pp. 9–45.

Clocchiatti, Emilio. *Leopoldo Alas "Clarín": Su crítica y estética*. Quebec, Canada: Ediciones La Crítica, 1949.

Davis, Gifford. "The Literary Relations of Clarín and Emilia Pardo Bazán." *Hispanic Review*, XXXIX (1971), 378–94.

Delogu, F. M. "Note su Leopoldo Alas (Clarín) 1852–1901." *Siculorum Gymnasium*, XIV (1961), 212–19.

Durand, Frank. "Characterization in *La Regenta*: Point of View and Theme." *Bulletin of Spanish Studies*, XLI (1964), 86–100.

———. "A Critical Analysis of Leopoldo Alas's *La Regenta*." Ph.D. dissertation, University of Michigan, 1962.

———. "Structural Unity in Leopoldo Alas's *La Regenta*." *Hispanic Review*, XXXI (1963), 324–35.

Eoff, Sherman H. "In Quest of a God of Love," in *The Modern Spanish Novel*. New York: New York University Press, 1961, pp. 51–84.

Esquer Torres, Ramón. "Las luchas del siglo XIX: El P. Blanco García y Leopoldo Alas 'Clarín.'" *Boletín de la Sociedad Castellonense de Cultura*, XXXVIII (1962), 241–55.

Feal Deibe, Carlos. "La anunciación a Bonis: Análisis de *Su único hijo*." *Bulletin of Hispanic Studies*, LI (1974), 255–71.

Fedorchek, Robert M. "En torno a una imagen de *La Regenta*." *Horizontes*, No. 38 (1976), 71–75.

Fernández Almagro, Melchor. "Crítica y sátira en 'Clarín'." *Archivum*, II (1952), 33–42.

———. "Leopoldo Alas y Clarín." *Insula*, No. 31 (1948), 1.

Ferreras, Juan Ignacio. "*La Regenta* ante un nuevo método." *Les Langues néolatines*, No. 169 (1963), 15–41.

Fishtine, Edith. "Clarín in his Early Writings." *Romanic Review*, XXIX (1938), 325–42.

García Pavón, Francisco. " 'Clarín' crítico en su obra narrativa." *Insula*, No. 76 (1952), 5, 11.

———. "Gentes humildes en la obra narrativa de 'Clarín'." *Arbor*, XXII (1952), 186–95.

García Sarriá, Francisco. *Clarín o la herejía amorosa*. Madrid: Gredos, 1975.

Gilman, Stephen. "La novela como diálogo: *La Regenta* y *Fortunata y Jacinta*." *Nueva Revista de Filología Hispánica*, XXIV (1975), 438–48.

Gómez-Santos, Marino. *Leopoldo Alas "Clarín": Ensayo bio-bibliográfico*. Oviedo: Instituto de Estudios Asturianos, 1952.

González Blanco, Andrés. *Historia de la novela en España desde el romanticismo a nuestros días*. Madrid: Sáenz de Jubera, 1909, pp. 495–535.

Gramberg, Eduard. *Fondo y forma del humorismo de Leopoldo Alas, "Clarín."* Oviedo: Instituto de Estudios Asturianos, 1958.

———. "*Su único hijo*, novela incomprendida de Leopoldo Alas." *Hispania*, XLV (1962), 194–99.

———. "Tres tipos de ambientación en la novela del siglo diecinueve." *Revista Hispánica Moderna*, XXVIII (1962), 315–26.

Gullón, Germán. " 'Clarín' o la complejidad narrativa," in *El narrador en la novela del siglo XIX*. Madrid: Taurus, 1976, pp. 133–48.

Gullón, Ricardo. "Aspectos de 'Clarín'." *Archivum*, II (1952), 217–26.

———. " 'Clarín,' crítico literario." *Universidad: Revista de Cultura y Vida Universitaria* (Zaragoza), XXVI (1949), 389–431.

———. "Las novelas cortas de Clarín." *Insula*, No. 76 (1952), 3.

Hatzfeld, Helmut. "La imitación estilística de *Madame Bovary* (1857) en *La Regenta* (1884)." *Thesaurus*, XXXII (1977), 40–53.

Ibarra, Fernando. "Clarín y Azorín: El matrimonio y el papel de la mujer española." *Hispania*, LV (1972), 45–54.

———. "Clarín y Rubén Darío." *Hispanic Review*, XLI (1973), 524–40.

———. "Clarín y el teatro político." *Romance Notes*, XIII (1971), 266–71.

Ife, Barry W. "Idealism and Materialism in Clarín's *La Regenta*: Two Comparative Studies." *Revue de littérature comparée*, XLIV (1970), 273–95.

Jackson, Robert M. " 'Cervantismo' in the Creative Process of Clarín's *La Regenta*." *Modern Language Notes*, LXXXIV (1969), 208–27.

———. "*La Regenta* and Contemporary History." *Revista de Estudios Hispánicos*, XI (1977), 287–302.

Kronik, John. "Clarín and Verlaine." *Revue de littérature comparée*, XXXVII (1963), 368–84.

———. "The Function of Names in the Stories of Alas." *Modern Language Notes*, LXXX (1965), 260–65.

———. "La modernidad de Leopoldo Alas." *Papeles de Son Armadans*, XLI (1966), 121–34.

Laffitte, G. "*Madame Bovary* et *La Regenta*." *Bulletin hispanique*, XLV (1943), 157–63.

Little, William, and Joseph Schraibman. "Notas sobre el motivo de la paternidad en *Su único hijo* de 'Clarín.' " *Boletín del Instituto de Estudios Asturianos*, XXXII (1978), 21–29.

Lott, Robert E. "El estilo indirecto libre en *La Regenta*." *Romance Notes*, XV (1974), 259–63.

Martínez Cachero, José María. "Adiciones a una bibliografía sobre Leopoldo Alas, 'Clarín'." *Archivum*, II (1952), 408–20.

———. " 'Clarín' y 'Azorín'." *Archivum*, III (1953), 159–80.

———. "Crónica y bibliografía del primer centenario de Leopoldo Alas, 'Clarín': Años 1951 y 1952." *Archivum*, III (1953), 79–112.

———. "Dos fragmentos narrativos de Leopoldo Alas." *Archivum*, XII (1962), 479–506.

———, ed. *Leopoldo Alas 'Clarín.'* Madrid: Taurus, 1978.

———. "Noticia de tres folletos contra 'Clarín.' " *Boletín del Instituto de Estudios Asturianos*, XIII (1959), 225–44.

———. "Los versos de Leopoldo Alas." *Archivum*, II (1952), 89–111.

Martínez Ruiz, José ("Azorín"), " 'Una novela': *Su único hijo*." *ABC*, February 1, 1950.

Mazzeo, Guido. "The Banquet Scene in *La Regenta*, a Case of Sacrilege." *Romance Notes*, X (1968), 68–72.

———. "La voluntad ajena en *Los pazos de Ulloa* y *La Regenta*." *Duquesne Hispanic Review*, IV (1965), 153–61.

Melón Ruiz de Gordejuela, Santiago. "Clarín y el bovarysmo." *Archivum*, II (1952), 69–87.

Meregalli, Franco. "Clarín and Unamuno: Parallels and Divergencies," in *Unamuno Creator and Creation*. Edited by José Rubía Barcía and M. A. Zeitlin. Los Angeles: University of California Press, 1967, pp. 156–70.

Montes Huidobro, Matías. "Leopoldo Alas: El amor, unidad y pluralidad en el estilo." *Archivum*, XIX (1969), 207–20.

————. "Riqueza estilística de *La Regenta*." *Revista de Estudios Hispánicos*, II (1969), 43–50.

————. "*Su único hijo*: Sinfónico avatar de Clarín." *Archivum*, XXII (1972), 149–209.

Navarrete, Rosina. "Análisis algebraico de un retrato." *Explicación de Textos Literarios*, I (1972), 125–28.

Nimetz, Michael. "Eros and Ecclesia in Clarín's Vetusta." *Modern Language Notes*, LXXXVI (1971), 242–53.

Noval Fernández, Francisco. "Vetusta, Clarín, Frígilis (Aproximación a *La Regenta*)." *Boletín del Instituto de Estudios Asturianos*, XXVI (1972), 743–63.

Núñez de Villavicencio, Laura. *La creatividad en el estilo de Leopoldo Alas, "Clarín."* Oviedo: Instituto de Estudios Asturianos, 1974.

Oleza, Juan. *La novela del XIX: Del parto a la crisis de una ideología.* Valencia: Bello, 1976, pp. 141–213.

Ortega, José. "Don Fermín de Pas: Un estudio 'de Superbia et Concupiscentia Catholicis.'" *Revista de Estudios Hispánicos*, IX (1975), 323–42.

Ortega, Soledad, ed. *Cartas a Galdós.* Madrid: Revista de Occidente, 1964.

Palls, Byron P. "El naturalismo de *La Regenta*." *Nueva Revista de Filología Hispánica*, XXI (1972), 23–39.

Panebianco, Candido. "Personaggi e problematica ne *La Regenta*." *Siculorum Gymnasium*, XXIII (1970), 158–74.

Penzol, Pedro. "Parentescos." *Archivum*, II (1952), 421–26. Repr. in *Escritos*. Vol. II. Oviedo: Instituto de Estudios Asturianos, 1974, pp. 205–10.

Pérez de Ayala, Ramón. "'Clarín' y don Leopoldo Alas," in *Supercheria, Cuervo, Doña Berta*. Madrid: Taurus, 1970, pp. 9–30.

Pérez Galdós, Benito. "Prólogo" to Leopoldo Alas' *La Regenta*, I. Madrid: Fernando Fe, 1901.

Pérez Gutiérrez, Francisco. *El problema religioso en la generación de 1868* (*'La leyenda de Dios'*). Madrid: Taurus, 1975, pp. 269–338.

Pérez Minik, Domingo. *Novelistas españoles de los siglos XIX y XX*. Madrid: Guadarrama, 1957, pp. 131–55.

Polo de Bernabé, José Manuel. "Mito y símbolo en la estructuración narrativa de *La Regenta*." *Papeles de Son Armadans*, LXVIII (1973), 121–40.

Posada, Adolfo. *Leopoldo Alas (Clarín)*. Oviedo: Imp. "La Cruz," 1946.

Proaño, Franklin. "Ascesis y misticismo en Ana Ozores." *Boletín del Instituto de Estudios Asturianos*, XXVI (1972), 765–82.

———. "Cambios de identidad en Ana Ozores." *Nueva Revista de Filología Hispánica*, XXIII (1974), 115–21.

———. "Dicotomías en los personajes de Leopoldo Alas." *Boletín del Instituto de Estudios Asturianos*, XXIX (1975), 65–75.

———. "Presencia y problemática del yo en los personajes de 'Clarín.' " *Boletín del Instituto de Estudios Asturianos*, XXVII (1973), 549–75.

———. "Tricotomías del yo en los personajes de Clarín." *Boletín del Instituto de Estudios Asturianos*, XXVIII (1974), 313–21.

Ramos-Gascón, Antonio. "Relaciones Clarín–Martínez Ruiz: 1897–1900." *Hispanic Review*, XLII (1974), 413–26.

Reiss, Katherine. "Valoración artística de las narraciones breves de Leopoldo Alas, 'Clarín,' desde los puntos de vista estético, técnico y temático." *Archivum*, V (1955), 77–126; 256–303.

Rice, Miriam Wagner. "The Meaning of Metaphor in *La Regenta*." *Revista de Estudios Hispánicos*, XI (1977), 141–51.

———. "Vetusta invertebrada: El particularismo en un contexto asturiano." *South Atlantic Bulletin*, XLII (1977), 67–75.

Richmond, Carolyn. "Introducción," in *Su único hijo*, by Leopoldo Alas. Madrid: Espasa-Calpe, 1979, pp. xi–lix.

———. "La ópera como enlace entre dos obras de 'Clarín': 'Amor è furbo' y *Su único hijo*." *Insula*, No. 377 (1978), 3.

———. "A 'Peristyle' Without a Roof: Clarín's *Su único hijo* and its Unfinished Trilogy," in *Studies in Honor of Ruth Lee Kennedy*. Edited by Vern G. Williamsen and A. F. Michael Atlee. Chapel Hill, North Carolina: Estudios de Hispanófila, 1977, pp. 85–102.

———. "La polémica Clarín-Bonafoux y Flaubert." *Insula*, No. 365 (1977), 1, 12.

Ríos, Laura de los. *Los cuentos de Clarín*. Madrid: Revista de Occidente, 1965.

Roberts, Gemma. "Notas sobre el realismo psicológico de *La Regenta*." *Archivum*, XVIII (1968), 189–201.

Rogers, Douglass. "Don Juan, *Donjuanismo*, and Death in Clarín." *Symposium*, XXX (1976), 325–42.

Round, Nicholas G. "The Fictional Integrity of Leopoldo Alas' *Super-chería*." *Bulletin of Hispanic Studies*, XLVII (1970), 97–111.

Rutherford, John. *Leopoldo Alas: La Regenta*. London: Grant and Cutler, 1974.

Sáinz Rodríguez, Pedro. "La obra de Clarín," in *Evolución de las ideas sobre la decadencia española y otros estudios de crítica literaria*. Madrid: Rialp, 1962, pp. 334–429.

Sánchez, Roberto G. "Clarín y el romanticismo teatral: Examen de una afición." *Hispanic Review*, XXXI (1963), 216–28.

———. "The Presence of the Theater and 'the Consciousness of Theater' in Clarín's *La Regenta*." *Hispanic Review*, XXXVII (1969), 491–509.

———. "Teatro e intimidad en *Su único hijo*: Un aspecto de la modernidad de Clarín." *Insula*, No. 311 (1972), 3, 12.

———. *El teatro en la novela Galdós y Clarín*. Madrid: Insula, 1974.

San Miguel, Luis G. *De la sociedad aristocrática a la sociedad industrial en la España del siglo XIX*. Madrid: Edicusa, 1973, pp. 131–49; 195–97; 217–59.

Savaiano, Eugene. *An Historical Justification of the Anticlericalism of Galdós and Alas*. Wichita, Kansas: University Studies No. 24, 1952.

Semprún Donahue, Moraima de. "La doble seducción de *La Regenta*." *Archivum*, XXIII (1973), 117–33. Also in *Papeles de Son Armadans*, LXXI (1973), 209–28.

Serrano Poncela, Segundo. "Un estudio de *La Regenta*." *Cuadernos Americanos*, CLII (1967), 223–41.

Sobejano, Gonzalo. "Clarín y la crisis de la crítica satírica," in *Forma literaria y sensibilidad social*. Madrid: Gredos, 1967, pp. 139–77.

———. "La inadaptada (Leopoldo Alas: *La Regenta*, capítulo XVI)," in *El comentario de textos*. Madrid: Castalia, 1973, pp. 126–66.

———. "Prólogo (Leopoldo Alas, la novela naturalista y la imaginación moral de *La Regenta*)," in *La Regenta*, by Leopoldo Alas. Barcelona: Noguer, 1976, pp. 11–58.

Solís, Jesús-Andrés. *Vida y obra de "Clarín."* Gijón: Imp. Gráficas Guinea, [1975].

Thompson, Clifford R., Jr. "Cervantine Motifs in the Short Stories of Leopoldo Alas." *Revista de Estudios Hispánicos*, X (1976), 391–403.

———. "Egoism and Alienation in the Works of Leopoldo Alas." *Romanische Forschungen*, LXXXI (1969), 193–203.

Torre, Guillermo de. "Clarín, crítico y novelista," in *Del 98 al barroco*. Madrid: Gredos, 1969, pp. 265–81.

Torrente Ballester, Gonzalo. *Panorama de la literatura española contemporánea*. Vol. I. 2nd ed. Madrid: Guadarrama, 1961, pp. 72–84.

Ullman, Pierre L. "The Antifeminist Premises of Clarín's *Su único hijo*." *Estudos Ibero-Americanos*, I (1975), 57–91.

———. "Clarín's Androcratic Ethic and the Antiapocalyptic Structure of '¡Adiós, Cordera!' " in *The Analysis of Hispanic Texts: Current Trends in Methodology*. 2nd York College Colloquium. Edited by Lisa E. Davis and Isabel C. Tarán. Jamaica, N.Y.: Bilingual Press, 1976, pp. 11–31.

Valis, Noël Maureen. "Fermín de Pas: Una flor del mal clariniana." *Explicación de Textos Literarios*, VII (1978), 31–36.

———. "The Landscape of the Soul in Clarín and Baudelaire." *Revue de littérature comparée*, LIV (1980), 17–31.

———. "Leopoldo Alas y los Goncourt: El alma neurótica." *Archivum*, XXVII–XXVIII (1977–78), 51–63.

———. "Leopoldo Alas y Zola: Paralelismos y divergencias temáticos." *Anuario de Letras* (Mexico), XVII (1979), 327–35.

———. "Romantic Reverberation in Clarín's *La Regenta*." *The Comparatist*, III (1979), 40–52.

———. "A Spanish Decadent Hero: Clarín's Antonio Reyes of 'Una medianía.' " *Modern Language Studies*, IX (1979), 53–60.

Varela Jácome, Benito. "Estructuración de *Su único hijo*," in *Estructuras novelísticas del siglo XIX*. Barcelona: Aubí, 1974, pp. 185–213.

Villavicencio, Laura N. "Reiteración y extremismo en el estilo creativo de Clarín." *Hispania*, LIV (1971), 459–69.

Weber, Frances. "The Dynamics of Motif in Leopoldo Alas's *La Regenta*." *Romanic Review*, LVII (1966), 188–99.

———. "Ideology and Religious Parody in the Novels of Leopoldo Alas." *Bulletin of Hispanic Studies*, XLIII (1966), 197–208.

Weiner, Hadassah Ruth. "*Su único hijo*: Desequilibrio y exaltación."

Boletín del Instituto de Estudios Asturianos, XXX (1976), 431–47.

Wiltrout, Ann. "El cosmos de *La Regenta* y el mundo de su autor." *Archivum*, XXI (1971), 47–64.

Zeda. "*Su único hijo*, por Leopoldo Alas (Clarín)." *Revista de España* (Madrid), CXXXV (1891), 498–510.

Other References

Alarcón, Pedro Antonio de. *El final de Norma*. México: Novaro-México, 1958.

Alvarez, A. *The Savage God: A Study of Suicide*. New York: Bantam Books, 1973.

Arjona, Doris King. "La Voluntad and Abulia in Contemporary Spanish Ideology." *Revue hispanique*, LXXIV (1928), 573–671.

Bachelard, Gaston. *The Poetics of Reverie*. New York: Orion Press, 1969.

Balakian, Anna. *El movimiento simbolista*. Madrid: Guadarrama, 1969.

Barbey d'Aurevilly, Jules. *Les Diaboliques*. Paris: Garnier, 1963.

Baudelaire, Charles. *L'Art romantique*. Paris: Garnier-Flammarion, 1968.

———. *Les Fleurs du mal*. Paris: Gallimard, 1965.

———. *Petits poèmes en prose*. Paris: Garnier-Flammarion, 1967.

Becker, George J., ed. *Documents of Modern Literary Realism*. Princeton, N.J.: Princeton University Press, 1967.

Bornecque, J. H., and P. Cogny. *Réalisme et naturalisme*. Paris: Hachette, 1958.

Bourges, Élémir. *Le Crépuscule des dieux*, in André Lebois' *La Genèse du Crépuscule des dieux*. Paris: Le Cercle du Livre, 1954.

Bourget, Paul. *Le Disciple*. Paris: Plon, 1928.

Cabezas, Juan Antonio. *Asturias: Biografía de una región*. Madrid: Espasa-Calpe, 1956.

Campbell, Joseph. *The Hero with a Thousand Faces*. Princeton, N.J.: Princeton University Press, 1972.

Carr, Raymond. *Spain, 1801–1939*. London: Clarendon Press, 1966.

Carter, A. E. *The Idea of Decadence in French Literature, 1830–1900*. Toronto: University of Toronto Press, 1958.

Charcot, J. M. *Clinical Lectures on Certain Diseases of the Nervous System*. Detroit, Michigan: George S. Davis, 1888.

Coloma, Luis. *Pequeñeces*. México: Porrúa, 1968.

Cram, Ralph Adams. *The Decadent: Being the Gospel of Inaction*. Boston: Privately printed, 1893.

Davies, R. Trevor. *Spain in Decline, 1621–1700*. London: Macmillan and Company, 1965.

Davis, Lisa E. "Oscar Wilde in Spain." *Comparative Literature*, XXV (1973), 136–52.

Díaz-Plaja, Fernando. *La vida española en el siglo XIX*. Madrid: "Prensa Española," 1969.

Dowson, Ernest. *Poems and Prose*. New York: Modern Library, 1919.

Flaubert, Gustave. *Madame Bovary*. Paris: Charpentier, 1923.

Frazer, Sir James George. *The Golden Bough*. Abridged ed. New York: Macmillan Company, 1960.

Gautier, Théophile. *Mademoiselle de Maupin*. Paris: Garnier-Flammarion, 1966.

———. "Notice," in Baudelaire's *Fleurs du mal*. Definitive edition. Paris: Calmann Lévy, 1900.

———. *Le Roman de la momie*. Paris: Garnier, 1963.

Gioanola, Elio. *Il decadentismo*. Roma: Editrice Studium, 1972.

Grout, Donald Jay. *A Short History of Opera*. 2nd ed. New York: Columbia University Press, 1965.

Hartley, Anthony, ed. *Mallarmé*. Baltimore, Md.: Penguin Books, 1965.

Hugo, Victor. *Notre-Dame de Paris*. Paris: Garnier-Flammarion, 1967.

———. *Cromwell*. Paris: Garnier-Flammarion, 1968.

Huxley, Aldous. *The Devils of Loudun*. New York: Harper and Row, 1971.

Huysmans, J.-K. *A Rebours*. Paris: Fasquelle, 1970.

Jackson, Holbrook. *The Eighteen Nineties*. New York: Capricorn Books, 1966.

Janet, Pierre. *The Major Symptoms of Hysteria*. 2nd ed. New York: Hafner Publishing Company, 1965.

Jullian, Philippe. *Dreamers of Decadence: Symbolist Painters of the 1890's*. New York: Praeger Publishers, 1974.

Jung, C. G. *Four Archetypes*. Princeton, N.J.: Princeton University Press, 1971.

———, ed. *Man and His Symbols*. New York: Dell Publishing Co., 1971.

Laín Entralgo, Pedro. *La generación del 98*. Madrid: Espasa-Calpe, 1970.

Legerman, David G., ed. *A Treasury of Opera Librettos.* Garden City, N.Y.: Doubleday and Company, 1962.

Levin, Harry. *The Gates of Horn.* New York: Oxford University Press, 1966.

Lida, Clara E., and Iris M. Zavala. *La revolución de 1868: historia, pensamiento, literatura.* New York: Las Américas Publishing Company, 1970.

Litvak, Lily. "La idea de la decadencia en la crítica antimodernista en España (1888–1910)." *Hispanic Review,* XLV (1977), 397–412.

Lukács, Georg. *Studies in European Realism.* New York: Grosset and Dunlap, 1964.

Martino, P. *Le Naturalisme français.* Paris: Armand Colin, 1965.

Meregalli, Franco. "D'Annunzio en España." *Filología Moderna,* Nos. 15–16 (1964), 265–89.

Mirbeau, Octave. *Le Jardin des supplices.* Paris: Charpentier, 1929.

Montesinos, José F. *Introducción a una historia de la novela en España en el siglo XIX.* Madrid: Castalia, 1955.

Neumann, Erich. *The Great Mother: An Analysis of the Archetype.* Princeton, N.J.: Princeton University Press, 1972.

Nordau, Max. *Degeneration.* New York: D. Appleton and Company, 1895.

Núñez de Arce, Gaspar. "Prefacio" to *Gritos del combate.* Madrid: Fernando Fe, 1914.

Ortega y Gasset, José. *España invertebrada.* Madrid: Revista de Occidente, 1967.

———. *Vieja y nueva política.* Madrid: Revista de Occidente, 1963.

Pardo Bazán, Emilia. *La cuestión palpitante.* Salamanca: Anaya, 1970.

Pattison, Walter. *El naturalismo español.* Madrid: Gredos, 1969.

Peña y Goñi, Antonio. *España desde la ópera a la zarzuela.* Madrid: Alianza, 1967.

Pérez de la Dehesa, Rafael. "Zola y la literatura española finisecular." *Hispanic Review,* XXXIX (1971), 49–60.

Pérez Galdós, Benito. *Ensayos de crítica literaria.* Barcelona: Península, 1972.

Petronius. *The Satyricon.* Trans. William Arrowsmith. New York: New American Library, 1959.

Praz, Mario. *The Romantic Agony.* New York: World Publishing Company, 1968.

Raitt, A. W. *Life and Letters in France: The Nineteenth Century*. New York: Scribner's Sons, 1965.

Richard, Noël. *À l'aube du symbolisme*. Paris: Nizet, 1961.

Ridge, George Ross. *The Hero in French Decadent Literature*. Athens, Georgia: University of Georgia Press, 1961.

Sainte-Beuve, Charles-Augustin. *Volupté*. Paris: Garnier-Flammarion, 1969.

Shattuck, Roger. *The Banquet Years*. New York: Random House, 1968.

Shaw, Donald L. "Armonismo: The Failure of an Illusion," in *La revolución de 1868*. Edited by Clara C. Lida and Iris M. Zavala. New York: Las Américas Publishing Co., 1970, pp. 351–61.

Sobejano, Gonzalo. *Nietzsche en España*. Madrid: Gredos, 1967.

Stromberg, Roland N., ed. *Realism, Naturalism, and Symbolism*. New York: Harper and Row, 1968.

Symons, Arthur. "The Decadent Movement in Literature." *Harper's New Monthly Magazine*, LXXXVII (1893), 858–67.

Thomas à Kempis. *The Imitation of Christ*. Trans. Ronald Knox and Michael Oakley. New York: Sheed and Ward, 1962.

Unamuno, Miguel de. "Sobre el marasmo actual de España." *En torno al casticismo*. Madrid: Espasa-Calpe, 1968.

Valle-Inclán, Ramón del. *Sonatas*. New York: Las Américas Publishing Company, 1961.

Van Roosbroeck, G. L. *The Legend of the Decadents*. New York: Institut des Études Françaises, Columbia University, 1927.

Veith, Ilza. *Hysteria: The History of a Disease*. Chicago: University of Chicago Press, 1970.

Villiers de l'Isle-Adam, Philippe Auguste. *Axël*. Vol. 4 of *Oeuvres complètes*. Genève: Slatkine Reprints, 1970.

———. *Contes cruels*. Paris: Pierre Belfond, 1966.

Zavala, Iris M. *Ideología y política en la novela española del siglo XIX*. Salamanca: Anaya, 1971.

Zola, Émile. *La Curée*. Paris: Fasquelle, 1969.

———. *La Faute de l'abbé Mouret*. Paris: Fasquelle, 1967.

———. *Nana*. 2 vols. Paris: Charpentier, 1928.

———. *Le Rêve*. Paris: Nelson, 1932.

Index

Afrancesamiento, 21
Agudiez, Juan Ventura, 77–78, 145
Alarcón, Pedro Antonio de, 115*n*,
  132
Alas, Leopoldo: literary internationalism, 6 and *n*; life-style, 12
—"Una medianía": abulic dreamer
  type, 4, 5; analysis of, 183–90
—*La Regenta*: Restoration society,
  4–5, 24–25, 46, 82 and *n*, 86, 92,
  103; psychological complexities,
  4; hispanization of French decadent sensibility, 5, 10, 105;
  Carter's naturalist phase, 15; decadent label, 23; debasement of
  religion, 24, 25, 86–87; romanticism, 24–25, 26–27, 48–51, 87;
  technique of contrast, 24–25;
  moral landscape, 25–26; and
  Notre-Dame de Paris, 27–30, 32–
  33, 40–42, 46, 47, 48, 51; sexually abnormal types, 29–33; Fermín
  de Pas, description of, 33–40;
  flowers of evil motif, 38, 40, 74–
  76; tower device, 42, 44, 46–48;
  devouring motif, 42, 53, 60, 65,
  73; conquest motif, 43, 46, 90;
  Siglo de Oro motif, 43–44, 87–89,
  90; spying, 44, 47, 72, 103 and *n*;
  Vetusta, description of, 44–46;
  indianos, 45–46, 50, 51; authorial
  viewpoint, 47, 51; Darwinian universe, 52–81, 90, 92; animal imagery, 52–53, 56; marketplace
  image, 53–57; underground
  image, 58–60; banquet motif, 60–
  71, 92; sensation-seeking, 72–81;
  vampire motif, 80*n*, 101–102,
  146–47; sickly soul, 81–105; split
  in self, 82, 85, 89*n*, 93–96; misnomers, 84*n*; pastoral motif, 89–
  90; lack of future, 91; hysteria,
  93–96; sickroom motif, 96–97;
  mysticism, 97–99; suicide, 100–
  101; self-concealment, 103–104;
  compared with *Su único hijo*, 107,
  108, 109, 142, 145, 146, 182, 187,
  191–93
—*Su único hijo*: Restoration society, 4–5; psychological complexities, 4; hispanization of French
  decadent sensibility, 5, 10, 105;
  decadent archetypes, 15, 16, 23,
  135–67; criticism on, 107–109; its
  classification, 108–10; time, 110–
  14; setting, 110, 114; romanticism, 111, 115, 132, 133, 135, 138,
  142, 146, 148–49, 167; medical
  allusions, 111–12; role of music,
  111, 112–13, 115–35; hysteria,
  112, 141; historical allusions, 113,
  114; melodrama, 115–35; point of
  view, 115, 120–21, 123, 131, 144,
  145, 161, 167, 173, 181; daydreaming, 124–26, 157, 161–62,
  164–66, 173–74; *femme fatale*,
  137, 138, 147, 152, 154, 155;
  heroism, 138, 162, 166, 168–71,
  174–75, 177, 178–81; misnomers,
  138, 162–63, 185; sickroom, 142;
  flowers of evil motif, 145; vampire motif, 146–47, 150, 151, 152;
  fatherhood, 161, 171–81; Bonifacio and the arts, 164–65; Bonifacio's "shadow," 176–78; regeneration, 182, 192–93. *See also*

Baudelaire, Charles; Decadent Movement; *Modernismo*; Symbolism
Alfonso XII, 18
Alpujarras War, 139
Alvarez, A., 101
Amadeo, King of Spain, 84
Anaphrodyte, 31, 74
Androgyne, 16, 150, 173
Anima, 173–74
Archetype, definition of, 110, 128–29, 151–52
Armonismo, 18
Ateneo, 185, 187, 188
Atila, 129
Azorín. *See* Martínez Ruiz, José

Bacchantes, 80n
Bachelard, Gaston, 173
Balakian, Anna, 134
Balzac, Honoré de, 7, 30, 68n
Bandera, Cesáreo, 123, 177, 179
Baquero Goyanes, Mariano, 107 and n, 109, 110, 111
Barbey d'Aurevilly, Jules, 12, 36–37, 77–78, 137
Bastiat, Frédéric, 54
Baudelaire, Charles: Alas' receptiveness to, 6; decadent viewpoint, 10, 11; decadent style, 12; perversion, 30; use of cosmetics, 36; flowers of evil image, 38; British style of dress, 40; sickroom image, 96, 97; vampire motif, 102; metaphysical decadence, 105; and Wagner, 132; and music, 134; parallels with Alas, 191 and n
Beardsley, Aubrey, 12
Becker, George J., 7
Bellini, Vincenzo, 112, 130, 131, 132, 153
Beser, Sergio, 183, 184
Beyle, Henri, 127, 136n
Blanco García, Francisco, 108
Bourges, Élémir, 9, 37, 80, 132–33, 137, 140, 154
Bourget, Paul, 9, 14, 15

Brandreth, Henry R. T., 13
Brunetière, Ferdinand, 20
Byron, Lord, 36, 149

Caciquismo, 19, 54, 169
Calderonianism, 88, 103
Campbell, Joseph, 174
Candelas, Luis, 148
Cánovas del Castillo, Antonio, 113
Carlist Wars, 113
Carlyle, Thomas, 170n
Carr, Raymond, 19
Carter, A. E., 14, 15, 40, 99, 135, 139, 140, 191
Cervantes Saavedra Miguel, 109, 167. *See also* Don Quixote
Charcot, Jean-Martin, 93, 94, 112
Clarín. *See* Alas, Leopoldo
Coloma, Luis, 10, 111n, 115n
Costumbrismo, 21
Crociato, Il, 129

Dame aux camélias, 124
Darío, Rubén, 12
Darwin, Charles, 44, 52, 56, 58, 59
Decadence as an obsession, 14, 15, 16
Decadence as a world view, 16
Decadentism. *See* Decadent Movement
Decadent Movement: Alas' attitude toward, 5, 6n; point of view, 10–11; decadent life-style, 11, 12; decadent style, 12–13, 14; definition of decadence, 12, 14, 15; and symbolists, 13; and Baudelaire, 105
Diana, 89
Diana enamorada, 89
Donizetti, Gaetano, 112
Donoso Cortés, Juan, 7
Don Quixote, 167, 168, 169
Dowson, Ernest, 12, 16
Dubois, Dr. Paul, 112
Durand, Frank, 42n, 52

Ellis, Havelock, 14

"Esperaindeo," 183
Espronceda, José de, 7, 149
Eumenide, 150, 152

Fernández Almagro, Melchor, 3
Fin de siècle: transitional age, 3,
    15–16; anti-materialism, 8–9, 20;
    mood of uneasiness, 9; "tired
    mood," 16–17
Flaubert, Gustave, 7, 10, 138
France, decadence of, 20
Franco-Prussian War, 9
Franz, M.-L. von, 177

Gautier, Théophile, 12, 14, 30, 36,
    78–79
Generation of 1898, pp. 19, 21, 188
Goncourt, Edmond, and Jules de,
    6, 10, 14, 96
Good Mother, 138, 152, 153
Götterdämmerung, 9
Gracioso, 32, 33
Gramberg, Eduard, 108, 114
Great Mother, 152, 160
"Great Round," 160
Grotesque, definition of, 28–29, 30

Hahnemann, Samuel, 112
Heliogabalus, 75 and *n*
Howe, Irving, 181
Hugo, Victor: *Notre-Dame de
    Paris*, 27–30, 32–33, 34*n*, 40–42,
    46–48, 51; maiden-victim, 136;
    idealized criminal, 149
Huxley, Aldous, 97
Huxley, Thomas, 44
Huysmans, J.-K.: decadent view-
    point, 10–11, 146; Des Esseintes,
    11, 14, 36, 80, 136, 139–40, 164–
    65, 189; decadent movement, 12;
    A Rebours, 12, 13, 14, 23; per-
    version, 30; use of cosmetics, 37;
    flowers of evil motif, 38, 75; dec-
    adent Rome, 66; vampire motif,
    102; decadent typology, 136, 137;
    and Zola, 140

Istúriz, Francisco Javier, 113

Jackson, Holbrook, 13, 14, 17, 73
Jackson, Robert M., 82*n*
Jacopone da Todi, 170
Janet, Pierre, 93–96
"Juanito Reseco," 183
Jung, Carl, 129, 151, 152
Juretschke, Hans, 6

Küpper, Werner, 110

La Mennais, Félicité Robert de, 7
Larra, Mariano José de, 7, 21, 187
Lewis, M. G., 36
Lombroso, Cesare, 99
Lorraine, Jean, 30
Loudun, witchcraft trial of, 97

Mademoiselle de Maupin, 69, 80
Máinez, Ramón León, 107
Mallarmé, Stéphane, 37, 96, 97,
    134–35, 150
María Cristina, Regency of, 113
Martial, 75
Martínez Ruiz, José, 107 and *n*,
    110, 187
Materialism, 7, 8, 70
Mazzeo, Guido, 65
Melpomene, 150, 151
Menéndez y Pelayo, Marcelino, 110
Meyerbeer, Giacomo, 189
Mirbeau, Octave, 30, 37, 74–75, 79,
    102
Modernismo: Alas' attitude toward,
    5; and decadence, 10; and dec-
    adent movement, 12
Monsieur de Phocas, 14
Moreau, Gustave, 13
Morel, B. H., 139

Nabucodonosor, 129
Naturalism (literary), 8, 10, 105
Nekyia, 179
Neumann, Erich, 83, 160
Nietzsche, Friedrich, 15, 143 and *n*
Nocturnal Mother, 161

Nordau, Max, 15, 99, 143 and *n*
Núñez de Arce, Gaspar, 19–20, 21

Odyssey, 179
Ortega y Gasset, José, 17, 18

Pardo Bazán, Emilia, 8
Patria chica, 19
Péladan, Joséphin, 30
Peña y Goñi, Antonio, 112
Penzol, Pedro, 41
Pérez Galdós, Benito, 8, 10, 20–21, 30*n*
Petronius, 66–71
Plato, 62, 66, 71, 89
Praz, Mario, 37, 135, 136, 137, 150
Proust, Marcel, 188, 189

Quevedo Francisco de, 39, 44

Rachilde, 30, 66
Radcliffe, Mrs. Ann, 36, 136
Realism (literary), 7, 8, 10
Realism (Spanish), 30, 39, 48
Redon, Odilon, 13
Revolution of 1868, p. 18
Richmond, Carolyn, 107*n*, 110*n*, 183
Ridge, George Ross, 9–10, 137, 147, 164, 185–86
Rossini, Gioacchino, 100, 112, 130

Sade, Marquis de, 69
Sagasta, Práxedes Mateo, 113
Sainte-Beuve, Charles-Augustin, 76–77, 136*n*, 165–66, 188
Salpêtrière, 93, 112
Samain, Albert, 66
Semiramide, 129
Shattuck, Roger, 65*n*
Spain: Restoration, 3, 18–19; regeneration, 17, 182; historical decadence, 17, 18, 20–22; Empire, 17, 18; "two Spains," 18; Reconquest, 45, 139, 182
Spencer, Herbert, 9
Stahl, Georg, 112
Stendhal. *See* Beyle, Henri

Surin, Father, 97
Sydenham, Thomas, 112
Symbolism: Alas' attitude toward, 5; and decadents, 13; and music, 132, 133–35
Symons, Arthur, 14

Taboada, Luis, 65
Taine, Hippolyte, 9
Teresa, Saint, 98
Teresa, 137*n*
Terrible Mother, 138, 152–53
Thomas à Kempis, 98
Tolstoy, Leo, 7
Turgenev, Ivan, 7
Turno pacífico, 19, 54, 92

Ulysses, 163, 179, 180
Unamuno, Miguel de, 22

Valle-Inclán, Ramón del, 12, 13, 30*n*
Van Roosbroeck, G. L., 15
Veith, Ilza, 93
Vélez de Guevara, Luis, 44
Verdi, Giuseppe: 111 and *n*, 112, 113, 118, 121, 122*n*, 123–24
Verlaine, Paul: decadent life-style, 11, 12; decadent movement, 12, 13; perversion, 30, 146; Roman decadence, 66; attitude toward music, 133–34
Villiers de l'Isle-Adam, Phillipe Auguste, 36, 165
Vinci, Leonardo da, 65, 67
Vogüé, E.-M. de, 8
Volupté, 76–77, 165, 188
Voluptuosidad, 75–77

Wagner, Richard, 9, 116, 132–33
Wallace, Alfred Russel, 44
Wilde, Oscar, 10, 11, 12, 23, 149*n*

Zola, Émile: *Nana*, 10, 20, 37, 76, 102; as naturalist writer, 10, 14, 15, 16, 52, 191; Rougon-Macquart

series, 20, 80; flowers of evil
motif, 38, 74, 75; *La Conquête
de Plassans*, 41*n*; physiological
degeneration, 80, 81, 104, 139;
dominating female, 136–37; *Le*

Rêve, 165. *See also* Huysmans,
J.-K.
Zorrilla, José, 91
Zutistas, 186
Zutistes, 186*n*